The Marketer's Guide to Selling Products Abroad

The Marketer's Guide to Selling Products Abroad

Robert E. Weber

Q

QUORUM BOOKS
New York • Westport, Connecticut • London

Library of Congress Cataloging-in-Publication Data

Weber, Robert E.
    The marketer's guide to selling products abroad / Robert E. Weber.
        p.   cm.
    Bibliography: p.
    Includes index.
    ISBN 0-89930-325-0 (lib. bdg. : alk. paper)
    1. Export marketing—United States—Handbooks, manuals, etc.
2. Exports—United States—Handbooks, manuals, etc.   I. Title.
HF1416.5.W43   1989
658.8′48—dc19   88-11316

British Library Cataloguing in Publication Data is available.

Library of Congress Catalog Card Number: 88-11316
ISBN: 0-89930-325-0

First published in 1989 by Quorum Books

Greenwood Press, Inc.
88 Post Road West, Westport, Connecticut 06881

Printed in the United States of America

The paper used in this book complies with the
Permanent Paper Standard issued by the National
Information Standards Organization (Z39.48-1984).

10 9 8 7 6 5 4 3 2 1

Copyright Acknowledgments

Extracts from *Samarkand and Beyond,* copyright © 1977 by James Wellard.
Reproduced by permission of Curtis Brown Ltd., London.

ICC No. 400, Uniform Customs and Practice For Documentary Credits/1983
Revision. Copyright © 1983 by ICC Publishing S.A.

Exhibit 8.1, The Air Waybill, is reprinted courtesy of American Airlines.

Exhibit 8.8, Air Package Express Combination Letter of Instructions and Customs
Declaration, is reprinted courtesy of Federal Express.

Every reasonable effort has been made to trace the owners of copyright materials
used in this book, but in some instances this has proven impossible. The publishers
will be glad to receive information leading to more complete acknowledgments in
subsequent prints of this book, and in the meantime extend their apologies for any
omissions.

To the memory of

E.B. (Bob) Smeed and Lois Dopp

Contents

PART I
DECIDING TO EXPORT

PART II
HANDLING DOCUMENTATION

PART III
MARKETING ABROAD

Illustrations

Preface

The American Widget Manufacturing Company is a large domestic producer of specialty widgets. It markets through a network of independent distributors who purchase for their own inventories. Terms are net thirty days and if an account becomes more than sixty days old, it is placed on credit hold. The company controls 40% of the available U.S. market.

Recently, the American Widget Company developed a process that enables it to increase its production by one third. However, the marketing department forecasts that the cost of increasing market share to absorb the increased production is prohibitive. What is executive management to do in this situation? It is confronted with the prospect of substantially increasing production, but frustrated by an inability to distribute the additional products to their traditional market.

The answer to the dilemma is export. Indeed, over the years the company has received numerous requests for its products from the far corners of the world. However, each time an inquiry was pursued, something always occurred to prevent the transaction from materializing. On one occasion the customer could not secure American currency: another time the actual product was shipped, but the letter of credit which was negotiated contained errors forcing the widget company to absorb unexpected expenses and generally raised havoc with its accounting department.

This time, however, the company was determined to export properly. Management reasoned, correctly, that because many American companies successfully export products, there was no reason why the widget company could not also be successful. After all, the product was good and considering the quantity of inquiries received from time to time, it seemed obvious that there was need for the product in other countries.

This book is intended for use by those companies which are similar to the American Widget Company or which have had similar experiences. It sequentially takes the reader from the obvious questions regarding when and how to export through nettling concerns such as documentation, product servicing, advertising, distribution agreements, patents, trademarks, political risks, to the best ways to travel the territory and the importance of foreign trade shows.

The author gratefully acknowledges the assistance of numerous persons whose time and effort helped make this book possible. Included among them are:

Mr. Neil Hesse, Trade Specialist assigned to the Dallas District Office of the U.S. and Foreign Commercial Service. Mr. C. A. (Onnie) Sumangil, Assistant Vice-President at First RepubliBank in Dallas, Texas. Mr. Ronald V. Thurman, Partner at Hubbard, Thurman, Turner & Tucker, attorneys specializing in Patent, Trademark, Copyright and unfair competition matters. Mr. Roy A. Wagman, Vice-President, The Boatmen's National Bank of St. Louis for his assistance in helping develop the forms used to illustrate the section on collecting accounts receivable.

Introduction

EXPORT, HOW IT ALL BEGAN

As soon as primordial man first set foot on the warm earth, certain commodities were needed to assure his survival. Among the items essential to him were food, shelter, and a means of protecting himself from his predators, including other men.

In this early inhospitable environment, some men, no doubt, were more adept at one discipline of survival than at others. It must have been evident from the earliest times that men could help one another by taking advantage of each other's specific skills. Thus, the excellent gatherer of fruits and berries could provide more items than he personally needed. Likewise, the hunter or fisher could kill more game than he personally could eat. When these two primitive people cooperated, they were able to trade items and help ensure their own and the other's survival, as well as to achieve an improved standard of living.

Thus, trade began from this imperspicuous foundation and it has followed man right into the twentieth century. Shortly after the first trade was conducted it must have occurred to one of the primitives that he did not have to give up his extra items if he could take or steal the other's commodities. Stealing certainly was easy, but these first primitives must have learned that with theft comes the probability of retaliation.

The earliest trades consisted of barter, such as exchanging meat for fish, or a handful of berries for some eggs that were foraged, and so forth. Trading was principally composed of agricultural items or animals which were hunted for their meat, fur, or hides. Exchanges of goods took place mainly on a chance basis because man was nomadic and followed the seasons. It was not until the New Stone Age that man began to domesticate animals and raise grains.

In the New Stone Age, the Bronze Age, and early Iron Age larger bodies of people, with a more complicated social organization, moving in an orderly way, driving their herds and transporting their belongings on pack animals or in wagons, found the line of migration blocked here and there by settled farming communities whose villages and cities were strong points which could be defended, and also centers in which artisans produced pottery, textiles, and later, metal wares, which could be used for trade as an alternative to war. Conversely, the settled peoples extended their territories as their population increased and developed them into kingdoms and states.[1]

As people began to settle and establish cities and states it must have become apparent that the actual trading of goods was not very satisfactory. Many times items of unlike value could not be traded simply because a like value was not perceived. Thus it was essential that a crude currency system be devised. The first system to evolve lasted at least six thousand years. No one can be certain when money was first coined, but the first know location seems to have been in what is present-day India.

The antiquity of money in India is confirmed by other ancient writings, by ancient epigraphic monuments, and by the existence of "punc-marked" coins of a purely Indian type, which though undated, are evidently older than the period of the Greek invasion, older than Buddhism, and . . . older even than the Vedic writings.[2]

The minting of currency was one of history's greatest achievements because for the first time, it enabled people to exchange goods and services for a common denominator. The first monies were produced using base metals such as copper, silver, and later gold. These currencies were always in the forms of coins. Among the earliest coins were those whose very shape reflected the specific object being traded. Thus, a coin in the shape of a fish represented the value of one fish. Some early coins even had the image of a person stamped onto the coin. It is speculated that this coin represented the value of one slave.

Later coins were issued by cities and/or states. These early nummular systems were stamped with the city's symbol or the ruler's image and were good for exchange anywhere within the particular city or state. Although this system was a vast improvement over direct barter trades, it was fraught with problems, such as forgery. It was a simple matter for unscrupulous persons to melt down coins and remold them into another city's coin. Also, because the cities lacked control of the natural resources for making their coins, anyone could make duplicates of the city's currencies by melting and molding the metal themselves. Moreover, the supply of metals from which to make coins was unpredictable because the ravages of war or disease frequently limited access to mines.

These problems with coinage were not satisfactorily solved until sometime between the fifth and tenth century B.C. in the states of Ionia,

Byzantium, Sparta, and Athens. During this period, the states issued money that was disk shaped and consisted of purposely rotted iron or copper. This currency, in and of itself, had no value. What gave currency its value was the fact that for the first time in know history a state decreed by law that its coins were legal tender for the payment of all debts, claims, purchases, and taxes. The state protected the coins from being counterfeited and limited their issuance. This was a great step forward because the limitation and the value of the coins was definitely know and guaranteed. Whatever the relation between the commodity or service, its value in currency was fixed. The value of the coins would not only be constant at the current time in history, but in the future as well.[3]

This system of currency was utilized for centuries and would probably still be in use today except for several flaws inherent in the system. First, the currency was only good as long as the state remained in existence because its value was only guaranteed by the state itself; the money had no intrinsic value in and of itself. Second, the problem with forgeries was never completely eliminated. And last, the currency was not flexible enough to allow for the expansion of commerce or credit.

The problems inherent with such currency were slowly addressed and over a great deal of time states were able to control the mining of the precious metals from which the coins were minted. They even controlled the number of slaves working in the mines so as to maintain consistent production and cost. The states also began to find ways to make the coins more complicated so they were increasingly difficult to duplicate. They were successfully able to alloy metals to further frustrate counterfeiters. In the process, though, they were able to legislate a way "to measure and determine value; and that its efficiency, precision, stability, and equitable operation depended largely, if not entirely, upon the strength, wisdom, and virtue of the government by whose laws it was created and regulated."[4]

The creation of a nummular system was essential for the establishment of foreign trade. Although actual items were bartered when the merchant returned to his homeland, it was essential that he be able to convert the items he traded in another part of the world for a currency. This not only assured him of a profit, it also enabled him to reinvest in additional items for his next journey. The early merchants were probably of either European extraction or from what we refer to today as the Middle East. Under the umbrella of the Greek city-states and later the Roman empire, trade routes to Asia were established. However, it does seem apparent that even prior to this period some organized trading was going on. During the Bronze Age tin from England was transported by the Phoenicians to the early Mediterranean empires in order for them to create bronze weapons. The Bronze Age flourished not only in the countries around the Mediterranean, but also in Central Europe and Scandinavia. All this was two thousand B.C. and because the creation of bronze occurred in so many areas separated by great distances, it follows that transport of goods and manufacturing processes must have occurred.

In order for these goods to be transported, a method of transport had to have existed. Transport actually occurred over land through the establishment of a system of roads and over water principally through the Persian Gulf and Indian ocean to India and China, which early traders referred to as *Seres,* the contemporary Chinese word for silk. During "the Bronze Age there was an established European road system. Four Amber Roads joined the Baltic with the Mediterranean. A Tin Road ran across southern Britain to Britainy [sic], and thence across France to Marseilles."[5]

During this time trans-European roads also existed. The oldest of these caravan routes were the Spice Road and the Incense Road. These roads existed until the Middle Ages and during this time they were also expanded to include the Gold Road into Africa, and the Silk Road which transversed over five thousand miles from its origin in present-day Italy to China. Traders were able to transit these great distances by caravan, being certain not to offend any of the rulers of territory through which they passed. Because trade was good for all parties concerned, most of the traders were allowed transit through many different states without hindrance. Most of the rulers did require a tribute to be paid for the right to pass trough their country. However, in return, the rulers usually protected the caravans from bandits. This method of moving goods from one geographical area to another was so successful that it continued uninterrupted until Marco Polo made the trip along the Silk Road to China 1,100 years later! In fact, such a trip today would probably be impossible due to the many different governments and their politics.

This early system of international trade is not much different from today's trade system. Although it is true that trade was usually for barter rather than currency, the transactions were identical with today's in that both parties shared the perception of value. Only the intervention of governments and bankers distinguishes today's trade from that of three thousand years ago.

The intervention of government into foreign trade was inevitable. As long as man has been uniting with his fellow man to form tribes, cities, and states, he has been subjected to war, usually over territory. Historically, in order for a government to finance a war, it was essential for it to collect taxes from its citizenry. One of the earliest ways governments learned to raise funds was by taxing imports. Thus the first tariffs were born and they remain with us today.

The introduction of tariffs to trade complicated what was heretofore basically a simple transaction between two individuals. It may be said that the development of tariffs was a conspiracy by government against its constituents. Tariffs create scarcity and when items are scarce, they frequently become coveted. The scarcity is caused when the tariff artificially raises the cost and therefore, the value of the item. If there were no tariffs, then goods would flow unencumbered according to demand. The concept of trade is that each entity, the buyer and the seller, perceives that he will benefit more from the trade than the other. Governments typically believe, however, that the needs of the state are more important than the needs of the individual. An illustration of this apparent dichotomy can be found in our own Revolution. Prior to 1776 the king of England decreed a tax on almost all items that were shipped to the American colonies. This tax was know as the Townsend Acts of 1767. The colonists were obliged to pay the taxes (read tariffs) even though they did not receive any benefit from them nor have a voice in establishing them. The money collected for the taxes was sent to King George in order for him to pay for his Seven Years War. These disguised taxes were greatly resented and resulted in the Boston Massacre and, later, the Boston Tea Party.

So opposed was the general populace to the establishment of taxes, that the new post-revolutionary government did not attempt to establish nor collect taxes. Instead it relied on each state's donating monies to the central government to pay for its maintenance costs. The result of the founding fathers' good intentions was chaos. The states balked at paying what many of them deemed unfair shares. Additionally, individual states set up protectionist tariffs and predatory pricing policies that hindered trade and fostered animosities among the various states.

In an effort to overcome these problems, many of the Continental Congress' members met in Philadelphia in 1787 to redefine the Articles of Confederation. What resulted was our present Constitution. In the Constitution under the powers granted to Congress, article eight specifically grants Congress the power to lay and collect taxes, duties, imposts, and excises, to pay the debts and provide for the common defense and general welfare of the United States. Furthermore it stated that all duties, imposts and excises shall be uniform throughout the United States.

The United States and most other countries have a dual type of tariff structure. There are *ad-valorem* duties and *specific* duties. Ad-valorem duties are taxes that are charged as a percentage of the value of the item being imported. Specific duties are taxes that represent a fixed amount for an item. An example of specific duties could be one dollar per pair of shoes or thirty-five cents per bottle of wine imported. Ad-valorem and specific duties can be charged on the cost of the item being imported either before or after transportation costs are included in the cost of the item.

The importance of international trade (export-import) among nations and their constituents cannot be overstated because it is essential to their well-being and important to the world's economy. Each nation must export those items that it can produce in excess of its needs in exchange for items that it cannot produce in adequate quantities. The uninterrupted flow of goods and services among nations can only serve mankind.

NOTES

1. Owen and Eleanor Lattimore, *Silks, Spices and Empire* (New York: Delacorte Press, 1968), p. 3.

2. Alexander Del Mar, *History of Monetary Systems* (New York: Augustus M. Kelley, 1969), p. 2.

3. Ibid, p. xxxiv.

4. Lattimore, op.cit., p. xxxiv.

5. James Wellard, *Samarkand and Beyond* (London: Constable and Company, 1977), pp. 38-39.

PART I
DECIDING TO EXPORT

Chapter 1
Export to Improve
Your Balance Sheet

This chapter discusses the various ways exporting can improve your economies of scale, extend the life of an obsolete product or service, and the governmental incentives for exporting.

IMPROVING YOUR ECONOMIES OF SCALE

Three areas of economies of scale may be identified when you first begin to consider exporting your products or services: production, marketing, and distribution.

Generally speaking, the more raw materials you can purchase, the less expensive the materials. Most manufacturers and fabricators will grant additional discounts for purchasing in large quantities. Additionally, you can usually save on the freight rate because the greater the weight and cube shipped, the lower the rate you will have to pay. These savings can enable you to reduce the selling price of your product or to increase your profit margin. If you can create a market for your product abroad, you will be able to increase your quantity purchases of material used to manufacture your product, and lower your unit cost.

Just as you can reduce actual material costs, you can achieve similar results in reduced marketing expenses. Your unit cost in producing sales literature can be significantly lowered by producing more literature to serve additional markets. Although it is true you may not want to produce all literature in English, considerable savings can result when halftones produced for your domestic program can be stripped in for your foreign language advertising. In this manner you will only have extra costs for overprinting text.

If your type of product is such that samples are occasionally utilized, the same economy of scale you gain on the purchase of raw materials will apply here.

Media purchases can be made through several firms that will correctly place you in applicable foreign media. This will increase your exposure and cost very little extra. In fact, measured in a response rate or in number of exposures to potential clients, your cost per response or exposure will be lower. There are many American trade publications available abroad. Advertising in these magazines can be cost effective because the magazine will usually do translations gratis if the periodical is published in a foreign language. The only caveat is that you should always have your own expert who is familiar with the language of publication read the copy before it goes to press. All too often the person doing the translating for the magazine is not familiar with the "buzz words" unique to your industry. Failure to do this may create a situation where Kentucky Fried Chicken's slogan, "finger licking good," becomes "Tastiness Until Licking Fingers."

All your marketing, public relations, advertising, and administrative costs can be reduced as a percent of total cost if you export. This is possible because your market will be larger and, therefore, your cost per exposure will be lower.

Similarly, your distribution cost will be lowered by implementing an export program. Your fixed costs become spread over more volume and, thus, your costs are reduced and your profits enhanced.

If your product has a seasonal nature, quite likely you can find a market for it in a different hemisphere, thereby reducing your slack period while improving production and profitability. If done correctly, exporting can only enhance your economy of scale.

In addition to the obvious gains in economies there are many government programs that may be available to you. These programs are typically in the form of payment guarantees or production loans. Your firm may be eligible for one or several programs provided to American exporters by various branches of government or quasi-governmental associations. The following is a list and description of the government programs available at the time this book was being written. As in the case with much government communication, it is cloaked in the code words of the bureaucracy. Each program has an acronym so it is not necessary (or probably desirable) to talk with the Department of Commerce's Trade Specialists using each program's complete title.

SMALL BUSINESS ADMINISTRATION (SBA)

The Small Business Administration offers three primary plans to assist individuals and companies interested in exporting. Export Counseling Services are provided at no cost to companies interested in commencing export. Assistance is given by utilizing executives, graduate business students, and professional consultants. Members of SCORE (Service Corps of Retired Executives) and ACE (Active Corps of Executives) will be pleased to share their expertise and offer advice regarding the potential for your product in foreign markets. Additionally, the SBA has arrangements with over 450 colleges and universities to offer counseling assistance.

Thirdly, the SBA offers its Call Contact Program. This program can put you in contact with technical consultants or management knowledgeable in sophisticated industries. These individuals can help highly technical companies realistically evaluate their export potential. They will even assist you by placing you in contact with attorneys, should you have any foreign legal questions.

Lastly, and most importantly, the Small Business Administration can place qualified companies into their Export Line of Credit (ERLC). The ERLC loan is not a loan in the literal sense. It is more accurately described as a guarantee of up to 90% of any loan you are able to secure from your own bank or other private lender. By guaranteeing the loan you should be able to qualify for a lower rate or secure a loan that might otherwise not be available to you. Because the ERLC is in the form of a line of credit, you can draw it as your needs arise.

In order to be eligible for this type of loan you must qualify as a small business by the SBA's definition and have been in business in the United States not less than twelve months. Additionally, you must be current on all payroll tax payments and have a depository plan for the payment of future withholding taxes. Funds from the line of credit cannot be used to pay existing obligations or to purchase fixed assets. However, they may be used for any other item or event that furthers your ability to export. For example, funds may be used to finance labor, purchase materials, provide export services, professional consulting, or foreign travel.

One other SBA program is currently in existence to assist the firm interested in exporting. It is a cooperative effort between the Small Business Administration and the Ex-Im Bank. The requirements for eligibility for participation in this program are the same as for the ERLC program, but the size of loans can be greater. Whereas the largest loan available directly from the SBA is $500 thousand, the Ex-Im/SBA loan can be as large as $1 million.

To determine if you qualify for either of these financial programs or just to gather information on how the SBA can help with its counseling services, contact

Office of International Trade
U.S. Small Business Administration
1129-20th Street NW
Washington, D.C. 20416
(202) 653-7794

EXPORT-IMPORT BANK (EXIMBANK)

Eximbank is an agency of the U.S. government that can grant direct loans or supplement financing by commercial banks for large projects that generate exports. There are several programs available to qualified companies.

The Working Capital Guarantee Program is to be used by companies that need to finance the build-up of inventories prior to actual sales. Eximbank will guarantee up to 90% of the principal of the loan. Therefore, the commercial lender is only at risk for 10%. The use of this program can also free up needed cash by reducing the lender's collateral requirements. It must be cautioned, however, that guarantees of this sort must be used for specific export-related activity and cannot be used for any other domestic needs or to acquire assets. Costs of these loan guarantees is similar to those of other commercial loans but security requirements are generally lower. Security is usually required of only 110% of the outstanding balance rather than the 150% to 200% typically required by a commercial lender.

In addition to working capital loans, Eximbank may offer you Commercial Bank Guarantees. These instruments are guarantees by Eximbank to your commercial bank against nonpayment by your foreign buyer. These are usually for medium term accounts receivable ranging from 181 days to 5 years. In order for Eximbank to guarantee the payment, it requires the foreign client to make a 15% deposit at the time he places his order with you. At this point Eximbank makes a distinction between *political risk* and *commercial risk.* Political risk refers to your risk due to the buyer's government changing policy, i.e., currency inconvertibility or expropriation or even violent political overthrow. Eximbank will guarantee payment of 100% of the receivable. However it will only guarantee 90% against commercial risk, such as nonpayment due to bankruptcy or insolvency of the client.

Because political risk is a serious reality in many parts of the world, the government only offers Commercial Bank Guarantees in the most secure countries. Currently there are 140 countries where coverage of this sort is available. Before relying on this program, be certain to check with Eximbank. The list of eligible countries changes from time to time.

A variation of the Commercial Bank Guarantees is Export Credit Insurance, which is available through the Foreign Credit Insurance Association (FCIA). The FCIA is an association of insurance companies that insures against nonpayment of obligations due to political or commercial default. Just as Commercial Bank Guarantees provide protection to the exporter's commercial lender, the Export Credit Insurance protects the exporter. Credit insurance will cover 100% of any losses for political reasons and as much as 95% for commercial losses.

Eximbank through FCIA has made available export credit insurance as a Master Policy to over two hundred banks so they can routinely insure their exporting clients. Additionally there are umbrella policies available to nonbanks such as freight forwarders, export trading companies, and regional or local economic development agencies.

For those companies that are new to export and have not sold more than $750 thousand worth of product abroad, there is Eximbank's "New-to-Export" program. This program will afford the new exporter better terms than the "old hand" at export would be offered.

Lastly, if your company is interested in large construction projects abroad or sales of large capital equipment items, the Eximbank will custom build a program combining appropriate elements enabling you to compete with foreign bidders on favorable terms.

The utilization of these programs should make exporting your products as safe as dealing with the company just down the street. The inability to finance or otherwise accept export orders should not be reason for passing up the sale. Your government wants you to export and it is willing to provide all the reasonable help it possibly can. If you have an interest in how one or more of these programs can work for you, call Eximbank's toll free number, 800/424-5201.

OTHER GOVERNMENT AGENCIES

Should you want to commence dealing with a Third World country, you can work with the Overseas Private Investment Corporation (OPIC). This corporation is an anomaly within our system of government in that it is an independent and financially self-supporting corporation wholly owned by the U.S. government. The purpose of OPIC is to offer financing insurance to U.S. companies that want to bid projects in Third World countries. Many underdeveloped nations require foreign project bidders to post performance bonds, usually in the form of stand-by Letters of Credit. The Overseas Private Investment Corporation will guarantee payment thus protecting U.S. contractors from arbitrary or unfair drawing against these letters of credit. Contractors may also obtain insurance against other risks often associated with the Third World, specifically, currency inconvertibility, confiscation of assets, confiscation of bank accounts, war, revolution, insurrection, and civil strife. In addition, should the host government fail to adjudicate a dispute in accordance with the contract, the OPIC insurance will assure you of payment.

If additional or more detailed information regarding the Overseas Private Investment Corporation's services is desired, its toll-free number is 800/424-6742.

The U.S. government is attempting to help many Third World countries pull themselves up by their own boot straps. A large part of this effort is in the form of bilateral economic assistance administered by the International Development Cooperation Agency (IDCA). This administrative body forms a part of the Agency for International Development (AID). AID, established in 1961 by Congress, was charged with responsibility for giving assistance to foreign governments who were friendly toward the United States but who were economically less developed than the United States and its industrialized allies. In total nineteen countries were eligible to receive funds. The list has not greatly changed since the program's inception. Under this program American exporters are eligible to receive payment guarantees for their participation. However, in order to participate, the exporter should be aware that the goal of the program is to encourage direct U.S. private investment in the underdeveloped country of interest. This proviso applies to licensing arrangements as well as to equity investments. Exporters who are receptive to establishing licensing or equity arrangements in a Third World country are required to make a proposal to IDCA. Their proposal must contain information demonstrating that the proposed activity will reasonably contribute to the development of the host country and that the host country has shown a willingness to promote the economic, political, and social concerns of its people. In other words, the host government must express willingness to take over the work of the U.S. exporter at some future date when it has demonstrated the ability to competently manage its own affairs.

The International Development Cooperation Agency implements its programs by making billions of dollars available in the form of loans to foreign governments, financing institutions, and to U.S. and foreign firms. These loans generally have a forty- year term with interest charged at 3%. However, should it be necessary to grant any grace periods of repayment, the interest drops to only 2%. Should a foreign government be the recipient of the dollars, it may reloan them to its local recipients at the prevailing rate within its own country.

Due to the sophisticated nature of this program, it is not recommended that the beginning exporter become involved with it, nor is it recommended for the faint of heart. However, the program is capable of doing a great deal of good for all parties if the need between business and government dovetails. As an example, during the late 1980s a new disease called Acquired Immune Deficiency Syndrome (AIDS) was discovered in the heart of Africa. The disease was being spread rapidly throughout the world. Because this particular disease has an incubation period recognized in the area of ten years, it is extremely difficult to test drugs and treatment that can cure the disease in less time than its incubation period. Therefore, it behooves research universities and drug manufacturers to test procedures and systems without the restraint of typical lengthy procedures mandated prior to research on human beings. During this timeframe, several firms and institutions have established operations in Zaire to test experimental drugs and procedures on human recipients. This is only being done because of the severity of the disease and the long incubation period associated with it. These programs, however, meet the criteria established by IDCA to benefit from U.S. funds. The programs will improve the education, technical, and professional skills, and the ability of the indigenous population. They are undertaking a major social development by attempting to control disease. They improve and expand existing institutions and organizations, which also will result in the improved life of the inhabitants. They will improve the physical facilities required for continued economic growth.

This is an excellent example of how our government and private industry can work together with underdeveloped nations for the benefit of all mankind. Additional information regarding IDCA loans can be acquired by contacting the Assistant Administrator, Bureau for Program and Policy Coordination at 202/632-0482.

A variation of the IDCA program is its Trade and Development Program (TDP). This program is similar to AID except it is directed at friendly middle-income developing countries. This program is designed to help finance planning services by these countries that will lead to the export of U.S. products or services. These programs center around grants rather than loans and are on a country to country basis. American exporters can only benefit from them by selling their goods or services to the recipient country. Recipients are required to use the loan money to purchase U.S. goods and services. The U.S. government is looking for a return of 75 to 100 times the amount of its grant to be spent with U.S. firms participating. For more information and to determine if there are any recipient countries looking for your type of goods, contact the Trade and Development Program International Development Cooperation Agency at 703/235-3663.

Of limited interest to the novice exporter are several programs sponsored by the Department of Agriculture. One such program is PL-480: Food for Peace. Under this program food is made available to those countries that cannot feed themselves and in those situations where disaster or emergency conditions exist, such as earthquakes and typhoons. In these instances loans or grants are given to the country in need with the provision that the funds be used to purchase food stuffs from American food merchants. Actual procurement is by competitive bid. In order to get on the bid list for projects as they come up from time to time, it is necessary to be named on the USDA (U.S. Department of Agriculture) list of potential vendors. For information regarding this procedure, contact the Director Kansas City ASCS Commodity Office, U.S. Department of Agriculture, 816/926-6301.

Also of interest to the beginning exporter of agricultural products is the Department of Agriculture's three programs that fall under the Commodity Credit Corporation (CCC)-Commercial Export Program. All three of these programs provide for short term financing of American agricultural products and, to a lesser extent of forest products. The first program is the Export Credit Guarantee Program (GSM). Under this program private U.S. commercial bank financing is guaranteed by CCC's borrowing authority. The second program is the Export Credit Sales Program (GSM-5). The only difference between this program and GSM-102 is in the interest rates and/or fees charged the importer or the importer's bank. This is an administrative function and is of little interest to the actual exporter. The third and last program is know as the Blended Credit Program. This is a blend of GSM-102 and GSM-5. Utilization of this program is recommended when specific commodities must compete with other exporting countries whose exports are subsidized. This program will help the American farm products exporter compete on a more equal footing with his world competition. Questions regarding these programs should be directed to the CCC Operations Division, Export Credits, Foreign Agricultural Service U.S. Department of Agriculture, 202/447-3224.

The remaining government programs are not designed to specifically guarantee the United States' exporter payment for his goods shipped abroad. Rather, they are designed to help other countries develop their own economies, usually by making loans available to these countries at low rates or on concessionary terms so as not to deplete their foreign exchange accounts. However, once loans or grants are given, the awarding group generally publishes a list of them and American exporters are encouraged to bid for this business. Should orders materialize, the exporter can normally employ one of the loan guarantee programs offered by the SBA, Eximbank, or the FCIA. Exporters should make themselves aware of all the opportunities their government makes available to them in order to increase their overseas sales.

Among the programs offered to other countries that may result in sales of U.S. products abroad, are three that are awarded under the auspices of the World Bank Group. First is the International Bank for Reconstruction and Development (IBRD). IBRD will extend loans to member governments, and to private or public companies within these countries. Should loans be made to private enterprises they must be guaranteed by the member government. These loans are granted on conventional banking terms and generally they are used for very high-priority specific projects, such as dams, construction, and so forth. IBRD projects almost always stipulate that procurement of goods and services for projects be by competitive bid and open to bidders from all member countries. Bidding invitations are generally issued to the member country's embassies located in the country in which the project will commence. It is up to each of the embassies to see that the invitations are disseminated to the appropriate bidders within their own country. If you would like to be made aware of any bids that are planned for the future write to:

IBRD & IDA
1818 H St. NW
Washington, D.C. 20433

Ask for the bank's "Summaries of Future Projects in Advance of Approvals." Should you like to know which loans have been approved, refer to the bank's press releases. These press releases contain the names and addresses of the contacts in the country where the project is going to occur. You can be placed on the procurement list by contacting the address mentioned.

The World Bank Group's second program is offered through the International Development Association (IDA). Like the IBRD this group's charter is to promote economic development of member countries. The difference between the two programs lies in their qualifying of recipients. The IDA deals with less-developed member countries (those countries where the annual per capita income is less than the U.S. $725). Loans are made on concessionary terms so as not to impact their balance of payments position. These loans carry no interest, but do charge a .5% administrative fee. Invitations to bid are handled in an identical manner to the bidding for IBRD projects, as is the dissemination of the bidding information. Everything you need to know about these programs is available by writing:

World Bank Publications Office
Room H-2167
1818 H St. NW
Washington, D.C. 20433

The World Bank's last program is administered by the International Finance Corporation (IFC). This is a unique program and differs from the bank's other offerings by being directed entirely towards the private businessman, rather than his government. The IFC encourages private enterprises to grow in member developing countries by making loans and noncontrolling equity capital available to qualified firms. They also will provide underwriting and stand-by commitments in order to attract outside financing. Interest rates for these loans are at market rate, whereas equity capital is sold to private investors as deemed appropriate. Because there are no formal procurement procedures for the IFC, it is necessary for interested firms to contact the U.S. Department of Commerce field offices or the International Finance Corporation. The IFC has offices in Washington and in New York City. The Washington telephone number is 202/477-1234 and the New York number is 212/754-6008. Persons at either office will be pleased to assist you with your inquiries.

There are two remaining international organizations that offer programs of interest to the U. S. exporter: the Inter-American Development Bank (IDB) and the Asian Development Bank (ADB). The IDB was established to help Latin American countries improve their economic well being. Every country in Latin America, except Cuba, is a member of this bank. The funds that finance this operation are derived from the members with Latin America contributing 53% of the capital.[1] As with the operations of the World Bank mentioned earlier, the purpose of the IDB is to provide funds for its members in the form of longterm loans on a commercial basis or on concessionary terms. The Inter-American Development Bank has the option to require that up to 50% of its procurement come from its members. This gives the U.S. exporter the opportunity to bid competitively on projects financed in whole or in part by the IDB.

Information regarding pending projects, as well procedures for getting on the bid lists can be obtained by writing the:

Inter-American Development Bank
External Relations Office

> 808 17th St. NW
> Washington, D.C.

or by telephoning the External Relations Office at 202/634-8087.

The Asian Development Bank is the mirror image of the Inter-American Development Bank dealing, obviously, with Asia. Information on projects pending and instructions for bidding may be secured by contacting the:

> Office of the U.S. Director and
> Chief Information Officer
> Asian Development Bank
> P.O. Box 789
> Manila 2800
> Republic of the Philippines

SUMMARY

Hopefully you now understand both why you should export your products and the many incentive programs designed to help you export. Through exporting you will improve your economies of scale by,

> Selling more product, thereby increasing your need for raw materials, which you can purchase for less unit cost because you are purchasing in larger quantities. This can increase your profit margin because costs are lowered across the board, not just on those items you export. If you choose not to increase your profit margin you can lower your selling price and therefore, perhaps, become more competitive in your home market.

> Reducing or eliminating your slack periods of production due to seasonal swings in demand. This not only will increase your sales, but it will also allow you to schedule your production more efficiently.

> Spreading your marketing costs over a greater potential market. By purchasing more media, your rate should also be reduced, yielding further savings.

> Distribution costs will become a smaller percentage of gross sales because your fixed costs will be spread over the greater volume exporting creates. The additional costs of export distribution will be abated by the resulting increased sales.

> Many U.S. governmental agencies and international entities

exist to protect your foreign accounts' receivables, while introducing you to new markets for your products.

With all the available incentives for you to export, it is well worth the effort to learn how to actually begin exporting. The increased sales and experience you will gain through impementation of an aggressive export policy will be rewarding to your company and to you personally.

NOTES

Source: *"A Guide for Exporters and Investors, "Official U.S. and International Financing Institutions* (U.S. Department of Commerce, 1985).

1. Arthur W. Goodearl, "Foreign Trade Documentation and Finance," *International Trade Handbook* (Chicago and London: The Dartnell Corporation, 1963), p. 502.

Chapter 2
Determining International
Need for Your Products

Now that you are convinced that you should be exporting, the next step in actualizing it is to be certain that a need exists for your product in foreign markets. This chapter introduces the many services available to help you determine the true need for your company's product(s) abroad:

* U.S. government assistance
* Private assistance
* Foreign government assistance

Once you decide to investigate the opportunities that exist for your products abroad, your first inquiries should be with the Department of Commerce trade specialist for your area. All major cities have a Department of Commerce office staffed with professionals who know how to help you start exporting. The government is extremely interested in encouraging American firms to increase exports. It is no secret that we have had a balance of trade problem for several years. This shortage of exports (or excess of imports, depending on your point of view) occurs because U.S. citizens purchase more foreign goods than American companies export. Ideally the government would like to see the same amount of exports as imports. Because the imports exceed the exports, U.S. currency is increasingly in the hands of our foreign trading partners. In order to get it back we must export more. Therefore, the government really goes out of its way to help make it easy for you to market your products abroad.

When you sit down with a Trade Specialist, one of the first things he will want to know is whether you have received any inquiries from abroad for your product. Among the reasons most firms decide to look into the possibilities of export is foreign inquiry about their product(s).

Typically about half of the companies that express a first time interest in exporting do it because they have been approached by someone who has seen their product at an American trade show or in use at another American company. If you have been contacted in such a manner, the Trade Specialist will want to help you determine the sincerity of the party's interest and help you get started selling to him if it is in fact a legitimate situation. No doubt he will begin by suggesting that you obtain additional information through the Department's *World Traders Data Reports (WTDR's)*.

When you order one of these reports, a commercial attaché assigned to the embassy or consulate in the country where your potential distributor is located will personally do research to assist you. Among the facts he will document is the firm's reputation and payment history within the country. He will seek out trade and credit references and offer his opinion as to the suitability of the potential trading partner. Furthermore, he will document the year of the business' establishment, the product lines currently carried, the number of employees on the payroll, the company's reputation, and determine with which other American agents or companies he is dealing.

It must be pointed out that attachés try very hard to do the best job possible for you. You should be aware, however, that the report you get will only be as good as the person who prepared it and, occasionally, you may not be satisfied with the information. If you are inquiring about a company that has a long history of importing from the United States, it is entirely possible that the firms you are interested in are already in the embassy's file. Particularly in Europe, where there is so much trade going on and the embassies are so busy, it should not surprise you to learn that your inquiries will not be personally researched at all. Rather, a photocopy of the firm's existing file may be the only research provided. This may or may not be adequate. Its usefulness will no doubt be tempered by how long it has been in the file. Also, when you are dealing with many of the Third World nations or nonindustrialized nations in general, it is likely that the Department of Commerce's World Trader's Data Reports may be your only avenue for checking out the potential importer. Frequently, in these situations the information you receive is sketchy at best. Many of these countries just do not have sophisticated information available in order to provide you with what American firms would consider adequate history. Should you choose to continue a dialogue with a company that cannot furnish you with enough information to enable you to make a favorable decision, be sure to read the section of this book dealing with credit and collections because there are ways to protect yourself even though you know little about your trading partner.

Dealing with Russia, Eastern Bloc countries, and certain Asian countries require that you do all the checking and verifying yourself. But in these situations you will have to deal with a state trading company anyway. Payment from these trading companies is always difficult to negotiate because they do not have much hard currency, and dealing with anything other than an irrevocable documentary letter of credit is certain to promise slow pay. In these situations the question is not usually, "will I be paid?"

but, "when will I be paid?" More information on dealing with Communist countries can be located in chapter 16 entitled, "Foreign Political Considerations."

If you want verification of a foreign importer or distributor's creditworthiness other than through the Department of Commerce, consider using Dunn & Bradstreet's International Credit Reports. These reports are compiled by D & B personnel throughout the Free World and are maintained on a current basis. Dunn & Bradstreet sells this service in modules of twenty-five units. Each report uses multiple units. For example, if you wanted a credit report on a company in Canada, it would cost you one unit. However, if you wanted one in Japan it would cost six units. European companies cost two and one half units each. Therefore, if you wanted to do a credit report on a potential distributor in Japan and had purchased Dunn and Bradstreet's minimum of twenty-five units, you would still have nineteen units left to use on other foreign credit reports. These report programs are valid for twelve months from the time you first purchase them and the minimum cost for twenty-five units is currently U.S. $1,150 or U.S. $46 per unit. On the other hand, if you will be looking at a number of distributors in several countries over twelve months, it may be to your advantage to order fifty units at U.S. $1,850, in which case your cost per unit shrinks from U.S. $46 to U.S. $37.30. If you will only require one report, the Department of Commerce's report service is quite inexpensive. The Commerce Department currently charges only U.S. $75 per report. Of course, this will add up if you are considering multiple reports.

Dunn & Bradstreet also publishes *Principal International Business,* which lists and qualifies all major foreign firms. Of slightly less interest is their directory, *Europe's 5000 Largest Companies.* From the publisher who brings the world the foremost publication on ships comes Jane's *Major Companies of Europe.* All three of these directories should be available at your local library and can be used to locate potential importers for your products. Unless you have a commodity item or a knock-off of a major product, don't be surprised if your potential importer is not among the giant foreign firms. This is not necessarily bad. In fact, it can be to your advantage. If you have a product that is relatively unique and positioned in the marketplace so it is not subject to scrutiny by the major companies, you can be relatively assured that they will not bother competing with you abroad. Many companies have become quite large private enterprises by building a strong domestic operation and then branching out overseas. Companies that are not household names but are nevertheless well-known to many persons both at home and abroad are Marsh, Avery, Fasson, and Signode.

The commercial section of foreign embassies and their consulates located in major cities generally compile and have available lists of firms in their country. They will confirm your inquirers' existence and tell you if he is considered reputable.

Armed with this information you should be able to determine the credibility of the company that wants to represent you abroad. Other chapters of this book deal with how to safely begin commercial relations with overseas companies.

If you are merely inquiring into the possibility of exporting in order to increase your market, the Trade Specialist will begin by familiarizing you with several publications, programs, and services offered to novice exporters by the Department of Commerce.

No doubt one of the first items your Trade Specialist will bring up is the Department of Commerce's Export Mailing List Service (EMLS). This service is available in two formats. One format known as Export Mailing Lists consist of on-line lists of potential importers for your products based wholly on your marketing criteria. These lists may be purchased for a nominal fee in the form of computer printouts, mailing labels, or computer tape. This information originates from Lockheed's custom "Dialog" program. The U.S. Department of Commerce has purchased the right to access this extremely complete data base in order to provide American exporters with comprehensive lists of interested foreign importers on a company to company basis. These lists do contain general importers but, more importantly, they identify those companies that are interested in importing or expanding their current lines in order to service their end-users more completely.

The information contained in the Dialog system is also available in the form of *Trade Lists*. These directories list companies either by country or by product grouping. Therefore you can look at a single industry around the world or a single country across all product sectors.[1]

The conscientious use of the EMLS service can provide you with comprehensive mailing lists enabling you to do your own search for prospective marketers for your products. Among the information spelled out in the lists is whether the companies listed are manufacturers, agents, retailers, service firms, or government agencies.

Until recently, the Department of Commerce could provide you with a lead service if you so desired. This service was called the Trade Opportunities Program (TOP). Due to budget limitations, this service was sold to *The Journal of Commerce* in August 1987. The information formerly contained in the TOP program is now available on a subscription basis through the Journal of Commerce. Persons interested in subscribing should direct their inquiries to *The Journal of Commerce and Commercial News*, 110 Wall Street, New York, NY 10005. Subscriptions at the time of writing were U.S. $195 annually.

The heart of this service begins with the gathering of information at the embassy or consulate level where commercial officers world wide seek information that they deem important to U.S. exporters. Local infomation is gathered and telexed daily to a computer center located in Washington, D.C., sorted and forwarded directly to the Journal of Commerce for publication the next day. The TOP Bulletin, now renamed *Export*

Opportunities, categorizes leads according to Standard Industrial Classification (SIC) as published by the Bureau of the Census.

For example, let us assume that you are a manufacturer of boats looking for export opportunities. A typical *Export Opportunies* listing would list "Boats & Boat Repair Services"; the countries that have expressed interest in looking at American exports of boats would be detailed as to the type of opportunity and given the notice number. In our example assume the opportunity is "Direct Sales to End-User" and the notice number is 056583.

This listing would then give you the name of the country making the inquiry, and a brief description of the need,

> Five ea. speedboats (twin screw diesel yachts). Buyer is a member of a reputable group of companies and plans to establish a touristic cruise fleet composed of up to five inboard powered cabin cruisers (length of each cruiser to be around 10 meters), to operate in Turkey's Aegean and Mediterranean regions. Interested U.S. suppliers should send catalogs and price info.

This description would be followed with specifics regarding to whom to reply, their address, and telephone number. It may also list their telex number if they have one and request a copy of your literature and other information to be forwarded to the commercial officer in the embassy or consulate responsible for creating the lead.

If a "rifle" approach is preferred to a "shot gun" approach, your Trade Specialist will want you to consider the use of the department's Agent/Distributor Service (ADS).

When you request an ADS search it will be necessary for you to provide the Department of Commerce with appropriate literature, video tape, or other material for presentation to potential overseas agents. You should also include a short benefits statement and a complete description of the type of representation you are seeking. Upon receipt of this information the Commerce Department will forward it to the embassy in the country in which you are interested in locating representation. The embassy, in turn, will assign your search to a commercial officer who will identify up to six potential representatives for you. The actual number of potential distributors or agents will depend on several factors including the competence of the commercial officer, the quality of the supportive information you provided, the local market conditions, and the demand for your product. If no possible representation exists, this information will also be passed on to you--although personally I would suspect this response.

Unless you have a product that is easily described, with obvious benefits, this writer has a problem with this type of service. My concern is that you will be relying on a quasi-disinterested third party to do your selling. You are depending on the commercial officer to totally understand

and adequately present your needs, frequently in English to a person or firm whose native tongue is other than English. You are relying on him to identify the only avenue of distribution for your product. For many potential exporters this approach leaves to much too chance.

As an example, consider that you manufacture a product that is traditionally sold through specialty stores in the United States. It is natural for you to assume that foreign distribution would be the same. However, it is a very real possibility that the country in which you are trying to establish commercial relations does not have any specialty stores. Perhaps the commercial officer will report that there is no market for your products in the country. However, if a more complete understanding of your product existed in the mind of the commercial officer, he might have been able to deduce that in this situation the proper avenue of marketing should be through pharmacies.

For those of you who have products or specialized distribution in the United States several other programs, such as trade shows, are offered by the Commerce Department.

If you want hands on participation in the introduction of your company's products abroad, exhibition in one of the many trade shows is a good route to take. There are hundreds of annual trade shows held throughout the world. The best way to determine which trade show to exhibit in is to contact the organizers of domestic trade shows in which you already participate. Generally, they will know many of the international shows that are similar to theirs. Once you have determined which shows are held in countries that are of interest to you, it is as easy as writing the foreign fair's organizing body for literature, demographics, and costs. Your participation in the fairs would certainly be welcome and the host country usually attempts to make it easy for you import your products into the country for the duration of the show.

However, as an alternative to direct entry into the show, you may want to contact your Trade Specialist at the Department of Commerce to determine if there will be a U.S. pavilion at that specific show. The Department of Commerce deems these fairs certified and assists American exporters with participation. Certified trade fairs are considered a leading international event with a minimum of twenty U.S. exhibitors. Commerce and embassy assistance is available to the exhibitor and staff can provide exhibit space, meeting rooms, translators, and hospitality suites. Embassy personnel will also promote the U.S. participants through marketing efforts including direct mail, publicity releases, and field contacts with potential distributors, agents, and end-users.

Participation in certified trade shows can be a great way to test the water for your products in a given foreign market. These shows are always heavily attended and most foreign buyers make an effort to stop by the American pavilion to see what is new. Participation in these fairs gives you firsthand experience in establishing relations with other commercial firms that may be distributors or agents for you. They also expose you to other

American companies already doing foreign business and the information they can impart to you can be valuable. The interaction you gain by actually talking and demonstrating your products to persons on their home territory cannot be equaled by sending literature to them or by third party presentations. No other opportunity will enable you to meet your local competition and assess it so easily.

This writer highly recommends that you participate in several international certified trade fairs in order establish commercial relations abroad. If funds are a limiting factor and preclude direct participation in trade fairs, the Department of Commerce can arrange for your participation in several special table top shows that take place from time to time in the major embassies around the world. Many of the embassies will have catalogue or video shows for particular industries scheduled throughout the year. If your product falls within the guidelines of a given show, you may exhibit your catalogues or videos. All leads that are generated during the show will be forwarded to you.

The cost of entering these shows is nominal and does not amount to much more than the cost of the literature and the postage to get it to the embassy. It should not, therefore, surprise you that the results are usually disappointing. Whenever you participate in trade fairs that have a broad appeal, your specific product will not have a good opportunity for maximum exposure. Many potential foreign distributors are busy and feel they do not have the time to travel to the American embassy to look at product literature that may or may not be applicable to their situation. Frequently, these people are bombarded not only with information on shows at American embassies, but also by information from shows at other foreign embassies. If you cannot justify entering an international show, you should seriously consider sticking with the Journal of Commerce's Export Opportunities program and the Department of Commerce's Export Mailing List Service for locating foreign representation. The only exception this author would suggest is if the country in which you are interested is a developing nation and does not have any trade fairs of international stature.

Another Department of Commerce service offered by your Trade Specialist is the Trade Missions Programs. These are really very well-organized tours of from five to twelve individuals representing their companies to several markets. The participants are always from one industry or several allied industries. These trips are beneficial to the beginning exporter in that they expose him to several countries, give him the opportunity to meet his peers, exchange information, and establish business relations in one or more marketplaces. There are two types of programs currently being offered: the United States Specialized Trade Missions and State and Industry-Organized Government-Approved (S&IOGA) Trade Missions.

Specialized missions are planned by the Commerce Department, which selects the industry and the itinerary based on its evaluation of maximum potential. Individual appointments between participants and prospects are scheduled on a hourly basis with keen attention to servicing the needs of both. In addition, foreign government officials involved with state purchasing and bureaucrats who make policy decisions are introduced to the participants.

The S&IOCA tours are similar to the Specialized Trade Missions except they are planned in concert with other quasi-governmental entities such as Chambers of Commerce, trade associations, and state development agencies. The Commerce Department takes care of the logistics and relies on the embassies and Foreign Commercial Service (FCS) for local promotion of the tours.

For those firms that would like to promote themselves abroad but feel the Trade Missions Programs are not technically oriented enough to fairly present their product offerings, there is the United States Seminal Missions. Again, this program resembles the Specialized Missions except in its thrust, which is toward foreign governments' questions regarding development or industrial problems occurring in the host country's economy. These missions are led by a "U.S. Seminar Team," which is made up of representatives of high technology industries. They give seminars on the latest developments within their industry and relate how these developments are germane to their hosts. This program has become popular with many large high-tech companies and may be of little interest to those that do not have a highly specialized nitch within high technology.

On a less sophisticated level, the U.S. & Foreign Commercial Service publishes *Commercial News USA*. As with other Department of Commerce endeavors, *Commercial News USA* represents another well-founded effort to promote exports from the United States. Generally, this small magazine only introduces new American products to overseas prospects. It is published monthly and a few interesting products are selected by the Voice of America for broadcasting.

Several times a year *Commercial News USA* also publishes an entire issue dedicated to the products of a single industry deemed interesting to its foreign audience.

The Commerce Department will tell you this publication is distributed to 240 embassies and consulates located in 96 countries and to over 200,000 interested foreign parties. Although this may be true, the majority of the copies probably never get into the hands of serious potential clients. The magazine is only printed in English and although a few of the local embassies may provide translations into native tongues, this activity is limited at best. It is a poor substitute for other more productive activities such as the TOP program and exhibition at trade fairs.

The Commerce Department has several other programs that it may recommend to you from time to time but, in general, they are redundant or just variations of other programs. Also, at the time of this writing the department is in the midst of attempting to upgrade all its reporting procedures from manual to computer. This has resulted in some delays and confusion regarding its standard offerings. The Trade Specialists are being trained in the use of computers, but until they are all trained and until all systems are up and running, there will continue to be problems. It is anticipated that it will be several years before they are completely on line with their computers in Washington. No doubt ultimately the computerization of the Department of Commerce will greatly improve the delivery of its service, but until that time, American exporters will have to tolerate some inconvenience and spotty programs.

The beginning exporter should also be aware of companies and individuals who appear to offer some of the same services that the Commerce Department does at a lower charge. Not all, but many of these operations are shams. Frequently, such firms will arrange to provide companies with leads for foreign representation, which they claim were generated by their own sources overseas. They also claim that the leads are more comprehensive than those of the Department of Commerce. Be cautious! More often than not these persons do nothing more than go through copies of TOP notices and TOP Bulletins and copy those that may be of interest to you. They can accomplish this because all the information printed in these notices and bulletins is not copyrighted and is considered to be in the public domain. This behavior can net a quick proft for unscrupulous individuals.

The United States has a long history of exporting agricultural products. Although this position has been challenged recently by other countries that are also able to produce surplus food, export still represents a tremendous opportunity for the American farmer and the companies that process or otherwise handle agricultural products.

Under the Department of Agriculture there exists the Foreign Agricultural Service (FAS). This service is made up of trade officers, commodity analysts, and marketing specialists. They have counterparts in many of the embassies and consulates around the world. As with most government services, one of the primary duties of these individuals is to gather facts and disseminate information. They also assist in arranging foreign contacts and provide promotional assistance on an as needed basis.

The Foreign Agricultural Services's Commodity and Marketing Programs (CMP) consist of six divisions that handle specific commodity-related information. These divisions are:

Dairy, Livestock & Poultry
Grain & Feed
Horticulture & Tropical Products
Oilseeds & Products
Tobacco, Cotton, & Seed
Forest Products

A telephone call or letter to any of these divisions will provide you with information regarding analysis of specific foreign consumption and also indicate what the Department of Agriculture can currently help you with in terms of support or marketing.

Through Agriculture's Export Programs Division (EPD) American agricultural products are promoted at trade fairs and trade groups. One of the problems that constantly faces exporters of branded products is the labeling requirements demanded by many overseas governments. EDP through its Label Clearance Program, can smooth the way by helping evaluate the acceptability of your existing labels and recommending changes if necessary so your product will comply with the foreign government's needs.

Foreign Agricultural Service's sales teams will invite five of six firms to work with them in particular markets that their research has shown to be particularly receptive to importing specific American agricultural products. A trade mission will be established with FAS handling all the details such as travel arrangements, preparation and printing of literature, rental of rooms, halls, and making appointments with appropriate buyers. Through their Export Incentive Program (EIP) they will even reimburse exporters for a portion of the expenses incurred in promoting their products abroad.

Just as the Department of Commerce publishes an abundance of material, so does the Department of Agriculture through the Agricultural Information and Marketing Services (AIMS) division. These publications include:

Foreign Contacts, a worldwide list of foreign importers who regularly handle specific commodities.

Product Publicity, a description of products that are new to export, distributed to over thirty five thousand foreign importers.

Trade Leads, leads that are acquired by agricultural officers stationed in embassies or consulates around the world. The leads come from foreign importers who have expressed a desire to import specific products from the United States.

International Marketing Profiles (IMPS), provides specific detailed statistical information on agricultural trade activity.

Buyer Alert Program, is a means of forwarding information regarding American suppliers to interested foreign buyers. This program operates very quickly utilizing the extensive telecommunications capabilities of the U.S. government.

Several other programs are sponcered by Commerce and Agriculture as well as other departments of the government. However, these programs are usually skewed toward firms that are familiar with export and with handling large construction projects. For example, the Agency for International Development finances large scale projects such as irrigation, hospitals, and so forth in underdeveloped countries. The Trade and Development Program funds studies and plans for large-scale energy projects, mineral and mining programs, large agribusiness, and basic industrial programs.

In addition, some assistance can often be realized through state and local government. Many states and cities have established policies to help their local industry export its products abroad. Most of these plans are geared toward Europe or Japan, but they can be a source of leads and some states and cities even maintain missions in foreign countries. These entities frequently work with foreign Chambers of Commerce and other business organizations to establish trade missions to the United States and specifically to their states and cities as a means of making direct contact with potential suppliers of American goods and services. The missions are especially popular in areas that have a concentration of specific industry such as Silicone Valley, Boston, Dallas, and Austin, which all exhibit high concentrations of electronic technology or defense.

While attempting to establish the need for your products abroad, do not overlook the value of your friends and business acquaintances who have export experience. You can learn a great deal from their dealings and experience. These persons may already have contacts from whom you can benefit. Many times the importer and marketer of one product can become a resource for a related product offering. If such a person or company is already known to a person you trust, you will be farther along in your search for representation than you would ever be starting from scratch. If you deal with one of the country's larger banks, have your banker introduce you to the international bankers within the bank. These people will be happy to inform you of any knowledge they have regarding other clients who are successfully exporting. They may even be able to provide you with a list of potential companies to contact. An extremely helpful banker will even offer to contact his correspondent banks in countries that are of interest to you and request a list of prospects.

Both freight forwarders and American Chambers of Commerce maintain offices abroad and are generally willing to help you locate distribution. Your library is also a source of information. Many trade associations and industry periodicals publish foreign editions or distribute their English language magazines abroad. There are also a number of international directories that list foreign representatives. *The Business Publication* lists most international publications; peruse it and determine to which publications you should subscribe.

The Business Publication
Standard Rate and Data Service
5201 Old Orchard Road
Skokie, Illinois 60076[2]

Another potential source is your advertising agency or any large agency with overseas accounts. Although these firms may have foreign clients or American clients advertising abroad, generally the account executives themselves do not have specific knowledge of your product or the markets in which you may be interested. However, they can be very helpful, if you need samples of magazines or literature prepared for foreign consumption and they will be very willing to talk with you about developing a program of marketing abroad. However, I believe that this type of assistance, though well-intentioned, is usually too premature for the beginning exporter. You must first determine the marketability of your product in specific markets before you begin to advertise. There is a strong need for literature prepared in your prospect's native language, but this is best handled by the company in the market in which you will be dealing. Later, when you become more sophisticated and are represented in several markets it will be time to begin thinking in terms of an international marketing program. Chapter 10 will discuss this process at length.

SUMMARY

Your greatest ally in getting started exporting your company's products is the U.S. government! Through the Department of Commerce and the Department of Agriculture numerous programs exist to help you determine the need for your company's products in foreign markets. These programs include:

> World Traders Data Reports (WTDR)
> Export Mailing Lists (EMLS)
> Trade Lists
> Agent/Distributor Service (ADS)
> Trade Missions Programs
> Specialized Trade Missions
> State and Industry-Organized Government-Approved (S&IOGA) Trade Missions
> Seminal Missions
> Commercial News USA
> Foreign Agricultural Service (FAS)
> Commodity and Marketing Programs (CMP)
> Export Programs Division (EPD)
> Label Clearance Program
> Export Incentive Program (EIP)
> Agricultural Information and Marketing Services (AIMS)

The selective use of several of these programs will launch you on the course to profitable exporting. Getting started is similar to conducting an orchestra. You must be certain to use all the instruments that are necessary to properly reproduce the sounds the composer envisioned when he wrote the piece. You must use all the resources available to you to determine which markets are best-suited for your initial thrust into the foreign markets. Then you must determine the best way to distribute your products within those markets. To do this, use your Commerce Trade Specialists or your Agricultural Specialists. Use your business associates' assistance, your bankers, your trade associations, your library, and your freight forwarders.

NOTES

1. As of this writing, trade lists are not "on-line." The information is approximately three to five years old. The companies referenced may still be in business, but no guarantees nor warranties are made by Commerce regarding these listings.

2.   U.S. Department of Commerce, *A Basic Guide to Exporting* (Washington, D.C., Superintendent of Documents, U.S. Government Printing Office, September 1986), p. 33.

Chapter 3
Alternatives to Establishing
Your Own Export Department

This chapter examines alternatives available to American companies that want to export but would like to test the water first. Specifically this chapter discusses the advantages and disadvantages of using the services of commission agents or export management companies.

Actually, if you manufacture a product that is a component of another product, you are probably already exporting. More than likely the product, of which yours represents a portion, is already finding its way abroad through your host's export.

COMMISSION AGENTS

Commission agents purchase products for export. They may represent foreign buyers who are looking for specific products or they may represent American companies that are seeking distribution without the cost associated with direct exportation. As a general rule, commission agents represent commodity items such as food stuffs, electric motors, appliances, and other items that are easily available on a competitive bid basis. In fact, many so-called commission agents are actually foreign government agencies. All the Communist countries function in this manner. Each East European country, for example, will have several agencies whose function is to provide specific needs for their government-run industries. These agencies usually have tongue- twisting names such as, Chemolimpex, Chentrotex, Ceskoslovenska Kermmika, and Schiffscommerz. Don't let the names intimidate you because they are usually quite descriptive of the commodities the agencies are responsible for purchasing. Chemolimpex imports chemicals for Hungary whereas Schiffscommerz imports nautical items for the German Democratic Republic (East Germany).

Because all Communist countries lack hard currency, they are limited on items they can actually import from the West; it literally requires an act of government. It is very difficult for you as an American businessman to create a market for your products in these countries. Almost exclusively, you will only be able to make a sale in such countries after they have come to you for a price quotation.

Consider the U.S. manufacturer of label printing machinery that invented and patented a machine for imprinting bibliographic cards used in libraries. The demand for this machine was great and the machines slowly found their way into the Eastern bloc countries. In the world of politics there are certain countries that have satisfactory relations with both the East and the West. One such country is Finland. It trades a great deal with Russia and other Communist bloc countries. It was natural for the distributor of this machine in Finland to sell some product to Russia, and because it was not against the export license requirements, there was no reason to object to these sales. However, because hard currency is so scarce and everyone likes a deal, some of the state trading agencies began to inquire about purchasing the machines directly from the U. S. manufacturer. A great deal of commerce developed that is still going on today, fifteen years later.

This story illustrates how you will most likely begin exporting to Communist-controlled countries. Other than state-controlled trading agents, commission agents are the proverbial middlemen. They locate products for their clients and receive a commission for their service. They do not buy for their own account, nor do they become involved in your payments.

As an alternative to direct exporting, sales through commission agents is not very attractive. The agents are usually limited in the commodities they represent and frequently do not have all the distribution they represent themselves to have. They do not like to handle competing product lines and unless the market for your product is very large, there is little opportunity for them to make substantial commissions.

Commission agents have done very well in the arms brokerage business. They frequently work with foreign governments to acquire weapons that cannot be purchased directly from another government. The arms merchant receives a commission based on his success or failure in acquiring needed weapons systems. Most of these types of agents are monitored and otherwise closely scrutinized by the United States to be certain they are not selling technology that would be detrimental to the United States or that is contrary to official government policy.

Unless you have a product whose potential customers the commission agent can easily identify, or a product from which he can make a great deal of money, you probably do not want a commission agent.

EXPORT MANAGEMENT COMPANIES (EMCs)

For the manufacturer who wants to market his products abroad but does not want to dedicate the time necessary to develop his own distribution, an export management company may be exactly what he needs. Export management companies come in many sizes and with many different expertises.

If there is such a thing as a typical EMC, it will be small and specialize in marketing noncompeting products to one country, region, or to one industry. Many export management companies function similarly to commission agents in that they may be compensated for their services by receiving a commission on the products sold. However, most will provide more services such as export documentation, freight forwarding, and occasionally, collection of accounts receivable.

Export management companies generally have a network of clients abroad and can offer the domestic manufacturer instant distribution of his products. Of course this only applies to those manufacturers who have a product for which there is an existing market. EMCs are not too effective at creating markets for new technology, or at establishing marketing programs to promote products abroad. This is because they see themselves as conduits for distributing products rather than marketing departments for corporations.

An export management company may be a viable solution for the manufacturer of farm implements. In this illustration the manufacturer can produce his standard product, offer it to an EMC that specializes in selling farm implements to countries with large agricultural bases or developing nations that need farm equipment in order to feed themselves. Here the export management company can offer your products to its network of importers and negotiate price and terms. The manufacturer need only concern himself with producing the equipment. On the other hand, however, the manufacturer of new devices for repairing printed circuit boards may not be satisfied with the efforts of an export management company because it will be necessary to instruct the prospective clients on the advantages and use of the repair kit before sales can be realized. When it is necessary to train or to convince a buyer that a product will benefit him, in general EMCs do not have the time or the desire to develop the sale. EMCs like to work with commodity items that do not require a great deal of marketing or product knowledge.

Export management companies, as stated earlier, may be compensated by commission or they may receive a discount and purchase for their own account and then export. In this latter situation, only the largest companies can afford the cash flow necessary to operate.

The history of the U.S. economy is such that large export management companies never developed to fill a need. This is because the United States is in itself such a large market. Only the largest firms have a tradition of export, whereas the smaller firms have been content to market only within the boundaries of America. On the other hand, the Japanese never had a large domestic population and their tradition was to export. Therefore, they developed very large EMCs known as trading companies. For them the indirect exporting system has been beneficial as a look around the typical American household will attest.

In 1982 the government became concerned enough with Japan's successes in establishing export trading companies that it decided to create the Office of Export Trading Company Affairs (OETCA). This department within the International Trade Administration was established under the Export Trading Company Act. The stated purpose of this act was to stimulate exports by encouraging the formation of export trading companies. To promote companies to form such entities, the act expanded the opportunities available to finance such operations, primarily by permitting bank holding companies to invest in them. The act also made a significant advance in fostering foreign trade by limiting a trading company's exposure to antitrust legislation: specifically the Sherman Anti-Trust Act and the FTC Act.

The new ability of bank holding companies to make direct equity investments in export trading companies has been a boon to the formation of such companies. However, to date their success has been limited as banks have hesitated due to the current uncertainties of foreign exchange.

A listing of export trading companies is available through OETCA in the form of the Contact Facilitation Service (CFS). This is a directory that is updated annually and lists the name and addresses of all export trading companies.

The Department of Commerce working in concert with the Department of Justice also will issue Certificates of Review, which enable the holder to be immune from prosecution for antitrust activities as long as the implementation of the activity does not compromise U.S. federal or state antitrust provisions. The certificates also reduce the potential liability from treble damages to single damages.

SUMMARY

Given all the advantages and disadvantages of indirect exporting, ultimately it will be up to you to decide which form of exporting will provide the greatest sales and profits for your company. If you manufacture a commodity product, it may not be necessary for you to export directly yourself. However, if you manufacture an item that requires marketing support and product training, you will probably want to establish your own export department and overseas marketing plan.

As far as the newly-founded Export Trading Companies are concerned, you would be best advised to procure a copy of either the *Export Trading Company Guidebook* or the *Contract Facilitation Service Directory,* both of which are available from the Department of Commerce.

Chapter 4
Methods Available to You for
Selling Your Products Abroad

In this chapter we discuss your options in selecting the type of representation you require abroad. We will examine the pros and cons of the following types of representatives:

Manufacturer's Agent
Export Merchant
Export Commission House
Export Broker (Food Stuffs)
Commission Representative
Distributor

MANUFACTURER'S AGENT

The overseas manufacturer's agent, also known as a manufacturer's representative, is very similar to the representative you might already be working with in the United States. Commercial arrangements with these types of agents can be either formal or informal. Formal relations require that you negotiate a contract between your company and the representative. Be very cautious before you sign any contracts with foreign agents. Most countries have laws that are skewed in favor of the agent and make it almost impossible to terminate relations with an unsatisfactory agent. This is particularly true in Latin America and in Japan. If you do not exercise caution before you cement your agreements, one day you may find yourself both unable to find new representation, and liable for paying severe penalties to the terminated agent. These penalties are usually in the form of compensation for several years after the commercial relationship ceases. If the country in which you are dealing has trade treaties with the United States, you may be sued in the United States for nonperformance of your contract. If no applicable treaties exist, you will, at the very least, be precluded from conducting any business in the future in this country.

This writer has personal knowledge of one firm that established a manufacturing facility in Japan. The company became dissatisfied with its partners, bought out its stock shares, thus making the business entity a majority-owned American company in Japan. However, the management of the company was never able to generate sufficient sales to satisfy the parent company, it was decided to close down the operation and fill the current need by exporting from the United States. To this company's surprise, upon being informed of the intended closing, the Japanese government notified them that to do so it would have to continue to pay its Japanese employees until they reached the retirement age of sixty-five. The American firm would also have to continue to be responsible for the social charges they were obligated to pay under their equivalent of a welfare program. Under the circumstances this firm had no real choice except to continue to operate a very unsatisfactory and unprofitable subsidiary. Fifteen years later the Japanese company is still limping along.

The moral of this story is for you to be certain of the implication of any agreement that you sign. You should consult with an appropriate law firm familiar with employment contracts, and agent contracts before you enter into agreements. There are numerous excellent American law firms doing business in Western Europe and Japan; any of them would be pleased to assist you. In countries that do not have any American law firms, contact a local attorney and get an opinion of any proposed agreements. If you need the name of a reputable local firm, first try one of America's largest firms. They will almost certainly have a list of suitable firms. Failing this, find out which larger American manufacturers are currently doing business in the subject country and contact them to determine which firm they used to establish their commercial relations.

Informal relationships are not fraught with as many problems as formal relations and frequently are advantageous to both parties. Informal relations imply that there is no written contract. In these situations the agent, as well as the exporter, is free to change lines whenever he chooses. The agent, however, does feel that he is at risk for nonpayment of his commission for sales made but not delivered until after termination. Likewise, the manufacturer is skeptical that while he is paying the agent commissions, the agent may no longer be working to promote his products. In this situation there is risk on both sides, but the exposure is limited to only a few months. Informal relations are not recommended unless both parties know each other well. Perhaps you have worked with the agent while he was representing another company and you were employed there. Internationally, as in your domestic dealing, there is no substitute for trust. Written contracts or not, if someone wants to take advantage of another he will usually find a way. Also, the lack of a written contract is no guarantee that the agent's country does not consider a long term relationship "as though there had been a formal contract."

Your best protection when dealing with agents is to be certain you completely understand what you are entering into. If this means seeking legal advice, by all means do so. If you have accurate information up front you will be less likely to "shoot yourself in the foot."

EXPORT MERCHANT

There are two types of export merchants: American and foreign. American export merchants are large companies that enter into exclusive agreements to represent you in one or several countries. Dealing with these types of firms is the same as dealing with a domestic customer. They will purchase from you under contract and pay you on your standard terms. In situations where you are using an export merchant you probably will not even know who your foreign client is because the export merchant will handle all arrangements for export. He will warehouse, repack, relabel, resell, reship, insure, and handle all documentation. This type of arrangement will generally give you quick sales volume but, of course, you lose control of all knowledge about your ultimate customer.

Selling your products via an export merchant works especially well with commodity items and not so well otherwise. For example, if your product ever requires service or warranty work, who will do it and at what cost? Failure to provide adequate product training or service could give your product a very bad image abroad. Worse, you may not even know that a problem exists because you, more than likely, will not really know your customers.

Foreign export merchants are not very different from American export merchants except that they may tend to feel they owe their loyalty to their clients in their home country, rather than to their American exporting client. Usually these firms will have offices and warehouses along one or two coasts of the United States where they assemble orders for export to their clients. Frequently these are foreign government-owned or sponsored and they are capable of helping American firms develop variations of their domestic products for sale abroad. For example, perhaps your product uses one or more electric motors. The foreign export merchant can help you evaluate motors available in the United States that can be substituted for their home market. They will also help determine which motors meet all their safety codes and electrical demands such as 220 volts 50 hertz with a special three-prong plug that is different from the three prong-plug used in the United States. Or, if you manufacture office seating, you may be unaware that in Germany it is mandatory that the base of the swivel-tilt chair consist of five prongs rather than the four-prong prevalent in the United States. West Germany also requires that an internal braking system be incorporated in the caster of its office chairs so that when a person vacates the chair, it will stay in the same place until it is occupied once again. In situations like this, external export merchants can be of great assistance as information resources.

EXPORT BROKER

An export broker is a specialist in arranging buy/sell agreements between domestic growers of food stuffs and foreign buyers. The export broker is usually a one man operation who assumes no liability for any parts of the transactions he helps to arrange. The broker is strictly the middleman. His stock in trade is that he knows buyers and he knows sellers and he can arrange deals; nothing more. Export brokers are compensated by receiving a commission on any transactions that result in a sale.

COMMISSION REPRESENTATIVE

The primary difference between a manufacturer's agent and a commission representative is the status of an "agent." When dealing with an agent you knowingly enter into contracts with the representative whereby he, in effect—if not actually—becomes an agent (read representative) of your company. With the commission representative you should be extremely cautious not to do anything that could be construed as appointing the representative as your agent. In fact, in your contract with the representative you should state that the representative, "is not an agent of (name) company." You must be very certain to inform the representative that under no circumstances is he to take any action to protect your patent or trademarks. He may be encouraged to report any possible infringements to you, but he personally should not take any action. These types of problems must be handled directly by your firm and your firm's attorneys. A commission representative must not be allowed to handle any advertising nor other marketing activities nor expenses. You should encourage his input regarding what you should do, but do not let him become personally involved in decisions nor action. If you fail to take these precautions, you could find yourself with an agent and not a commission representative should the day come when you want to change distribution forms or to just change representatives.

Commission representatives are usually paid quarterly or semiannually. They are never paid commissions on items that you have not yet shipped and received payment. Should you ever have a problem with a delinquent account, you should expect the assistance of the representative to collect the debt. When establishing a new account, the commission representative is expected to provide you with enough information to enable you to make credit judgments. Typically this information will include bank references, other commercial references, history of payments to other foreign vendors, and the representative's evaluation of the potential client's creditworthiness. The actual responsibility for shipment and payment remain with you, the manufacturer, and the client who actually receives and effects payment; not the representative.

It is usual for the exporter to provide literature, pamphlets, instruction sheets, and other printed promotional material to the representative, usually at no charge.

DISTRIBUTOR

The establishment of a network of foreign distributors for your products is this writer's preferred method of distribution. When you decide to establish distributors for your products around the world, you are making a commitment to stay in various foreign markets for a long period of time. Distributor arrangements are not to be taken lightly because the distributor is in fact representing you in the marketplace. Changes in representation should not be made indiscriminately as many foreign nationals are offended by frequent changes. A distributor becomes your company in the eyes of the foreign client. To him a change in distributors is tantamount to a change in vendors. Therefore, before you establish distributor relations, be certain that your selection is going to last for many years.

Unlike other forms of representation mentioned in this chapter, the distributor must be financially able to import your products for his own account. He must be able to maintain an adequate inventory of all new products and replacement parts as well. He should have a service organization that is fully trained in servicing your products. He must be able to ship or deliver your products throughout the territory that you have mutually-agreed he will service. He is in fact your agent and as such he will undoubtedly want to prepare literature and other media for local consumption. Certainly it is to your advantage to have selling materials in the local language because it helps promote the image that you are reliable and dependable. It will help your distributor build confidence with his clients that you are committed to the market and that you will not pull out of the territory and abandon him at some unforeseen future time.

Many authors will insist that you have a written contract with any distributors that you establish. Whereas it is always a good idea to have a written document stating each party's rights and obligations, in over fifteen years of establishing and working with distributors in eighty three countries this writer has found that a written contract was never necessary or even desirable. Contracts are always subject to interpretation. Interpretation is always a source of controversy, but when the contract is in a foreign language it is subject to even more misunderstanding. Do not make the assumption that, for example, because the British speak English the nuances and application of terms are the same as they are in the United States. Frequently the same words have different interpretations and the way ideas are phrased is different. Without a doubt the best contract is based on mutual respect between the parties. As long as this mutual respect exists, and as long as both parties in the arrangement believe it is mutually beneficial to do business, the relationship will prosper. Treat all your distributors fairly and evenly and you will not experience any serious contractual problems.

Many years ago this writer wanted to hold a distributors' meeting in Berlin for all the company's European distributors. My superior was adamantly opposed to this idea on the grounds that all the distributors would compare notes and find that their terms were not identical. He felt that to bring them together would create dissension. When pressed as to which distributors were being treated differently from the others, my superior realized that he could not find a single issue where such inequity existed. The meeting was held after much cajoling and discussion. It became the prototype for many subsequent meetings. The problems envisioned never occurred and the opportunity for the distributors from the various areas of Europe to meet and discuss common problems far outweighed any perceived minor inequities.

SUMMARY

The form of distribution with which you choose to begin exporting is not necessarily the same channel for distribution you will want for the long term. Your initial decision regarding form of distribution will be affected by the type of product you are exporting and the strength of your commitment to foreign markets.

The strongest commitment you can make regarding the establishment of commercial relations will be with a distributor. Distributors are financially capable of purchasing for inventory and for maintaining spare parts for service. The next strongest form of distribution is the manufacturer's agent. Although this type of program does not include purchasing for inventory nor stocking spare parts, it does imply that the chosen individual or firm is an extension of your company. This occurs because the agent usually has a contract that stipulates the terms of your agreement, including protection of your patents and trademarks. Usually,the agent will arrange for advertising and marketing on your behalf in the country that comprises his territory.

The commission representative differs from the agent in that he contractually and in fact has no voice in any of your company's affairs. He is not the guardian of your patents or trademarks. He does not involve himself in your marketing or advertising programs. Frequently, what begins as a commission relationship grows into an agency relationship. This can happen accidentally because the exporter has not paid attention to what the representative has been doing. Later he may find out that he has, in effect, developed a partnership with his representative. Also, many commission representatives distinguish themselves so well that the manufacturer decides that it is in his best interest to change the relationship to that of agency. Many times if the product is right and the representative or agent performs exceptionally well and a trust develops, the arrangement will grow into a full-fledged distributorship. If this is the direction the manufacturer and the representative feel will be beneficial to both parties, it is an excellent way to phase yourself into long-term marketing of your products overseas.

Export merchants and export brokers fill a nitch in many companies' overseas marketing programs. They are inexpensive because very little commitment is required. The export merchants generally handle commodity items that are sold to the merchant's established clients. In these types of arrangements, price becomes a very serious factor. If your product is priced higher than a comparable product, its marketability will be diminished.

Chapter 5
Determining Your
Primary Markets

This chapter deals with the steps you should take in formulating a comprehensive plan to export. We deal primarily with long-range planning (strategic) and short-range planning (tactical), as well as review resources available to you for fulfilling your goals and objectives.

ESTABLISHING A LONG-RANGE PLAN

Once you are convinced that exporting will benefit your company and that there is a market for your products outside the United States, you must establish a long-range and a short-range plan. It cannot be overemphasized how important the establishment of a plan will be to your ultimate success. Just as a ship at sea cannot find its ports without charts and compass, you cannot tap foreign markets without thorough knowledge and plans. Consider your strategic plans as the captain of a ship would his charts and consider the tactical plans as he would his rudder. The strategic plan points to your ultimate destination and the tactical plan is what causes you to steer a straight course. Like ships at sea, you will find that your tactical plans will have to be adjusted from time to time because of storms, tides, and currents.

Your long-range plan should cover from ten to twenty years and take into account not only the current products you offer, but also any products that you anticipate introducing in the future. This is a time when you can *imagineer*. Let your knowledge and imagination wander and try to conceive of all the changes not only within your industry but globally, that may occur over the next decade. Strategic plans represent the broad strokes that will govern how you will implement your tactical plans.

A good place to start your long-range plan is to review your current domestic plan. (You do have one, I assume)! Begin to think how international sales will impact this plan and then make the necessary adjustments. Just as your plan takes into account domestic sales, your new plan needs to consider foreign sales and how they will be managed. How is your company currently structured? What changes will you have to make to accommodate international sales and marketing? How will research and development be impacted? What about purchasing, accounts receivable, management information systems, personnel, benefits, payroll, and a myriad of other departments? All segments of your business must be reviewed in light of your greatly widened horizon.

How do you plan to achieve increased sales and distribution? In planning for international sales it is better to use a rifle approach rather than a shotgun! You do not want to go running off in several directions at once. Choose your markets carefully and plan on their development one market at a time. As you grow and gain experience, you will be able to handle more than one area at a time and your growth will be geometric rather than linear as was necessary in the beginning.

The first question you should ask in your long-range planning sessions is, "Where do we want to be internationally ten years from now?" The answer to this question will certainly be found in your product and also in your company history. If you will analyze how you have been able to grow enough to arrive at the point of considering overseas sales, you should be able to divine how to do the same abroad. Who are your customers in the United States? The profile you have of your customers domestically probably will not be much different abroad. How do you traditionally market your products at home: direct sales, distributors, commission representatives? Do you want to maintain the same form of distribution abroad? Did your method of distribution change over the years? Do you want to start with one type distribution and then change it later? Is your product seasonal? Will it have the same seasonality abroad? Is your product used in heavy industry? Is your product high technology? All these questions will influence your plan and must be addressed in its actualization.

In your planning you should start by recognizing the various geopolitical sections of the earth. First, the world, obviously, is divided into continents: North America, South America, Australia, Africa, Asia, Europe. These continents may be further divided into three camps: Free (also known as the West), Communist (the East), and others. In addition to describing a country as free or Communist, persons frequently refer to them as friendly or not friendly toward the United States. It must be obvious that you will not want to attempt trade relations with countries that are not friendly toward the United States. Your marketing plan should be directed toward the friendly countries. If you are going to be marketing primarily to agricultural countries, your plan must be adaptable to recognize that most agricultural countries have limited financial resources and that their usual goal is to become an industrialized nation. In other words, their goal may be in conflict with your goal. This should not necessarily be discouraging, because the realization of the country's goal may take several generations and that is too distant even for your long range plans.

Because the industrialized nations of the world are generally more prosperous than the agricultural countries, if you sell your products in their market U. S. currency will be readily available to pay for your goods or services. Communist and agricultural countries both have the chronic problem of earning enough foreign exchange to purchase Western goods.

After you have chosen the type of major market (industrial or agricultural) for your long-range plan, you will begin with your need to identify the target countries and the order in which you will penetrate them. You also should decide on a timetable for each step of the plan. For example, if you have a product that is used in industrialized countries, you should think about beginning in Canada, Western Europe, and Australia. There are several other countries that could be on this list except there are political barriers that, although while not necessarily blocking you from their markets, do require some determination and, in this writer's opinion, experience before attempting to do business there. These countries include, Mexico, Japan, South Korea, Singapore, India, South Africa, the entire Middle East, and all of South America.

After deciding that you will consider only those industrialized nations that are liberal in allowing imports, your next consideration should be ease of doing business. This has to mean ease of dealing in one language. Because your language is English, you should begin by considering Canada, England, and Australia. Because Canada is right next door this would be a perfect place to start, followed by England. England should be your second choice for two reasons: first, a common language, second its proximity to the European continent provides a jumping-off spot for expansion into the rest of Europe. Australia's location almost halfway around the earth from your offices means that you will have to deal with long lead times and spotty communications due to the difference in time zones.

After penetrating the English-speaking countries, you should turn your attention to those countries that have a history of satisfactory trading relations. Although English is not the national language in most of these countries, you will find that English is in fact, the lingua franca of the world. There are very few places with which you will be trading where English is not known to a comfortable degree. However, in our example we are talking about industrialized countries and therefore, for your next step, you must consider Europe. Here you will want to consider market size and the potential share you can obtain. The biggest market for industrialized products in Europe is West Germany, followed by France, Italy, and Benelux (Belgium, Luxembourg, and the Netherlands). The specific order in which you go into these markets is probably of little importance. You may find that through your participation and successes in England your products will already be known to a few Europeans and they will contact you about obtaining your product. Frequently, this is how initial contact is made with representatives or distributors. As your export market grows so will your experience and reputation, making expansion easier and faster.

You must determine a timetable for growth and expansion because no one else will be in a position to know all the facts necessary to determine that growth. For example, most persons consider competition as a rival firm that takes business away from your firm. Consider that as you expand abroad your competitor can be your ally because between the two of you are creating a previously nonexistent demand. In other words, expansion of your market can grow faster with the help of your competition. Without competition it would take you longer to penetrate foreign markets. Once you are established in the market, your task will be to increase market share rather than to create demand. The purpose of your expansion into foreign markets will have changed. This will occur on a country by country basis and, no doubt, will be influenced by your traditional competitors and some local competition. Through it all your sales and profits will grow. You also will learn a great deal from marketing abroad. Local uses or needs for your products will spur new uses and new applications further vindicating your original judgment to go international.

Once you are in a foreign market, how you market your product may be different from how you market it at home. In the United States television is considered a must for marketing consumer products. In England as well as in many other countries the government controls television and restricts commercial advertisements. In these situations you will have to use alternative advertising methods, such as print and radio. There are also opportunities to take advantage of marketing techniques that are not available to you in the United States. As an example, in France and much of Europe, condom advertising has been permitted on television long before AIDS became a problem for the general public. No doubt this enhanced the profits of the condom manufacturers more than would have been possible by placing them on the back shelf of a local pharmacy!

As you begin to gather market share in foreign countries it is also important to realize that the per capita consumption of various items will vary from country to country so your plan will have to take these variables into consideration.

Your strategic plan should include provisions on how to staff and manage your growth overseas. Even if you plan on dealing exclusively with commission representatives, the job of expanding overseas is too great to attempt to handle without increasing your domestic staff. You will have to consider your personnel needs as well as the experience and talents they will require in order to realize the goals you will be setting for yourselves with your long-range plan.

How will you organize yourselves? Who will report to whom on your organizational chart? Perhaps you will begin by placing your domestic sales manager in charge of foreign sales. This will work temporarily, but if you are aggressive and educated to overseas development it will not be long before you will have to appoint someone to be responsible only for foreign sales. In fact, your plan should lay out your expected staffing requirements as you reach various plateaus or landmarks. Eventually you will need a division to oversee your foreign sales. This division will probably consist of a vice-president of overseas sales, and several managers by region or country. Perhaps you will want to set up management by product rather than by region. This task is more difficult abroad than it is domestically because of the added complication of language. However, never make a decision to hire a manager strictly on the strength of his knowledge of another language. Most everyone speaks English and because you are the manufacturer it is most important for you to be sure you oversee everything in English. Also be skeptical of candidates looking for jobs who are natives of the country in which you would assign them if they have been in America for a long time, that is, several years. Many of these people have become accustomed to the American lifestyle and will not be in touch with the changes that have taken place in their own country. They may even be considered Americans by their compatriots. Furthermore, they may want to implement ideas that are perfectly acceptable in the U.S. but that are not acceptable in the host country.

At one time this writer hired a Japanese national to become the vice president of a Japanese subsidiary company. This person had an excellent understanding of English and the "American way of business." Because I had experienced trouble with the former manager whose his English was lacking, it seemed imperative that I hire someone with a strong background in English. The fact that he had previously worked in Los Angeles for ten years was considered a bonus at the time. However, it was not too long before I discovered that the Japanese staff in Tokyo did not respect his judgment because he failed to understand how the product they were selling was traditionally marketed in Japan. For example, he purchased company cars for all the salesmen so they could get around the country and carry their demonstration equipment. Unfortunately, only one of the salesmen had a driver's license. In Tokyo salesmen have historically used the subway to go on their appointments. They would sold from literature and if there was substantial interest in the product, the prospect would go to the office for a demonstration or the salesman would arrange for a delivery service to deliver the demonstration equipment to the prospect's office at a later date. Using an automobile in Tokyo is almost impossible. Most of the streets are much narrower than in the United States and parking can be impossible. After a short time the cars were sold and the salesmen went back to selling the way they had before the advent of the new manager. Equally important, the new manager insisted on changing the way the product was to be sold . In America a typical salesman calls on his clients, frequently the purchasing agent. In Japan much purchasing is done by individuals who no longer work at their former company. As a form of retirement some persons are given a particular commodity to purchase on behalf of the former company. It is understood between the company and the individual that the price he negotiates will be the lowest possible. They further know that a discount or commission will be paid by the vendor to the person doing the purchasing. This discount or commission is to be split between the client and the purchasing individual. All attempts by the manager to circumvent this purchasing system failed. After a great deal of wasted time the salesmen went back to selling the way they knew best and the new manager was replaced. Frequent changes in management are always difficult, but it is even more difficult in markets that are far removed from the home plant where cultural differences become magnified. Thus, it is important that your plan reflect sound judgment with regards to the personnel assigned to responsible positions.

Your long-range plans must take into consideration potential political changes within some of the markets where you will be conducting business. Many American firms lost a great deal of money when Lebanon became involved in war with Israel. On the flip side of the coin, the Republic of China was not open to Western businessmen until recently. Examples abound of countries whose political situations have shifted causing problems for various international businesses. In fact Hitler's rise to power in Europe can be partly attributed to shifts in political and economic changes in Latin America. Prior to the 1940s South and Central America's traditional trading partners were the United States and various European countries. However, the inflation we all associate with South America today was rampant then too. South America did not have the foreign exchange to purchase all the items it needed from abroad and was on the brink of collapse until Germany agreed to provide manufactured materials for raw material, such as light bulbs for steel. Latin America, although opposed to the atrocities of the war, nevertheless did not forget how Germany had helped it out of its economic morass and allowed a great many Nazis to immigrate.

Political risk is a fact of life once you expand beyond your borders. Risk, however, can be minimized by the form of distribution you select for those parts of the world that you want to be in but where you do not want to risk hard assets. In areas suspect of political change, do not establish any direct operations. Instead, work through commission agents, export marketers, or distributors. By structuring yourselves in such a manner, the risk can be minimized.

Just as there is risk due to political crisis, there is an everyday risk of foreign exchange. This risk is small for the average exporter because he is paid in U.S. dollars and the risk for currency fluctuation falls on the shoulders of the importer, be it a commission agent or a distributor. However, exchange can affect how well your product will do in a market. If your distributor or other agent cannot land your products within his market and be competitive or prove value, he will not be likely to continue to purchase from you. For planning you should use constant dollars to determine sales. The same factors you use to allow for inflation should apply to your export figures.

If you are an exporter of a product that is not manufactured (such as agricultural products or construction projects), your exposure to currency fluctuations is greater and you should be sure to use some of the insurance policies offered by the Department of Agriculture or Commerce mentioned in Chapter 1.

ESTABLISHING A SHORT-RANGE PLAN

Your short-term or tactical plan should be for one year or, at most, eighteen months. The plan should detail the specific countries you will be exporting to during the next year and the order in which you will begin to export to them. You will want to itemize the products that you will offer to each market and determine what circumstances need to be present in order to take advantage of different opportunities as they occur.

Hypothetically, you may decide that the first country you will export should be Canada. Once you have decided this, the next step should be to determine which products will be exported and when the exporting will commence. The first short term plan you write may have a timetable similar to this:

1. Meet with Trade Specialist at Department of Commerce to initiate inquiries about exporting to Canada. Allow two weeks to decide on method of making contacts with Canadian representatives, agents, or distributors.

2. Allow sixteen weeks for replies from potential Canadian representatives.

3. During sixteen week waiting period, contact local freight forwarders to asses how they can help export by providing documentation services.

4. Respond to inquiries received from Department of Commerce efforts and establish dialogue as determined by responses. Allow eight to ten weeks.

5. Conduct personal interviews with potential representatives in their home market. Allow one week after preliminary determination of satisfactory applicants.

6. Meet with bankers to seek advice on payment terms.

7. Check with Department of Commerce to determine type of license needed for export of products. Allow two weeks for determination.

8. On advice of freight forwarder, meet with shipping and packaging personnel to determine proper way to pack and address cartons containing products for shipment to Canada. Determine ways to shunt products consigned for export out of the mainstream of packing and shipping procedures. Allow four weeks. Begin to make inquiries about export

opportunities in another country, probably the United Kingdom. Begin this approximately six to eight weeks after having initiated inquiries about Canada. Establish similar timetable for the UK as for Canada. (However, you will probably not be able to personally interview potential representatives unless they are willing to come to the United States).

9. Report monthly to upper management re: progress and adherence to the timetable.

10. Commence exporting to Canada.

In your long-term plan you assigned particular importance to the personnel you developed to control your overseas expansion. In the short-term, personnel selection is equally important. The long-term program will guide you in your overall strategy. For the first few years the short-term must be controlled by persons more suited to clerking duties, rather than by international specialists with a command of several languages. You will want the type of person who is detail-oriented and very focused. This export manager should develop a staff of similar-minded persons who can immerse themselves in the documentation process that is so very important.

During the first two or three years of exporting, documentation and packaging will probably be the source of your largest headache. It is imperative that you select staff that will be capable of focusing on the minutiae that is such an intricate and important element of export. Part II of this book deals at length with documentation; suffice it to say here that your initial (tactical) success in exporting will depend to no small extent on how well your documentation is completed.

After several years of successfully building a world market for your products, you will want to become more heavily involved in foreign distribution and perhaps assembly or even manufacturing abroad. When this time comes, you will need people with different skills from those who have handled export so competently for you. The characteristics that make for good export personnel are not the same ones that make for good international executives. The export management phase of your development calls for clerking skills. The international development of your company will call for executive skills such as the ability to communicate in two or more languages, to organize large organizations, and to recruit qualified people who are experts in their fields. In Chapter 6, selection of export personnel is dealt with at length.

In your long-range plan you will have specified which products you want to export and approximately when you want to commence exporting them. In the short-term plan it is important for you to indicate exactly which products you will be exporting year by year and back it up with knowledge of why the products you have selected have been chosen and what you expect to accomplish from each product. It is not enough to decide to export your products. You must qualify which ones are appropriate and why you believe they will do well in each specific country of export. This may be a simple common-sense decision or it may be more elaborate calling for detailed market studies before the actual exporting can commence.

Consider the purpose for beginning to export: Are you trying to increase your earnings? Are you trying to extend the life of a product that is becoming obsolete in the United States? Are you going to be exporting a product that may only be marketable in specific countries for one reason or another such as the development of technology? Does your product only appeal to undeveloped nations? Do you have a product mix that will appeal in part to some societies and another part that will deal with other segments of society? You will have to analyze your immediate objectives and tailor your exporting to those objectives.

In order to illustrate this important point consider an American manufacturer of library systems. In the industrialized nations of Europe and Asia, computer-driven systems that automatically check out library books and track their return would be valuable, because all these nations manifest all the conditions that are conducive to using such sophisticated equipment. They have an educated population that can be trained to use the equipment; they have a need for speed to improve checkout procedures; they have sufficient volume of transactions to be attracted to the savings in man-hours such a system will provide.

Less-developed Third World nations, however, will not have the same level of sophistication in their libraries that is evident in the industrialized countries. They will still have libraries but they will neither have the volume of books nor the volume of transactions. These countries still represent potential business to the American library equipment manufacturer because the manufacturer will no doubt still have the older manual systems that it probably developed to go into business in the first place. By selling different products to these two different markets, the exporter will accomplish several things that will benefit himself and his clients. He will gain several economies of scale by marketing his computer equipment in those markets that can support it and he will extend the life of an obsolete product while it continues to produce revenue by selling to the less-developed markets. Also, in most cases involving the exportation of technologically obsolete products, the development costs that were amortized years ago produce greater profits than they did when they were state-of-the-art in the United States. Thus, your short-term plan should carefully consider which products will be best suited for which markets. Then you should build your export program to address the needs of the different markets.

The needs of different markets should dictate the method of distribution. Usually companies choose distribution methods based on the way they historically have distributed their product in the United States or, less frequently, on consideration of distribution costs. Realize that this approach, although it may work, may not be successful in all markets. You must also consider what is traditional in the various countries. For example, in a country of 100 million persons there may be enough potential market for specialized distribution, but in a country of only ten million, the potential volume may be too low and you will have to select a distribution method that will take these population differences into consideration.

The dichotomy of export is that although the documentation is very specific and inflexible, the distribution and marketing may be general and variable.

An extreme example of this may be found in the exportation of alcoholic beverages. The procedure for exporting is very specific as dictated by the U.S. government and by the recipient country. However, the marketing may be very different. In countries that have a history of alcohol consumption, the advertising and marketing may be quite similar to that of the United States. In Moslem countries, however, advertising and marketing may be limited or not permitted. Some importation may be allowed by these countries if the alcoholic beverage is only for foreign consumption within their borders or perhaps for certain medicinal uses. The point of this message is that you must carefully consider your foreign clients' needs and then tailor your advertising and marketing to conform to that need. What works at home may not work abroad. Your best chance for achieving success abroad will come from sound planning, both long and short range.

SOURCES OF INFORMATION TO FACILITATE PLANNING

There are many individuals, agencies, and businesses that can help you plan for a successful embarkation into export. The Department of Commerce can be a great source of information that will assist you in determining which countries to consider for exporting and in which order you should approach them. The Department of Commerce publishes *Overseas Business Reports,* which can help you review specific countries' economic and business situations. These publications cover such items as best export prospects, industry trends, transportation and utilities, distribution and sales channels, licensing and franchising, advertising and research, credit, and trade regulations. The *Overseas Business Reports* also will list several publications that you can acquire to further hone your market research.

Through their embassies and consulates foreign governments can provide information regarding their countries' imports. How much information you receive will depend to a large extent on the sophistication of the information accumulated by the foreign government. You can expect to garner more information from countries in Europe than you will from countries in Africa or Latin America. Additionally, there usually is more information available in the native language than there is in English, so you may be restricted in some cases by not having certain language abilities within your company. You cannot, however, expect to have language abilities for every language spoken, so concentrate in those areas where the common languages are used, if not in everyday speech, at least in commerce. For example, English is the language of commerce in such faraway places as India, South Africa, the Philippines, Hong Kong, and Fiji. Likewise, French is spoken in many islands of the Caribbean and the South Pacific, as well as in Algeria, Lebanon, and Mozambique.

Banks know perhaps more about opportunities that exist in individual countries than sources other than their governments. (Today there are many branches of foreign banks in New York and other principal cities of America such as Chicago, Los Angeles, Houston, and San Francisco). These banks are anxious to have your business in the form of letters of credit, cash against documents, and so forth; they will happily assist you in locating information about opportunities for your products in their country. Many of these banks are controlled by their governments and in effect the information they can provide will be a reflection of government policy.

Major cities all have foreign trade associations or trade clubs that can assist you in your planning by providing information about specific countries as well as providing insight into what products have been successful in certain markets. The members of these associations or clubs will frequently include banks, export merchants, commission representatives, and agents. Just like the Rotary or Lions Club, these groups tend to use the association as a networking tool to promote their services and to identify potential clients. However, there is never any obligation and the individuals who make up these groups can be knowledgeable; you may find that you even want to use some of them for specific parts of your plan.

Freight forwarders and insurance companies can also help you with your planning by providing background information on markets. They also usually have a good sense regarding the future of the countries in which they do the majority of their business. They deal with them on a daily basis and are aware of many of the subtleties that would not be apparent to the casual observer. Because they would like to earn the opportunity to work with you in shipping your products abroad, they generally will go out of their way to assist you with your requests for information. The most help for your plan from these people will be in the form of providing you with rates, transit times, port delays, alternative methods of transit, and documentation costs. Although these are not the burning issues of international commerce, they are grass roots and will become important to your newly founded export division. The companies that help you the most during the formative stages of your enterprise will likely be the ones with which you form the most secure and comfortable relations that will remain with you for much of your exporting experience.

Your local Chamber of Commerce may also be of some assistance to you in developing your plans. At the very least they will be able to put you in touch with other local companies that are currently successfully exporting. The local chamber may also be able to put you in contact with foreign companies because they may have had some trade missions to countries with which you are considering export relations, and they may be aware of specific accounting or legal firms that have offices in other countries as well. If the city in which you are located is presently in some form of economic decline, it may be able to provide you with incentives to export because the expansion could create additional jobs in the area. This could be an important planning tool because it might financially help you with your decisions regarding how fast your export plans can materialize and how extensive they can be.

Large accounting firms and legal firms can also assist you in your planning, as well as in assisting you in developing procedures for exporting. Most of the larger firms have a foreign presence both in the form of offices abroad and in the form of foreign nationals working within their domestic offices. These operations can provide valuable information regarding taxation, trademark and patent protection, contract negotiation, and in certain instances they can help you weave through the governmental bureaucracy with regard to licensing for export of certain products, such as defense items.

Many of these firms also have foreign clients and frequently are in a position to introduce you to firms in other countries that can help in the marketing of your products.

SUMMARY

Comprehensive long-range and short-range plans are critical to your success in exporting. The long-range plan should encompass at least ten years. Because you will be dealing with many different cultures and languages, you must plan on a longer pay-back period from your export activities than you would from domestic activities. This is the reason you should look at a ten year period rather than the more traditional five-year period on which most corporations base their long-range plans. For the same reasons, your short-range plan must be one year or more. This is particularly true during the first year when you will be struggling to establish initial distribution and organize the export procedures that will help you realize your long term plans.

You must chose your primary markets carefully. Language, ability to service the market, and ease of doing business in the foreign land should be your most compelling reasons for entering the first few export markets. A mutual trust should be established early in your commercial relations. Trust is the essential commodity that must have dominance over any written contracts or mutual understandings. Without mutual trust it will become increasingly difficult to conduct business, particularly given the long distances involved.

As you embark on your journey into international commerce, think of your long-range plan as the objective and your short-range plan as the means by which you will reach your objective. These plans are separate fabrics held together by the thread of people working in concert to achieve the final results of increased profits and, ultimately, a better lifestyle for those touched by your efforts. This lofty ideal is really what getting up and going to work each day is all about.

Chapter 6
How to Staff Your
Export Department

In the previous chapter, personnel needs were briefly discussed in relation to the long-term and the short-term business plans. This chapter deals with the personnel needs of a newly formed export department or division. We discuss the specialties and quantity of people necessary to get the job done, as well as sources for acquiring such individuals.

THE EXPORT MANAGER

The size and expertise of the personnel that will make up your export department will, of course, depend on how aggressively you elect to enter foreign markets. However, it appears to this writer that most companies that begin to explore export markets for the first time are generating domestic sales somewhere in the area of $1 million to $5 million. Companies of this size usually are not in a financial position to launch large, expansive foreign marketing programs. Generally speaking, companies of such size are well-advised to move positively, but with caution. Caution for most manufacturing firms will mean not hiring nor transferring more than three or four persons into an export department; this is an adequate quantity. Indeed for the first six months to one year, many can get by with only one person who generally will assume the title of export manager.

The export manager preferably should come from within your own ranks. You will be far better served by selecting a loyal employee who knows your business and wants the challenge of starting something new than by going outside the company and hiring an expert. Talents such as language and experience will become important traits later as you progress from this humble beginning to full-scale international sales.

In many firms the mantle of export manager is given to someone in sales who has distinguished himself in managing other salesmen either at the home office or at a distant branch. The selection of a person with experience in managing other salesmen is important because this individual will be responsible for selecting nominees for your first several foreign agents, distributors, and so forth. Among the most critical problems your first export manager will have to confront is a lack of product knowledge by the foreign nationals. If you choose your markets wisely, language will be a minimal problem and certainly of far less concern than the necessity to pass along product information. Foreign representatives first need product information, and second, they need your experience in selling your products domestically. These individuals will not necessarily parrot everything you have done that proved successful in the United States but they will want to adapt and emulate many of your techniques. They will customize your statement of benefits to conform with their country's unique needs.

This writer dislikes bringing up the subject of gender with regards to qualifying persons for any job. I would, however, feel derelict in my duties not to mention that usually, though not always, a man is more acceptable abroad than is a woman. All the countries of the world do not place the same esteem on ability that we do in the United States. Unless you have a truly exceptional woman who can fill the position of Export Manager, do not create problems for yourself. It is tough enough getting started without hindering yourself with a manager who may not be acceptable to your foreign representatives and clients.

Religion, too, can be a consideration in your export marketing. The United States does not tolerate discrimination because of race, creed, religion, or national origin, but many other countries do. The Moslem countries are particularly sensitive about religious preference and unless you have a product that they absolutely feel compelled to own, they will not do business with you if they feel your company or the persons who represent it are anti-Moslem. Many of these Moslem nations will state in their orders for your products that you must certify that the product does not contain any components that were made in Israel and that trans shipment through Israel is forbidden. The U.S. government expressly forbids any American firms from doing business under these circumstances. A lengthy discussion of the anti-boycott and restrictive trade practices is covered in Chapter 16.

In addition to product knowledge and company loyalty, the export manager you appoint must be flexible and capable of influencing people. The quality manager must also be capable of persuading other people within your domestic operation to be flexible enough to accept deviations from their practiced norms. The shipping manager who has been at his job for ten or more years may be ill disposed to making exceptions to his procedures in order to properly execute an export order. He may fail to comprehend the demand for precise and exact markings on its packaging. He may resent the fact that he has to package in specific sequences and do it in advance of the actual packing itself. This practice is required because most export documents require identification of contents by package. Because it is a lengthy process to complete all the documentation, the export department must know in advance exactly how the items being exported are packaged and each package must be marked to specifically identify its contents.

Your export manager must be able to infer what is meant in many personal conversations and in daily overseas correspondence. Because English will be a second language for many of your foreign representatives, their phrasing and sentence structure may sound strange or even unintelligible to a person who does not have the patience nor desire to understand. Many persons writing in a foreign language incorrectly transfer their own language's nouns and verb patterns into the second language. It usually is not difficult to comprehend what the writer means, but many people do not have the patience to understand what is needed. For example, in English we would say, "I broke the dish", but a Spanish speaking person might say, "the dish broke itself".

The duties and the responsibilities of your new export manager may include locating and recruiting foreign representatives. This initial selection process, however, may fall on the shoulders of the general manager or the domestic sales manager. Later, as your sales abroad grow, the responsibility will undoubtedly fall to a Vice-President of international sales. The export manager will be responsible for educating, training, and encouraging your foreign representatives in the sale and promotion of your products abroad.

He will be responsible for providing the foreign representatives with samples, literature, manuals, and all matter of marketing tools needed for the representatives to successfully promote your products.

It will be the export manager's responsibility to see that the documentation that must accompany all foreign shipments is done in a timely and professional manner. He must ensure that all products consigned overseas are packaged appropriately, shipped correctly, and insured adequately.

The export manager must be responsible for the collection of all foreign accounts receivable and make certain the terms and conditions of all sales are met. At first management may want to dictate the terms and conditions under which all foreign sales are made. As the manager's skills grow, however, this responsibility should be transferred to him. There are many sound reasons why it may be to the advantage of both parties for payment to be in the form of cash against documents rather than an irrevocable documentary letter of credit. These judgments should be made by the export manager in cooperation with your company controller and the advice of your bank.

The export manager should be responsible for the hiring of domestic staff in order to provide the necessary services to complete his export orders. Most start-up operations will require the addition of at least one clerk typist to perform the actual documentation processes.

The export manager must have the authority necessary to make demands on your shipping department with regard to how orders are picked and how they are packaged. For example, shipments via ocean freight must be packed in wood or metal containers. Usually waterproof wrappings must be used to protect the cargo from moisture and the contents from developing rust. The addition of silicate gel is also normally included in the packaging. Wood crates must be made in your own shop or ordered from an export crate manufacturer. In order for these crates to be manufactured, the dimensions of the contents must be known in advance of the actual packaging. This is not usually a problem if you are manufacturing a product that is always the same and always has the same quantity to a package. If, on the other hand, the products vary in size and quantity you will have to develop someone within your organization who can mentally assemble the freight and determine the correct size crates that will be needed. Furthermore, the skids on the bottom of the crate must be capable of being handled by the fork lift equipment used on the docks. These skids differ from what you may be using domestically.

The export manager must have some authority over your plant's expediters because from time to time he will have his feet to the fire to get a shipment out on or before a specific date. Time is usually imperative when dealing with exports because most commitments for payment state both specific times that items must be shipped and documents that must be presented for payment. Failure to meet these deadlines can result at worse in cancellation of orders, or at best in negotiating an amendment to them. Timely shipment of goods is always the most expedient method for handling your foreign orders.

Your export manager should have authority to negotiate with freight forwarders and foreign transport companies. If you are located anywhere in the United States other than at a port city or international airport, it will be necessary to ship domestically from your factory or warehouse to the port of embarkation. Therefore, it is to your advantage to make certain that the least possible delay occurs. If a ship's sailing is missed, a great number of difficult problems must be dealt with and you also will find payment delayed.

During your department's early years, it may be necessary for your export manager to travel abroad occasionally in order to train your representatives on certain products or to encourage them to increase sales. Sales and product training will typically fall on the shoulders of the export manager unless you have a regular company trainer. If you do have a trainer, he should be capable of handling your international needs.

THE EXPORT CLERK

As with your new export manager, you should be able to find someone in your organization who would make a fine export clerk. Many of the same qualifications that were identified as desirable in the manager are equally desirable in the clerk. The person to whom you offer this opportunity should be familiar with your product line and the procedures you use to place orders domestically. Export clerking requires a keen sense of detail. Every t must be crossed and every i dotted. It is impossible to stress enough how important this detail orientation is. In export documentation the verbiage used must be identical throughout the documents. This is necessary because many times the customs officer inspecting the goods and the documents will not be fluent or even acquainted with English. Many times he will simply compare the wording from one document to the other. If discrepancies exist, entry into the country may be denied. Similarly the banks that process the payment documents may think they find discrepancies between the bills of lading and the payment documents if all descriptions do not agree. Should this happen, payment may be denied.

If your export department is only a two-person operation, then it will be necessary that each person is capable of doing the other one's job with respect to documentation and expedition of orders. If one of the individuals is ill or called away and a question must be answered, then it will become the only remaining person's burden to handle. You must cross-train your export manager and export clerk to perform one another's job so orders can be processed when unexpected events occur.

Your export clerk must be able to complete documents without mistakes because errors or strike-overs can be cause for denied entry of goods into another country or nonpayment. Unfortunately, export documentation does not easily lend itself to computerization. Each country requires its own forms be completed, usually in multiple copies and, therefore, this precludes the use of computerized forms. In order to make a computer work for you, it would be necessary to have a software program for each document. Then you would have to load and reload each time you had to make a change in forms. Obviously, if you generate enough volume this may be acceptable, but most small companies will not process enough documents or make the software investment to make it worthwhile to purchase forms in a continuous format.

Your export clerk should be a notary public in order to properly perform his job functions. Many countries require that their documents be notarized and frequently it will be among the last things to do prior to actually shipping the goods. In these situations it is helpful if the documentation clerk can do the notarizing rather than relying on someone else in the company who may not be available when needed.

DESIGNATED EXPORT PICKER AND PACKER

Many companies find it advantageous to designate one or more individuals to exclusively pick and pack export orders. Experience has shown that persons who have responsibility for picking and packing domestic orders as well as international orders frequently do not do as conscientious a job on international orders as they do on domestic orders. The reason for this appears to be a resentment on their part because of the demands placed on them with regard to the export order. As pointed out earlier in this chapter, the requirements for international shipping are different from domestic. International shipping requires attention to detail and an almost individual packaging per order. Persons who are comfortable with rote situations simply may not function as well when they are required to do something out of their ordinary routine.

Because the flow of regular export orders is usually intermittent, the designated picker and packers may not always be present to perform the necessary functions. When these situations occur, the regular staff will have to be pressed into service. In these instances the export manager or export clerk should always double-check the work to be certain it complies with international requirements.

Over time the export picker/packer should become familiar with estimating which products can be combined and in what quantities so that they become quite proficient at estimating the required cubic feet of space necessary for containers or wood crates. They also will become used to the demand of export and often catch errors that may have been made by the export clerk. In other words, you should strive to build a team that works well together and whose members support one another. If everyone on the team is striving for the same goals, fewer errors will occur and you will have developed an excellent export organization.

EXPORT PERSONNEL TRAINING

If you select your own personnel to begin your export department, it obviously will be necessary to train them in how to process export orders. The entire second section of this book will deal with training. In addition, however, there are commercial trainers who tour the United States on a regular basis and who deal strictly with export. Many of their courses are very informative and you are advised to enroll both your manager and your export clerk in one of these classes.

Major banks usually offer classes several times each year in the collection of overseas accounts. Attendance in these programs is also encouraged. Your bank will also work closely with your export personnel to answer questions as they come up on an individual case by case basis.

Freight forwarders will answer questions regarding overseas shipments. They will generously spend several hours with your people instructing them in document completion.

All these courses and specialists' assistance will greatly help you get your people up to speed. The best sources of information after they have a working knowledge of the terms inherent to their new profession, are found in several books that literally spell out which documents and procedures need to be followed for each country to which they will be shipping. This is covered in detail in Part II.

If you should determine that there is no one within your organization who can possibly take over the export function and you have to go outside of the company for personnel, one of the first places to look is among your competition. Competitors who are already exporting should have developed a staff of competent people to handle the functions. If you can induce them to move to your company, then you will only have to train them in your procedures and products to make them productive. This option is not as desirable as promoting from within, but it can be successfully employed if necessary.

Another source of personnel is freight forwarders. In most instances these persons are trained in the ways of export but know little or nothing about your business. You will have to train them on your products and your procedures as you would someone from your competition. In addition, persons of this ilk may not have any knowledge of how to work within a manufacturing environment. It may be difficult for them to move onto a factory floor and urge someone to rush an order so that deadlines can be met. Many of the freight forwarders do not handle more than one form of transportation. In these cases you will also have to be sure they receive training in the other methods of transportation you may use. For example, if you hire a clerk from an ocean freight forwarder, it is entirely possible he will have no knowledge about air freight, land transport, insurance documentation or collection procedure. The same could also be said if you were to recruit from a bank's international collection department. Such recruits would not have knowledge regarding the other disciplines needed to prepare an export order.

BEYOND THE EXPORT DEPARTMENT

As your sales develop to encompass more than three or four countries, you will need to restructure your export department into an international division. At this point in your development you will find that your representatives, agents, or distributors will need more services than your export department can provide. Your expanded sales will require attention to items that hitherto had not been a source of concern, but which now will have become more and more time-consuming: items such as patent protection, trademark registration, licensing agreements, royalties, budgets, advertising and marketing, international taxation, and protection of trade secrets.

Your export department will become an operating group within your international division. It will be necessary for you to place someone in charge who has knowledge of how to perpetuate the growth that your increased foreign market penetration has brought about. There are only a few schools that graduate students in international trade: Georgetown, Johns Hopkins, Harvard Business School, and the American Institute for Foreign Trade. Most competent individuals in positions of authority in international trade grew into their positions. Formally they were domestic sales managers, controllers, marketing managers and the like. Many heads of international groups are persons of foreign birth. The reason for this appears to be that foreign universities train more international businessmen than do U. S. universities and foreign students tend to have greater language proficiencies than American students. This should not be surprising because most of the countries of the world are smaller geographically than the

United States. In order to improve their individual financial situations, it is usually necessary for these people to become fluent in other languages, almost always including English.

It would be unlikely that the person you select to become your export manager would be able to grow into the position of manager or vice president of an international division. The very qualities that made him your selection for export manager will auger against him when the scope of the position changes. For the manager of the international division you will want someone with a broad overview of the entire international business process and a good understanding of the general principles of business. You will want a generalist rather than a detail person. Many executives can competently move from strictly domestic positions into international positions. However, this writer feels it is important that a competency in at least one foreign language is essential. French or Spanish is preferable because with either of these two languages business can be conducted in almost all situations.

After you grow some more, you will need specialists to be responsible for specific markets such as Europe, the Far East, and so forth. For these positions specific language skills will be advantageous. For example, the Far East manager should be able to read and write Japanese or Chinese and the Latin American manager to be fluent in Spanish and/or Portuguese.

A typical job description for the manager or vice-president of an international division should read similarly to the one printed below:

> Preservation and increase of sales and profits of the company and its foreign subsidiaries in all territories of the world.
>
> Long-range planning for increased sales and profits of all products, know-how, and proprietary interests.
>
> Management of the use and protection of all international patents, trademark, and trade secrets.
>
> Management, overseeing, and negotiation of all international licensing agreements, royalties, and joint ventures.
>
> Management of all international financial details including the establishment of budgets, preparation of financial statements, and assignments of quotas.
>
> Establishment and maintenance of all foreign factories, sale outlets, agents, and distributors so as to meet overall management's corporate objectives.

Direction of and advice to the corporation regarding trade law regulations and customs of all foreign countries in which the corporation has an interest or does business.

Frequent travel in the territory so as to gain firsthand knowledge of the market.

Collaboration with domestic management in the use of sales promotion, manufacturing processes, and research development and/or development of such modifications in material as will best suit territorial needs.

Establishment of price and credit practices acceptable for each international operation.

Assessment of performance of distributors, agents, sales, offices, and manufacturing plants.

SUMMARY

When staffing the newly formed export department, try to promote from within. The importance of becoming established by using loyal persons who are familiar with your products is more important than language or prior experience. There are many training classes available to help your new staff learn the documentation procedures for exporting.

In addition to an export manager, you will need an export clerk and a picker/packer. The clerk should be cross-trained in the manager's job in the event the manager is ever ill or unavailable when needed. The clerk should be a notary public because many documents require notarizing. The picker/packer should be one or two persons who are especially trained in filling export orders.

As your export department grows, you will need to increase personnel to ensure the continued growth of your international sales. The person you place in charge of your international division should be capable of seeing the overall picture and have the support of corporate management. He should be fluent in at least one language other than English. The export manager should report to the Manager or Vice President of the international division of your company.

PART II
HANDLING DOCUMENTATION

Chapter 7
The Pro Forma

In this chapter we examine the proper way to respond to requests for quotations received from abroad. The pro forma is in many ways one of the most important export documents you will be called upon to prepare. This chapter reviews completing the form, various export terms incidental to completion, and the essential need for specificity. A list of export terms in common parlance is included.

PREPARING THE PRO FORMA

Even before you establish trading relations with agents, representatives, or distributors you will probably be asked for some pro formas. A pro forma is best described as an invoice in advance of a sale. The pro forma represents all the descriptions, quantities and charges that a shipment of goods abroad will entail. The pro forma must be accurate because its recipient will, most likely, need it in order to procure an import license and/or arrange for credit terms, such as a letter of credit.

When you are having discussions with potential representatives of your products, the inquiring party will want to know what his actual costs of importing will be so he can determine if there is a market for your products. Unlike your domestic fepresentatives, the foreign agent must consider numerous additional costs. The importing agent must consider the additional costs of duty, value added tax, transportation, insurance, packaging charges, and miscellaneous charges associated with clearing goods from customs. The best way for him to determine his real costs is by providing him with sample pro formas of typical shipments, or even actual shipments, which may include the original stocking order.

Certain of the items included in the pro forma are approximations, such as freight charges and the exact units of packaging. It is generally understood that some deviation from the actual will occur because the pro forma is compiled prior to the actual assembly of goods. A pro forma should not be considered a commercial invoice that has been renamed. At the bottom of the pro forma, a signed statement must be made indicating that each pro forma is a representation of a potential action.

If your company has a standard invoice form that is not too detailed and contains mostly white space, you may be able to press this form into service as a pro forma. If, however, your usual forms contain terms, conditions, and specific locations to place information, then you will probably have to design a new form just to be used as a pro forma. The simplest forms usually perform the best for this function because, at least in the beginning, you will find that you will have to respond to different requests regarding content; the more flexible you can be, the better.

A typical pro forma will contain all the standard information any of your commercial invoices or letterheads would such as your company name, style of business, i.e., partnership, sole proprietorship, corporation, street address, post office box if applicable, telephone number including the area code. You should also include a cable address, telex, or TWX number if you have them. Note that if you have a telex or TWX on your international stationary and other documents of correspondence such as pro formas, you should include your answer-back code. Unless your correspondent knows your answer-back he cannot be assured of reaching the right company in his telegraphic correspondence.

The body of the pro forma should include the current date and a reference to the originator of the request for the pro forma. If you code your responses be certain to include the code on your pro formas as well. Also, when you indicate the date spell out the month in words. This is advised because it will eliminate any possibilities of confusing the days with the months. In the body include your terms of sale such as letter of credit, cash against documents, and so forth and the name and address of the ultimate consignee. The ultimate consignee is defined here as the person or company that will actually take title to the goods. Unless you want to plant both of your new export legs into a mire of bureaucracy, avoid shipping through third countries until you have gained more experience. Indicate the shipping address if it is different from the consignee's office address. Just as all invoices have numbers assigned to them, make certain you include a pro forma number. This number should be significant to you and it may be preprinted or assigned sequentially, whichever system is more suited to your individual operating style.

After the usual commercial information is presented, it is typical to include a statement such as, " We hereby quote as follows" or similar statement followed by the quantity, model, description, unit price, discount (if applicable), and price extension. The price extension is summed and the summation line spells out at which point the extended price applies. In domestic transactions you may sum your quotes and on the reverse side of the quote state that the prices quoted are with or without freight included.

How you quote your prices internationally is more complicated and may take you a little while to become accustomed to because there are many different ways to indicate total price. The safest way to quote price is to do it several different ways at different points in your pro formas. For example, if the summation of your extended prices does not include any freight of any kind and represents the selling price in U.S. dollars if the client were picking it up at your shipping dock, you should state "total ex-works" or "ex-factory." The term ex as used in export means "point of origin." It is also imperative that you always state your figures in U.S. currency, i.e., U.S. $100,000. Failure to respect this rule of exporting can result in your being paid in Cruzeiros or Dinar or whatever the local currency is in the country to which you are exporting. Murphy's law dictates that if this situation arises the currency in which you will be paid will be worth less than U. S. currency. Mistakes like this are not always intentional on the part of the foreign client, either. Many times he is as naive as you are in the intricacies of international dealing and he may incorrectly assume that you have quoted him in his currency.

When dealing with international commercial transactions, do not leave anything to chance. Always be very specific in what you say and in what you do. This caution will be repeated many times throughout this book. It is necessary in order to keep you from making assumptions based only on experience with domestic transactions. This is why the careful selection of your export manager and your export clerk is so important and why it was stressed that you need detail-oriented people.

All the expenses that the actual merchandise will incur should be included. Next you should include all charges for export packaging. There will usually be a fee for crating the merchandise so it can be handled by the ship's loading equipment, as well as to assure that it arrives in salable condition. Most companies do not make a profit on this transaction. They just pass along the actual cost of the wood, nails, and carpenter's time. Of course, it is entirely up to you whether or not to mark-up these services.

Occasionally you will have to acquire consular invoices or Chamber of Commerce legalization for shipments. If this is the case, you may be charged a fee by the consulate or even by the Chamber of Commerce. It is usual to pass along these fees to your buyer.

The next line items on your pro forma will deal with the method of transport you select or the transport requested by your foreign client. From your factory or warehouse the items being quoted will have to be transported to a point of disembarkation. In the case of heavy shipments this will most likely be a wharf or ship. In lighter shipments it may be parcel post, air freight, or one of the newer air messenger services such as Federal Express, Purolator, and so forth. You must indicate the form of transport and the next destination point in the movement of your goods and the cost for this service. If you are going to ship via ocean freight, you will need to indicate that the goods will be picked up at your shipping dock and delivered to (1) a particular wharf or dock, and (2) a ship.

In order to determine which of these two ways you will quote, it will be necessary to telephone your usual domestic freight forwarder and get a rate. Probably your freight forwarder will only be able to quote a rate from your dock to the wharf, not to the ship. This is because he will not be familiar with the fees the wharf will charge to transfer the goods from land to the ship. If you quote in this manner, your pro forma should state "Total inland freight to dock" or "F.O.B. dock." If there is any question as to which city the dock is located in, this writer advises that you detail the city and the location of the specific dock to which you will deliver. In a city the size of New York for example, there are many docks spread throughout the waterfront and the freight rates will vary from one point to the other. A preferable way to quote the inland freight is, "Total inland freight F.O.B. Pier 23 New York City." Like "ex" F.O.B. is a very common export word, it means free on board and, in other words, it represents all the charges incurred until the point specified.

Should you elect to quote all inland freight including delivery onto the deck of the ship or into its hull, you should call an export freight forwarder and get a rate. Tell the forwarder you want to quote "F.O.B. shipboard" and he will make certain all the charges include transfer from land to the ship. You also may request a detail of those charges if you wish.

International forwarders will charge a fee for their services, as well as a handling fee. These charges should be detailed as another line entry, not included in the freight fees.

While you are acquiring all this information from various sources such as the inland freight forwarder, crate builder, and so forth, you should be building a file for each quote containing the detail relating to the proposed transaction. Failure to do this may result in an inability to duplicate the same figures later when you are ready to make the actual shipments. Because of the long time period that may elapse between the time you request rates for shipment and the actual shipping date, it is prudent to ask if any rate increases are anticipated. If some are anticipated, they should be included in the quote.

The next line on your pro forma would be for the actual ocean freight. You can ascertain this amount by talking with your freight forwarder. In order to quote a figure for ocean freight, he will have to know which harbor is closest to the freight's destination. If you are shipping to Paris, France, the port of disembarkation must be stated because Paris is a land-locked city. Prior to establishing the port where the freight is to be delivered, you should inquire of your client if he has any preference. Foreign clients usually do have preferences. They usually know if one harbor or the other is currently slow because of an abundance of freight coming into it or if there are labor problems. Some ports cannot handle containers and if you are planning on using containers to ship, naturally you will want to land the goods at a port that is capable of unloading them.

Ocean freight rates are determined in part by the distance between the point of embarkation and the point of disembarkation. It is possible that your client may want you to ship to one point rather than another because the rate will be lower.

The last rate you should include in your pro forma is the insurance. It will be necessary to insure the goods for its value only. It is not advisable to attempt to recover any implied costs such as documentation fees, handling costs, and so forth. There are several policies available to the exporter that will be dealt with later in this book. For the purpose of illustrating how a pro forma is prepared, our discussions will center around the "Open Cargo Policy." Open policy cargo insurance is available in certificate form from any of the many companies that underwrite marine insurance. Your export manager should arrange for an open policy that you can automatically attach to shipments. This type of policy is ongoing and the rate can be negotiated before any actual shipments commence. You will only be charged for those shipments that you actually make.

The pro forma is now almost complete. You will have the C.I.F. price when you add all the costs: extended unit prices, less any discounts; crating costs; inland freight; handling costs, loading costs to put cargo on board; miscellaneous charges; ocean freight; and insurance. C.I.F. means, "Cost, Insurance, Freight." This is the figure that is ultimately meaningful to your client. It tells him what his costs for your products will be up to delivery to a harbor in his country. In addition to these costs he will have to add landing costs and inland freight to determine what his actual costs will be. It is not unusual in export for the landed cost of the goods to the importing entity to equal the selling price of the products in the United States. Therefore, you can be assured that the selling price of your products in another country will be substantially higher than they are in America. This implies that for your product to be successful abroad, it must provide perceived value to the user.

The last item on your pro forma will be the weight and dimensions of the freight. Weight and cube should be expressed in both American and metric weights and measures. Here again is another situation where you have to be careful about how you interpret common terms such as *net* and *gross*.

What is the true net weight? Is it the weight of the items without any packing? Or is it the weight of the item in its domestic package, but not in the export packing? *Net* weight is the weight of the item without any packaging, domestic or otherwise. The weight of the item plus its domestic packaging is called its *legal* weight. The weight of the item, its domestic packaging, any other packing such as excelsior, wood crate, and so forth is the *gross* weight.

It is not recommended using the term *legal weight* unless you have written or spoken with the consulate in the country to which you will be exporting and received their definition of legal weight. The problem is that some countries consider legal weight to be only the first container an item is placed in and they will use this weight to assess duty and other taxes. Then again, some countries consider it to be the item, its first package, and the other intermediate packing such as the excelsior mentioned previously. Failure to correctly state the weight can result in fines and increased customs duty.

Tare is another term used frequently and you should know that it means the difference between the weight of the goods with its internal packaging and the weight of the external packaging. Thus, when you are quoting weight in a pro forma you should first quote the net weight (weight of the item(s) itself), weight of the item and all its packaging (gross weight), and the tare (weight of the packaging alone). You should also state the cubic volume. You must do this for each container or crate that will be shipped. This information is not only important to your overseas client, but it is also important to your freight forwarder so he can determine which rates to quote to you. The majority of the freight charges are based on weight and cube.

At the very bottom of your pro forma make sure you print a statement validating the pro forma for a specific period of time, usually sixty to ninety days. State that any increases in shipping fees or insurance rates are for the account of the foreign buyer. Lastly, state the estimated shipping date and base it upon a significant event such as receipt of a satisfactory letter of credit.

Illustrations 7.1 and 7.2 are two examples of pro formas. A list of export terms and their meanings is found in illustration 7.3.

These export terms are presented as a quick reference guide. However, because these terms are used so extensively, following is a more detailed explanation of each as well as some of the caveats regarding their useage.

The term *F.O.B.* should always raise a red flag in your mind. You should be cautious in your application of it. For example, you may receive a request for a quote F.O.B. Miami. You must consider whether to actually quote F.O.B. the vessel or F.O.B. the Miami docks. There will be a difference in the price. In the former example, all freight charges and the land portion of the handling charges will be included. The statement "Miami docks" in your quote will not include delivering the freight from the docks to the ship. Similarly the quote "ex-dock"
does not specify which dock should be considered as the point of origin: Does it mean the shipping dock at your factory or the dock from which your freight will leave the country? Always try to avoid situations where you have to make a judgment and never use terms such as *ex-dock*.

You should also be careful with the term *F.A.S.* Free along side means next to the ship or truck, <u>not</u> on it. The term *C & F* is infrequently used and that is why you may mistakenly read *C.I.F.* However, it is used in those rare situations where the foreign client has arranged for his own insurance. He may do this if he believes he can purchase it for less than

7.1. The Pro Forma Invoice

August 20, 1988   Pro Forma Invoice # 1001

BILL TO: **SHIP TO:**

Roger Deselles   Same
Cartographic and Travel Publisher
31 King Rd., Brentford, Middlesex TW8 0QP
England

Terms: Irrevocable documentary Letter of Credit in our favor drawn on a U.S. bank; all charges to your account.

We hereby quote as follows:

Qty.	Title	Unit Price	ext.
500	The Greatest Ski Resorts in America	U.S. $8.52	U.S. $4,362.24
	TOTAL EX-WAREHOUSE, DALLAS, TEXAS,		U.S. $4,362.24

Pick-up Charges		27.36
Air Freight		496.80
Airport Transfer		13.80
Insurance		17.20
Handling Charges		25.00
	TOTAL CIF LONDON	U.S. $4,942.40

Net Weight: 597 lbs. (10.4 k)
Tare: 11 lbs. (5.0 k)
Gross Weight: 608 lbs. (276 k)

This pro forma is valid for 30 days. Estimated shipping date is 10 days from receipt of satisfactory letter of credit.

7.2. Example of a Pro Forma Prepared for Shipment via Parcel Post

AMERICAN WIDGIT MANUFACTURING COMPANY
1234 North Preston Road Fort Worth, Texas 76101

Tel: 817/931-0716   Telex: 886504   Cable: Widgit, Ft.Worth 76101

Date	Pro Forma	Terms
December 12, 1987	1235-CR	Sight Draft

Bill To: **Ship To:**

Ensal S.A.   Ensal S.A.
Correo 872-2000   Calle 9 Av.
San Jose   San Jose
Costa Rica   Costa Rica

We hereby quote as follows:

Quantity	Model	Description	Unit Price	Extention
1	TU-3	Polypropalene Tape	U.S. $100	U.S. $100

TOTAL EX-FACTORY U.S.	**$100.00**
Parcel Post Charges	6.00
Chamber of Commerce legalization	2.50
TOTAL C & F SAN JOSE U.S.	**$108.50**

Net Weight:	23 Lbs. (10.4 k)
Tare:	3 Lbs. (1.4 k)
Gross Weight:	26 Lbs. (11.8 k)

This proforma is valid for 90 days. Estimated shipping date is 10 days from receipt of order.

7.3. Export Terms of Sale

Terms	Definition
C & F	Cost and Freight
C.I.F.	Cost, Insurance, Freight
Ex	*Point of Origin*
Ex-Factory	*Point of Origin* is the factory where the goods are actually manufactured and shipped.
Ex-Warehouse	*Point of Origin* is the warehouse where the goods are stored and shipment is made.
Ex-Foundry	*Point of Origin* is the foundry where goods are actually cast and shipped.
F.O.B.	Free on Board Named inland carrier at named inland point of departure. Named inland carrier at named inland point of departure freight prepaid to named point of exportation. Named inland carrier at named inland point of exportation. Named inland carrier at named point of exportation. Named port of shipment. Named inland point in country of importation.
F.A.S.	Free Alongside[1]

you can provide it. Perhaps he is importing such large quantities from the United States that he commissions his own cargo ship and takes consignment of the entire cargo. In this case he may only want an F.A.S. or F.O.B. (name of vessel).

SUMMARY

The pro forma is used by the importing party to arrange payment for the merchandise with his bank. This is the method most commonly used in international trade to inform both the client and his bank of the amount his purchases will total. Because the pro forma is used to ensure that enough currency is available to pay you in U.S. dollars, accuracy is essential. All costs that will be incurred in the movement of the merchandise from your shipping dock to the client's borders must be noted. Failure to accurately forecast costs may result in insufficient funds being available to pay your account and cause, at best, delays in payment.

The terms you use to describe how your costs are incurred regarding freight must be accurate and include all elements necessary to effectively move the goods. This means that all your pro formas should be totaled C.I.F. (Cost, Insurance, Freight) unless instructed otherwise by your client.

All measurements should be in both the English inch-boot system and the Continental metric system.

NOTE

1. Gerard R. Richter, *The Export Price Quotation*, International Trade Handbook (Chicago: The Dartnell Corporation, 1963), pp. 85-93.

Chapter 8
Methods of Transport

With the exceptions of Canada and the countries of Central America, all shipments abroad must be transported by Ocean Freight, Air Freight, Parcel Post, or Air Package Express. Of these various methods, ocean freight is the most involved. Due to the extra packaging required to insure the safe passage of merchandise over great distances and through potentially hazardous conditions.

OCEAN FREIGHT

The principal document you will need to prepare for an ocean shipment is the ocean Bill of Lading (B/L). Although you are probably familiar with bills of lading used by trucking companies, railroad carriers, and air lines, the ocean bill is different because it is usually the document that controls title to the goods. Ocean bills of lading have evolved over a long period of time and have been tested frequently in the world's courts. A great deal of precedence has been built up, and for this reason, little change has been made to make them more contemporary. Fear of creating new and untested law is the prime motivating factor mitigating against change.

Even though all ocean B/L's are documents of title, they are not all capable of conveying unrestricted title. The ability to convey unrestricted title is important if the goods are going to be paid for by a bank, such as with a letter of credit. If the bank cannot procure title it is obviously not going to pay on the letter of credit. It is, therefore, extremely important that you understand which bills are negotiable and which are not.

Nonnegotiable bills of lading are referred to as Straight and negotiable bills are referred to as To Order. To order or negotiable B/L's are protected by the Negotiable Instruments Law. This law protects the bearer of the bill of lading. Even the unpaid manufacturer or shipper can repossess the goods from an innocent third party who has paid for the merchandise if he has in hes possession the To Order B/L. This is important because banks will only consider negotiable bills of lading as collateral and only if they are free from claims against the merchandise or the shipping company. In order to effect this, title is transferred by way of "blank endorsement," which, in turn, makes the bill of lading "bearer paper." Once a bill of lading is blank endorsed it is transferable without further endorsement and can be freely traded.

Ocean bills of lading are prepared in three originals. This means that there must be three original documents each signed by an authorized officer or agent of the exporting company. One original is sent with the goods, the other two are sent under separate cover to the bank in the client's country that will be responsible for paying for the merchandise. The carrier will not release the shipment without receiving the consignee's original bill of lading as proof that the goods should be released.

There is some potential liability by blank endorsing the B/L. If you do not know with whom you are dealing, it is possible for the bearer of the negotiable B/L to be a fraud. For some years now there have been problems with Nigeria. Typically an American company will receive a large order with terms calling for an irrevocable documentary letter of credit. These L/C's are generally drawn on a Nigerian bank or even a bank located in Europe. To the unpracticed eye they appear to be legitimate. However, caution is advised because experience has shown that these L/C's are frequently drawn on nonexistent banks! Once your goods have left their U.S. harbor with a blank endorsed B/L, you will have lost them with no recourse. Always be certain the bank you are dealing with has a correspondent bank in the United States through which you can verify the legitimacy of any letters of credit you receive.

A way to safeguard your investment is to use a special endorsement for all the bills of lading which you endorse. There are three types of satisfactory endorsements that will protect your accounts receivable. They are:

1. To the order notify (insert name of shipper)

2. To order of shipper, blank endorsed

3. To order of negotiating bank

By endorsing as per one of these examples, the transaction is essentially completed within the United States. The Bs/L can, therefore, only be of value to the specific party for whom they are intended. Any legitimate bank will not pay or allow its letter of credit to be drawn on without receiving all three clean, original Bs/L.

A clean bill of lading is one in which there are no exceptions made to the acceptable condition of the goods and its packaging. If the bills contain any notations such as: rattle in package #3, water damage to package #1, or received in damaged condition, they are said to be "foul."

Generally banks are particular and will not accept Bs/L that are stamped "received for shipment Bs/L," which is the traditional way a ship's master signs for cargo. However, in order to be sure the L/C issuing bank will honor the Bs/L when they are submitted, insist that they be stamped "on board S/S (name of vessel)." This insures that the cargo has been placed on a specific vessel, further protecting the bank from any possible misconsignments or misdirected ships.

It is usual for the shipper to prepay the freight, both ocean and inland. In fact, most banks will not accept shipment on any other basis, so you must be sure that the Bs/L are stamped in this manner. Banks also will not accept *stale* Bs/L. Stale Bs/L are those bills that have not been received by the L/C issuing bank ahead of the actual cargo. Such Bs/L are not considered as acceptable collateral.

When preparing your Bs/L for an export shipment, be careful to prepare them in three originals; use the negotiable or to order form and properly endorse them. These are the three cardinal rules you will need to remember with regard to ocean bills of lading. The other items that you will need to complete the Bs/L are self-explanatory on the form itself but are mentioned here for the sake of clarity and continuity.

Ocean bills of lading must contain the following information:

1. The name of the company from whom merchandise has been received, i.e., the shipper.

2. The place where merchandise has been received, i.e., the port of embarkation.

3. The place to which the merchandise is to be transported, i.e., the port of disembarkation.

4. The name of the vessel that will transport the merchandise, i.e., the ocean carrier.

5. The name of a specific consignee to whom the merchandise will be delivered.

6. The name and address of the party who is to be notified of the merchandise's arrival.

7. A description of the merchandise.

8. A consular declaration. This is not required by all countries.

9. The U.S. government destination control statement.

10. The signature of the carrier.

11. The date the bill of lading has been issued.

12. A short form of receipt, i.e., almost always on the reverse side of the B/L form.

13. A short form of contract, i.e., almost always on the reverse side of the B/L form.

The straight form bill of lading, although not negotiable, is used in those situations where you will be shipping directly to your client abroad. In other words, no banks are involved in the transaction. When you elect to ship in this manner, remember that you are allowing the merchandise to be transferred by assignment and not by endorsement. Therefore, the wording of the line "consignee" just states the name of your client. On the negotiable bill of lading the line will read, "to the order of...." If you are going to be shipping on a regular basis to an overseas client using the straight form of bill of lading, you may also consider the use of a "through export bill of lading." This B/L can be issued by your domestic carrier who will pick up the merchandise at your company's shipping dock. The use of this form will eliminate your having to prepare separate bills of lading for the inland portion of the journey and the ocean portion.

THE DESTINATION CONTROL STATEMENT

The U.S. destination control statement is required by law to be included on all copies of bills of lading, commercial invoices, and the export declaration. The destination control statement is designed to eliminate the possibility of U.S. merchandise's falling into the hands of unfriendly countries or governments. There are two satisfactory statements that must used: For goods that are shipped under the authority of a *general license,* "United States law prohibits distribution of these commodities to Cuba, the Soviet bloc, North Korea, Cambodia, and Viet-Nam, unless otherwise authorized by the United States." For those items that are shipped under a *validated license,* "These commodities licensed by the United States for ultimate destination: (insert name of country). Diversion contrary to U.S. law prohibited. Or, "These commodities licensed by the United States for ultimate destination in (name of country) and for distribution or resale in (name of country). Diversion contrary to United States law prohibited."

Validated licenses are granted on a country by country basis. However, unless you are going to be sending medical products or humanitarian items, you should consider Libya and Nicaragua as prohibited. In practical terms shipments to these two countries are also prohibited because the review process of your application for a license will become so burdensome that commercial transactions will be virtually impossible.

AIR FREIGHT

Air freight's equivalent of an ocean bill of lading is called the *air waybill* (illustration 8.1). Air waybills are not negotiable and cannot, therefore, be used as collateral. The information required on the air waybill is almost identical to the ocean bill of lading and does not require amplification here. The major difference between air and ocean cargo is, of course, the speed by which goods are transported. Although air rates are higher than surface rates, there are some sound reasons why air freight should be considered. If your product is relatively small and you are shipping only a few pieces to any one destination, the speed in which you can get them to their destination may nullify the additional cost. In countries that assess duties based on gross weight, the fact that you do not have to crate commodities for air transport can effectively reduce the overall cost of the item to your foreign buyer.

Most air freight movements are effected by an international air freight forwarder. International freight forwarders are licensed by the Civil Aeronautics Board as indirect air carriers. Their principal purpose is to consolidate shipments from many small shippers into larger movements and book them with an international airline. They can offer their clients lower rates by consolidating freight than the client could negotiate by dealing directly with an international airline. International air freight forwarders can also issue through air waybills which enable the shipper to complete only one air waybill for both the domestic and the international parts of the transport.

Air freight forwarders generally offer services in addition to consolidation such as door to door pickup and delivery, documentation services, and collection or COD delivery.

INTERNATIONAL PARCEL POST

International parcel post is very useful to those exporters who ship small quantities of items and items of small size to different locations around the world. The service is reliable and inexpensive. Parcel post is governed by bilateral parcels agreements with various countries or by the Parcel Post Agreement of the Postal Union of the Americas and Spain. It differs from Postal Union mail which, is governed by the Universal Postal Union Convention and by the Convention of the Postal Union of the Americas and Spain. Postal Union mail includes letters, packages, and cards which are paid at the rate of postage, post cards, and air grams. These types of post are referred to as LC mail. The LC is derived from the French *lettres et cartes*, which in English translates as letters and cards.

8.1. The Air Waybill

AIRPORT OF DEPARTURE
001-13213734

001-13213734

SHIPPERS NAME AND ADDRESS	SHIPPERS ACCOUNT NUMBER
. . . .	
. . . .	

Not Negotiable
Air Waybill
(Air Consignment note)

American Airlines, Inc.
P.O. BOX 61616 D/FW AIRPORT, TEXAS 75261 U.S.A.
Copies 1, 2 and 3 of this Air Waybill are originals and have the same validity.

AA
Member of International
Air Transport Association

ROUTE TO

CONSIGNEE'S NAME AND ADDRESS	CONSIGNEE'S ACCOUNT NUMBER
. . . .	
. . . .	

PCS.	UNIT #	BY	EXCPTN.	SUPV.

ISSUING CARRIERS AGENT NAME AND CITY

ALSO NOTIFY NAME AND ADDRESS *(OPTIONAL ACCOUNTING INFORMATION)*

CORPORATE IDENTIFICATION NO.

AGENTS IATA CODE	ACCOUNT NO.

GBL/GTR NO.

AIRPORT OF DEPARTURE (ADDR OF FIRST CARRIER) AND REQUESTED ROUTING

SHIPPER REFERENCE NO. | CONSIGNEE REFERENCE NO.

ROUTING AND DESTINATION

TO	BY FIRST CARRIER	TO	BY	TO	BY

CURRENCY | CHGS CODE | WT/VAL PPD COLL | OTHER PPD COLL | DECLARED VALUE FOR CARRIAGE | DECLARED VALUE FOR CUSTOMS

AIRPORT OF DESTINATION	FOR CARRIER USE ONLY FLIGHT/DATE	FLIGHT/DATE

AMOUNT OF INSURANCE | INSURANCE - If shipper requests insurance in accordance with conditions on reverse hereof, indicate amount to be insured in figures in box marked amount of insurance. | TC

HANDLING INFORMATION   These commodities licensed by US for ultimate destination. . . . .

NO. OF PIECES RCP	GROSS WEIGHT	Kg lb	RATE CLASS COMMODITY ITEM NO.	CHARGEABLE WEIGHT	RATE / CHARGE	TOTAL	NATURE AND QUANTITY OF GOODS (INCL. DIMENSIONS OR VOLUME)
. . . . .	. . . . .		. . . .	. . . .	. . . . . .	. . . .	. . . .
. . . . .	. . . . .		. . . .	. . . .	. . . . . .	. . . .	. . . .
. . . . .	. . . . .		. . . .	. . . .	. . . . . .	. . . .	. . . .
. . . . .	. . . . .		. . . .	. . . .	. . . . . .	. . . .	. . . .
. . . . .	. . . . .		. . . .	. . . .	. . . . . .	. . . .	. . . .
. . . . .	. . . . .		. . . .				

PREPAID	WEIGHT CHARGE	COLLECT	P-UP ZONE	PICKUP CHARGES	ORIGIN ADVANCE CHARGES	DESCRIPTION OF ORIGIN ADVANCE	ITEMS PREPAID
A.			B.		K.		
VALUATION CHARGE			DEL ZONE	DELIVERY CHARGES	DEST. ADVANCE CHARGES	DESCRIPTION OF DEST. ADVANCE	ITEMS COLLECT
D.			C.		L.		
TAX			SHIPPER'S R.F.C. (AMOUNT TO BE ENTERED BY SHIPPER)		OTHER CHARGES AND DESCRIPTION		
I.			J.		F.		

TOTAL OTHER CHARGES DUE AGENT

TOTAL OTHER CHARGES DUE CARRIER

Shipper certifies that the particulars on the face hereof are correct and that insofar as any part of the consignment contains hazardous materials/dangerous goods such part is properly described by name and is in proper condition for carriage by air according to applicable national government regulations, and for international shipments the current International Air Transport Association's Dangerous Goods Regulations.

G. COD →	CURRENCY	

SIGNATURE OF SHIPPER OR HIS AGENT

TOTAL PREPAID	TOTAL COLLECT	EXECUTED ON

CURRENCY CONVERSION RATES	TOTAL COLLECT IN DESTINATION CURRENCY	(Date) (Time) at (Place)	SIGNATURE OF ISSUING CARRIER OR ITS AGENT

FOR CARRIERS USE ONLY AT DESTINATION	CHARGES AT DESTINATION	TOTAL COLLECT CHARGES	COPY 8 (FOR FIRST CARRIER)

ALL COLLECT CHARGES IN DESTINATION CURRENCY

AA FORM AC 135 PRINTED IN USA

Another class of Postal Union mail is referred to as AO, which is also derived from the French meaning *autres objects*, or other articles. Included in this class are printed matter, books, sheet music, second-class and controlled circulation publication, matter for the blind and small packets.

Before any attempt is made to export via parcel post, you must obtain a current copy of *International Mail* published by the United States Postal Service in Washington, D.C. This is a lengthy publication that contains all the detail necessary in order to use the international mails and parcel post services. The publication is divided into sections that deal with every country of the world. For example, consider that a shipment to England is contemplated and you want to know what the requirements will be in order to effect shipment. First you will notice that England does not appear to be listed. This is because the correct term is Great Britain, which includes England as well as Scotland, Wales, the Channel Islands, and Northern Ireland. The first few pages deal with Postal Union mail and include references to tables that define which articles fall under this jurisdiction. Descriptions of prohibitions and restrictions as well as the rates are included in this section. A list of special services is also included. Next is the section dealing with parcel post. The first item under parcel post is the "Conditions for Mailing." The first thing that you should do when you review this section is check the prohibitions and restrictions to make certain the product you are planning on shipping is not on this list. Once you have assured yourself your merchandise is not prohibited, you should look up the rates for surface parcel post. Under the heading "Postage Rates" you are referred to appendix A, table 3-14, col. B. Flip through your handbook and locate this appendix. Upon reviewing this appendix, you will find that the rate for the first two pounds is given, as well as the rate for each additional pound or fraction thereof. From this information it is easy to determine what your freight cost will be. You can put the appropriate amount of postage on the parcel using stamps or printed tape from your postage meter.

Continuing with the instructions, the next item you will notice is the weight limit which is 44 pounds. The majority of foreign countries will accept parcels weighing up to 44 pounds, but there are a few that will only accept up to 22 pounds. Therefore, you must check each country before dispatch. The next item to be determined is which form you will need to effect export. The directory will tell you that in our example you need form 2966-A, Parcel Post Customs Declaration, and that one copy will be sufficient (illustration 8.2). This form, as well as all forms used for parcel post exports, is available from your local post office. Finally, you must verify the conditions for mailing and the directory refers you to appendix A, table 3-16 for summary conditions. If you find after reviewing these conditions you need detailed instructions, you are referred to section 320, "Conditions for Mailing." In the appendix you will find the size limitations for the parcel, preparation requirements, forms required, and marking and

8.2. Parcel Post Customs Declaration, Form 2966-A

United States Postal Service	No. 950237

FROM Expéditeur	Sender's Instructions if parcel is undeliverable: Dispositions de l'expéditeur En cas de non-livraison ☐ **Return to sender** Renvoyer à l'origine (NOTE: Parcel will be returned by surface and at sender's expense.) ☐ **Forward to: Réexpédié à**
TO Destinataire	
	☐ **Abandon** Abandonné

QTY.	Itemized List of Contents Please Print	VALUE (US $)

Signature of Sender	Date

Insured No./Numéro d'assurance	Weight/Poids
	lbs.	ozs.

Insured Amount (US$)	Gold Francs	SDR/DTS	Postage

PS Form 2966-A, June 1986   **Parcel Post Customs Declaration**
C2/CP3   **Colis de Poste Déclaration en Douane**

endorsing requirements if any. Shipping by parcel post is as simple as being capable of reading the international mail manual.

Without referring to the international mail manual, there are a few generalities that may be stated regarding international parcel post. The address surface of the parcel should measure at least 5 1/2 inches in length and 3 1/2 inches in width. The greatest allowable length is 3 1/2 feet, and the greatest combined length and girth allowable is 6 feet. To determine combined length and girth, measure the length once, the width twice, and the depth twice. Add the figures together and you will have the combined length and girth. For odd shaped parcels, the measurements should not exceed 64 inches. Odd shaped parcels are usually anything that is not square or rectangular.

If the product you will be shipping abroad is a liquid, be certain to include enough absorbent packing material to wick the spill should the product's container be broken in transit. Fragile articles must be packaged in corrugated capable of withstanding 350 pounds pressure and surrounded by a minimum of 2 inches of soft packing material.

Letters and other forms of personal communication are forbidden as enclosures in parcel post. Should you include this type of correspondence in a parcel, it will not be delivered and will be returned. You may, however, include commercial invoices with your shipments or old correspondence such as files.

If the country to which you are shipping requires only one postal form (such as in our example of Great Britain), you are correct to use forms 2966-A. If the country to which you are shipping requires multiple copies, however, you should use form 2966-B, Feb. 1985 (illustration 8.3). Form 2966-B is actually an export declaration and it should be completed in ink or typed. Accuracy in describing the contents is essential to avoid delay or even return. The actual information required is self-explanatory so it will not be dealt with here except to mention that there is a space where you can instruct the post office to abandon the parcel if it is undeliverable. You should check this box if the contents are not worth the cost of the return.

Some countries require a dispatch note (illustration 8.4) with parcel post shipments. The dispatch note is known by its form number 2966-E. This form is actually an envelope. All three copies of form 2966-B, July, 1986 should be inserted into the envelope.

Forms 2966-A and 2966-B are almost identical. The difference is that 2966-A is a pressure sensitive label that can be affixed to the package directly. Form 2966-B, Feb. 1985 is a three-part form that is designed so it can be inserted into an envelope that is attached to the form itself with a perforation. Form 2966-B, July, 1986 is similar to 2966-B, Feb. 1985 except that it is a separate form, which comes with an envelope known as form 2966-E and is overprinted with the legend, "Dispatch Note, Customs Declaration Enclosed."

8.3. Parcel Post Customs Declaration and Dispatch Note, Form 2966-B

PS Form 2966-B Feb. 1985

USA Parcel Post Customs Declaration and Dispatch Note

Read Carefully Before Completing Form

All parcel post items mailed to other countries are subject to the customs regulations in the country of destination, and must bear a customs declaration completed by the sender. It is essential that the declaration be completed fully, accurately, and legibly, otherwise, delay and inconvenience may be caused to the addressee. Moreover, a false, misleading or incomplete declaration may lead to the seizure or return of the package. It is the sender's responsibility to assure compliance with domestic, international, and individual country rules and regulations for mailability. The U.S. Postal Service accepts no responsibility for the delay, return, seizure, or charges, arising from the foreign country's import laws or internal regulations to which the contents of the parcel are subject.

Instructions

- Sender must complete all items except shaded areas (shaded areas for postal use).

- Use ballpoint pen and **Press Hard** — You are making 3 copies.

- Your signature on the front of the declaration certifies that the particulars given are correct and that the parcel does not contain any dangerous articles prohibited by postal regulations.

- If parcel is to be insured, state insured amount to the postal clerk. Postal clerk will complete the appropriate blocks on the form.

  NOTE: Do not separate the Forms until the postal clerk has entered the weight, amount of postage, insured amount, if applicable, and applied the postmark in the spaces provided.

- When completed, detach forms, remove stubs and insert Copies 1, 2, and 3 in envelope pocket. Peel off backing sheet and affix declaration envelope on the address side of the parcel.

FROM Expéditeur

Sender's Instructions
If parcel is undeliverable:
Dispositions de l'expéditeur
En cas de non-livraison

☐ **Return to sender**
Renvoyer à l'origine
(NOTE: Parcel will be returned by surface and at sender's expense.)

TO Destinataire

☐ **Forward to:** Réexpédié à

☐ Abandon   Abandonné

Customs Duty Droit de douane	Customs Stamp Timbre de la douane	Mailing Office Date Stamp Timbre du bureau d'origine
For Official Use Only		

Signature of Addressee Récepissé du Destinataire		Date

Signature of Sender	Date

Insured Amount - Words/Valeur déclarée - lettres

Insured No./Numéro d'assurance		Weight/Poids
		lbs. ozs.

Insured Amt.	Gold Francs	SDR/DTS	Postage

PS Form 2966-B Feb. 1985
CP/2

Parcel Post Dispatch Note Bulletin d'Expédition   Copy 3

DETACH FORM SET HERE

86

8.4. Dispatch Note, Postal Form 2966-B and Its Envelope Form 2966-E

DETACH STUB BEFORE MAILING

☆ U.S. GOVERNMENT PRINTING OFFICE: 1986—160-436

United States Postal Service	No. 161395

FROM Expéditeur	**Sender's Instructions** **If parcel is undeliverable:** Dispositions de l'expéditeur En cas de non-livraison ☐ **Return to sender** Renvoyer à l'origine (NOTE: Parcel will be returned by surface and at sender's expense.)
TO Destinataire	☐ **Forward to:** Réexpédié à ☐ **Abandon** Abandonné

QTY.	Itemized List of Contents Please Print	VALUE (US $)

Signature of Sender	Date

Insured No./Numéro d'assurance	Weight/Poids	
	lbs.	ozs.

Insured Amount (US$)	Gold Francs	SDR/DTS	Postage

PS Form 2966-B, July 1986   **Parcel Post Customs Declaration**   Copy 1
C2/CP3   **Colis de Poste Déclaration en Douane**

If more than one parcel is being sent to the same consignee, you must complete a separate declaration for each parcel and you must invoice each parcel separately as well. Should you fail to do this, substantial delays may result for your client. Customs will hold parcels that are combined on one commercial invoice until **all** the parcels arrive. They will not clear partial orders so if each parcel is effectively a separate order, it may be claimed as it arrives at its destination.

For shipments valued in excess of U.S. $250, an export declaration form number 7525V must be completed. These forms are available from your local post office at no charge unless you will be using them regularly. If regular use is anticipated, they may be purchased from the Superintendent of Documents, Government Printing Office, Washington, D.C. 20401.

Under no circumstances are these export declarations to be used on Postal Union mail! Should you want to send your merchandise via Postal Union mail you should use the green form 2976 (illustration 8.5). This is the correct form for dutiable merchandise and dutiable printed matter. It contains space for a description of the merchandise or printed matter. If you do not want to disclose on this form the contents (perhaps because of its high value), you may affix only the upper portion of the label on the outside and place the lower portion within the package. However, if you choose to do this, you must then complete form 2976-A (illustration 8.6). Place this form inside the container. You should refer to illustration 7.9 for details on the information required on this form.

8.5. Postal Union Mail Customs Form 2976

```
CUSTOMS–DOUANE C 1

May be Officially Opened
(Peut être ouvert d'office)
- - - - - - - - - - - - - - - - - - - - - -
    SEE INSTRUCTIONS ON BACK
Contents in detail:
Désignation détaillée
du contenu: _____
_____
_____
_____
_____

Mark X here if a gift . . . . . . .(  )
Il s'agit d'un cadeau

or a sample of merchandise . . .(  )
d'un énchantillon de merchandises

Value: _____ Weight: _____
Valeur        Poids
PS Form 2976, Jan. 1986
```

8.6. Postal Form 2976-A, Customs Declaration

C2

UNITED STATES OF AMERICA
Etats-Unis d'Amérique

CUSTOMS DECLARATION
Déclaration en Douane

SENDER'S NAME AND ADDRESS
Nom et adresse de l'expéditeur

SENDER'S REFERENCE NUMBER *(If any)*
Eventuellement numéro de référence de l'expéditeur

MARK X HERE IF A   Il s'agit d'un

☐ GIFT   ☐ SAMPLE OF MERCHANDISE
Cadeau   Echantillon de marchandises

ADDRESSEE'S NAME AND ADDRESS
Nom et adresse du destinataire

UNDERSIGNED DECLARES THAT THE STATEMENTS HEREIN ARE CORRECT

PLACE AND DATE
Lieu et Date

SIGNATURE

OBSERVATIONS

NOTE: Your signature affirms that your item does not contain any dangerous article prohibited by postal regulation.

COUNTRY OF ORIGIN OF MERCHANDISE
Pays d'origine des marchandises

COUNTRY OF DESTINATION
Pays de destination

TOTAL GROSS WEIGHT
Poids brut total

lbs.   oz.

CONTENTS IN DETAIL
Désignation détaillée du contenu

	TARIFF NO. *(If known)*	NET WEIGHT Poids Net		VALUE Valeur
		LBS.	OZ.	

NOTE: BEFORE COMPLETING, READ INSTRUCTIONS ON THE BACK ◄─

PS Form **2976-A**
Dec. 1979

☆ U.S. GOVERNMENT PRINTING OFFICE: 1980-651-159/1914

Air parcel post is treated similarly to surface parcel post with the principal difference being that airmail label 19 (illustration 8.7) should be placed on the address side of the parcel to the right of the country name. If a dispatch note, form 2972, is also required, an airmail label 19 must be placed on it as well.

8.7. Postal Form Air Mail Label 19

AIR PACKAGE EXPRESS

The concept of shipping abroad via an air package express company is relatively new. Prior to the 1980s the only way to quickly ship commercial products abroad was either to use air freight, air parcel post, or air mail. If documents had to be delivered faster than the post office could provide, the only way available to international traders was to use a messenger and book him on an airline to hand deliver them to the foreign consignee. Today, however, there are several firms to choose from (including the U.S. Post Office) that offer door to door delivery of everything from correspondence to merchandise. This new service is really a great boon to exporters because it is easy, fast, and without great complication. Air package express companies such as Federal Express, Purolator, and Burlington Northern offered delivery in over eighty countries at the time this book was going to press. These firms, however, are constantly increasing their coverage and no doubt one day will be available virtually everywhere.

Air package express provides two distinct services: one service is similar to air mail in that it will ship documents and correspondence, whereas the other service is for packages or merchandise. You can even ship dangerous goods to most service points, although the carrier usually needs to be notified at least one day in advance for cargo of this type. Whether you are sending correspondence or shipping cargo, the heart of

8.8. Air Package Express Combination Letter of Instructions and Customs Declaration

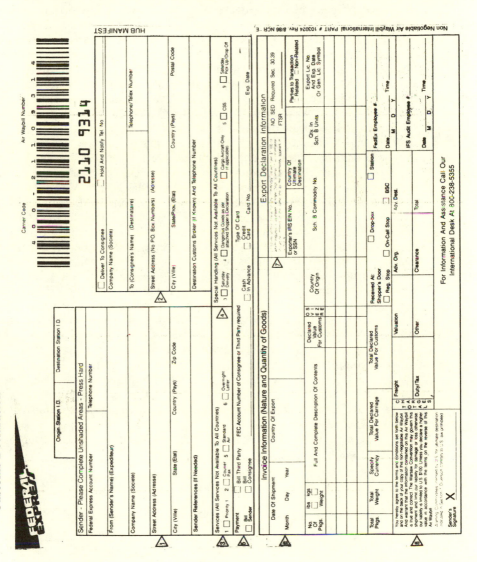

your transaction will be the air waybill. Air waybills are available from each air package express company at no charge. In fact, most will even imprint them with your name, address, and account number at no charge. Unlike ocean freight Bs/L, the international air waybill can also serve the combined purpose of export declaration and letter of instructions to the shipper (illustration 8.8). The typical air waybill is divided into eight sections. The first section deals with the shipper's information and contains his name, address, phone number, account number, and purchase order or invoice number may be used to identify each shipment. Section two usually deals with the consignee and provides space to complete his name, address, and phone number. The consignee information may also ask the shipper to instruct the air package express company to either deliver the package(s) directly to your consignee or hold it for his pick up. In some countries the delivery capabilities of the air express company may be limited, and, therefore, you may have to depend on their telephoning your client upon the freight's arrival at a terminal. For example, if you are going to be shipping some freight to a client in Virgin Gorda, British Virgin Islands, you will probably find out that the only city served by the air express companies is Road Town on the island of Tortola. To get to Virgin Gorda would require a small ship or aircraft, neither of which is currently available. However, there is regular commerce conducted between the two island and private local delivery is readily Aavailable. most overseas transactions, collect freight is discouraged and difficult to effect so most of your billing instructions will be applied to your account. Either you will have established an account with an air express company and will be billed to that account number or to a third party. For those that ship only occasionally, most companies will also accept credit cards such as Visa or Master Card. Special handling also must be noted on the air waybill. In order to complete this section you may need some assistance from the air package express company. Special handling is required for all "dangerous cargo" and certain other commodities may not be carried on passenger aircraft. Be sure to check with your express company before consigning questionable goods abroad.

The main body of all air waybills deals with the invoice information. You will have to provide the following information:

1. Date of shipment

2. Name of the country of export (assumedly the U.S.A.)

3. Number of packages

4. Weight of each package in pounds or kilos

5. Complete description of the each package's contents

6. Total number of packages being shipped on this air waybill

7. Total weight of all the packages on this air waybill

8. Currency used to determine the declared value, i.e., U.S. $

9. Declared value for customs

10. Declared value for transport (cannot exceed value for customs)

11. Country of origin.

The declared value for customs must not exceed U.S. $100 for correspondence. Likewise, the declared value for transportation is usually limited by the carrier to a specific per pound amount.

Although it may seem obvious that the country of origin is the United States, it frequently is not. Numerous exporters import products from another country, perform some added value service to the items, and then export them to a third country. In these types of situations you should always indicate the country in which the article was originally manufactured.

Air package express companies' air waybills provide space for you to complete an export declaration. This declaration is required on all shipments that exceed U.S. $1,000 or which require a validated export license. Schedule B numbers must also be provided. Schedule B numbers will be dealt with later in the section dealing with governmental documentation requirements.

The last item called for on all air waybills is the signature of the shipper. The bill must be signed by someone in your organization authorized to sign shipping documents. Failure to sign the air waybill will be cause for the company to refuse to ship the commodities.

All overseas shipments, whether air express or other, must be accompanied by a commercial invoice. The invoice should be your own invoice form containing corporate indicia. If you do not have such a form, then you will have to have some printed. The information on the invoice should be the same as appears on the export declaration. If the detail of the information on the invoice is too great to fit onto the export declaration, then the condensed information contained on the declaration should make it obvious to anyone comparing the two documents that the information is essentially the same. Unlike domestic invoices, you must sign the commercial invoice. It is expedient for you to try and always have the same individual who signs the commercial invoice also sign the export declaration.

SUMMARY

The methods of transport available to you for your overseas shipments include ocean freight, air freight, parcel post, air mail (correspondence only), and air package express. For ocean freight two possible types of bills of lading may be used: straight or to order. The straight form B/L is nonnegotiable and title to the merchandise is passed by assignment. The to order B/L transfers ownership of the merchandise by endorsement. To order Bs/L should always be used if you are going to effect payment through a bank or other fiduciary entity. All Bs/L should contain a destination control statement; certain commodities will also require a validated export license which is granted on a country by country basis.

Air freight bills of lading are called air waybills and they are always nonnegotiable. The information required on air waybills is almost identical to the information required on ocean bills of lading.

International parcel post and air parcel post do not require bills of lading. They do require that certain forms accompany all shipments, though. In order to determine which documents you need to accompany all international parcel post shipments, consult a current copy of the "International Mail" manual available from the Superintendent of Documents. Parcel post contains size and weight restrictions that you must be aware of before attempting to ship overseas. Letters and other forms of correspondence must not be included in parcel post shipments. In order to send items of this type, you must use international mail.

International mail is available either in surface mode or air mode. You must specify which type of transport you prefer. The forms required for description of goods used with international mail are different from those used with international parcel post.

Regardless of the type of carrier selected, you must include copies of your commercial invoice with each movement and you must include an export declaration, a destination control statement, and the schedule B number.

Air package express is a quick door to door alternative to shipping via air freight. The air waybill is a single document that incorporates the export declaration and letter of instructions to the shipper in a single document. Because air package express companies are freight consolidators, their rates may be lower than those of the scheduled air lines. The principal advantage these companies offer is a willingness to ship door-to-door thus taking responsibility for clearing customs and controlling the movement of goods.

Chapter 9
Other Documents

This chapter deals with documents that will be needed in order to export merchandise to other counties. Whereas the pro forma is created prior to any actual shipment of goods, this chapter deals with those documents, other than bills of lading, that will be needed in order to actually effect shipment.

The commercial invoice, export declaration, schedule B number, export license, letter of instructions, and other specific documents will be discussed in this chapter.

THE EXPORT SHIPPING MANUAL

Before discussing the various documents needed to effect an export shipment, it is important that you become familiar with the use of an export manual. The Bureau of National Affairs publishes the *International Trade Reporter,* which every export department should have. This manual is sold on a subscription basis with weekly updates of all the data. In order to demonstrate the manual's value, a review of one of its listing follows. In this example the writer has selected Ecuador, current as of July 25, 1978. Even though the information may not be up-to-date, it will suffice for the purpose of explanation.

The manual is thumb-indexed by countries making it easy to locate the country which you are researching. Ecuador includes the Galapagos Islands and the first page of the subject's section deals with Market Data: population, language, area, wights and measures, electric current, principal cities and population, currency, major banks, synopsis of trade—including exports to the United States, and principal export items. There is a map of the country, a list of government information and business information offices. The manual provides detailed instructions regarding all forms of shipping including prohibitions and restrictions. Telephone, radio, cable, and telex rates are included as is the time differential between Ecuador and the east coast of the United States (there is none). Holidays and business hours are noted; ports and shipping routes, and the tariff system are explained.

Preferential duties, customs surcharges, and indirect taxes are discussed, as are fines and penalties. Import and exchange controls are explained. The section on Ecuador includes information regarding trading procedures such as distribution channels, government procurement, and transportation. Note that at the time of publication port facilities were overburdened, causing delays and loss through pilferage.

The last section of the report on Ecuador is perhaps the most important for the exporter because it is a summary of the documents required. If we were going to be making a shipment to Ecuador, the first thing noted would be that documents containing erasures or amendments might be rejected by customs officials. We would also note that an import permit must be procured by the importer and its number must be noted on all documents. In other words, your client must go to the Ecuadorian government and receive prior approval to import your products into his country. Approval is given in the form of an import permit. A copy of the permit or at the very least their import number must accompany his actual order to you for merchandise.

The summary details the commercial invoice: two copies in Spanish are required along with certification that the prices being charged are the current export prices and that the origin of the goods is the United States. This certification must be performed by your local Chamber of Commerce. Usually the Chamber of Commerce will want an additional copy of the commercial invoice for its file so, in fact, three copies of the commercial invoice will be needed.

A certificate of origin is required in duplicate on a general form sold by commercial printers (illustration 9.1). As previously stated, the certificate of origin must be certified by the local Chamber of Commerce.

One copy of the bill of lading is required and the import license number must be shown on it. The original bill of lading should be posted ahead to the importer.

Additionally, a pro forma may be required. If this example were an actual shipment, it would have been necessary for your client to request a pro forma in order for him to receive an import permit. You should be starting to understand the relationship among the various documents by this time. Each document has a specific purpose and it is important that you understand how each builds on the other.

Some commodities have even more specific requirements. Some products may require certificates of purity or sanitation or a phytosanitary certificate. All pharmaceuticals, cosmetics, food, and similar products will require a certificate of analysis that must also be certified by the Chamber of Commerce. A list of products that require extraordinary handling includes items such as alcoholic beverages, rayon, fertilizer, oils and fats.

The balance of the report lists Ecuador's consulates in the United States and the consular holidays, document details and special data such as samples, advertising matter, labeling, marking, packing, entry, reexport, warehousing, and free trade zones.[1]

9.1. Example of a Typical Certificate of Origin

CERTIFICATE OF ORIGIN

For general use and for use in the following countries

BRAZIL	IRAN	EGYPT	SURINAM
SWEDEN	UGANDA	YUGOSLAVIA	ZAMBIA

The undersigned_____
(Owner or Agent)

for_____
(Name and Address of Shipper)

that the following merchandise shipped on S/S_____
(Name of Ship)

on_____consigned to_____
(date)

_____are product of the United States of America

Quantity	Marks and Numbers	Weight in Kilos	Description

Dated at_____on the_____day of_____19_____

Sworn to before me this_____day of_____19_____

_____
(signature of Owner or Agent)

_____, a recognized Chamber of Commerce under the laws of the state of _____, has examined the manufacturer's invoice and according to the best of its knowledge, find the products named originated in the United States of America.

Supervisor_____

This book, or one similar to it, is a must for every export department. To try and operate without one would be like trying to till a field without a tractor. There will be more information included in the chapters dealing with each country than you will ever need at one time, but there will also be much information that you will absolutely come to depend on.

THE COMMERCIAL INVOICE

Every export transaction must be accompanied by a commercial invoice. A commercial invoice in foreign trade is essentially the same as in a domestic transaction except it will contain more detail. The insatiable demand for detail required by various governments around the world makes it extremely difficult to automate the documentation process. If you will only be shipping to several countries, you may be able to satisfactorily add the documentation process to your computer, but if you are going to export to many different countries, the demands of each will probably auger for individual typing of the documents. The commercial invoice is a case in point. The commonalities between you domestic invoice and your export invoice will include:

1. Corporate name and address
2. Telephone number
3. Corporate indicia
4. Telex and cable address
5. Item number
6. Quantity
7. Unit price
8. Total price

The differences will probably include:

1. Country of origin
2. Country of destination
3. Marks and numbers
4. Weight (gross, net, legal, tare)
5. Measurements
6. Importer (if other than consignee)
7. Date of Exportation
8. Destination control statement
9. Statement certifying export pricing is current
10. Date payment is due and in which funds (U.S. $)
11. Destination if different than consignee address
12. Agreed shipping charges
13. Insurance costs
14. Consular fees
15. Signature of exporter

Additionally, your domestic and your overseas commercial invoices are different in that the overseas commercial invoice will need to be flexible enough to allow adequate space for more complete descriptions of the commodities. It may be necessary to describe the product in another language; weights may have to be stated in pounds and kilograms; volume may have to be included; the terms of payment will be different (letter of credit, cash against documents, draft, open account); and the name and address of the consignee may be much longer than would be normal in domestic transactions.

Should it be necessary for you to prepare your commercial invoice in a foreign language, it is advisable to forward a copy of your proposed English language invoice to your foreign agent or representative and ask him to prepare a replica of it in his language. This is recommended rather than hiring an interpreter because duty will be assessed on the description of the goods. If an interpreter does not completely understand your product, he may not select the correct foreign language equivalent word and, as a result, your client may have to pay duty on an incorrect description. Prior to actual shipment you can mail a list of descriptive words that will be used in your commercial invoice to your representative and he will be pleased to translate them for you. When it comes to actually typing these descriptions on the commercial invoice, errors can occur easily and may not be caught even by the most conscientious proofreader. If you have a memory typewriter or computer, it is advisable to key the correct verbiage into memory and then recall it as needed. This will greatly reduce the errors than can cause even the simplest transactions to be delayed and fines or penalties assessed. If you do not have this type of equipment, have your typewriter modified to include at least a tilde ($\sim$), a circumflex ($\char94$), a cedilla (ç), a pound sterling symbol (£), and a yen symbol (¥).

Illustration 9.2 is an example of a commercial invoice.

THE EXPORT DECLARATION

The export declaration is the document used by the U.S. government to record all transactions occurring between U.S. companies and foreign companies or governments. It is prohibited to ship any merchandise overseas without including an export declaration. On the reverse side of the declaration the laws governing its use are enumerated. Briefly, however, they state that it is illegal and punishable by fines and imprisonment to knowingly make false statements or misrepresentations on the export declaration. A declaration must be presented to a customs director or postmaster at the merchandiser's point of exportation before vessels or aircraft will be allowed to be cleared. Occasionally a bond may be posted with customs in lieu of an export declaration, but this is so rarely used that it will not be covered in this book. If additional information regarding the

9.2. Example of a Commercial Invoice

AMERICAN WIDGIT MANUFACTURING COMPANY
1234 North Preston Road Fort Worth, Texas 76101 U.S.A.

Tel: 817/931-0716 Telex: 886504 Cable: Widgit, Ft. Worth

December 12, 1987

BILL TO   **SHIP TO**

Hans Müller Organisation   Hans Müller Organisation
Postfach 339   D-57 Darmstadt
Burenstraße 45   Burenstraße 45
West Germany   West Germany

Your Order: 623   Our Order: 1234   Invoice Number 345
Terms: Irrevocable, documentary L/C drawn on a U.S. Bank

Marks	Qty.	Description	Price	Extension

△

Bremen
| 1/1 | 3 | Shrink Wrap Mach | 1,500 | 4,500.00 |
| | 1 | Blister Pack Mach | 800 | 800.00 |

TOTAL EX-FACTORY U.S. $ 5,300.00

One wood crate	150.00
Inland freight to Port of Houston	155.00
Handling Charges	125.00
Insurance	26.50
Ocean Freight	322.36

TOTAL C.I.F. BREMEN U.S. $ 6,078.86

Net Weight: 1,080 lbs. (590 k)   Dim: 70" x 45" X 54"
Tare: 321 lbs. (145.6 k) (177.8 cm X 114.3 cm X 137.2 cm)
Gross: 1,401 lbs. (635.5 k) 98.4 cubic ft. (2.78 cubic m)

These commodities licensed by U.S. for ultimate destination:
West Germany. Diversion contrary to U.S. law prohibited.
The above prices are current export pricing.   Manufactured in
the U.S.A.

American Widgit Manufacturing Co.

_____

Export Manager

posting of bonds is required, consult with a U.S. Customs office located in major cities.

When an export declaration is presented to customs officials, the exporter is affirming that the commodities being exported have a validated export license or general license and that all statements made on the declaration have been furnished for the purpose of effecting an exportation in accordance with the export control regulations. The exporter also affirms that he is authorized under the validated orgeneral export license identified in the declaration, and that the statement contained in it is identical in all respects with the contents of the validated export license or the terms, provisions, and conditions of the applicable general license.[2]

The shipper's export declaration (Commerce form 7525-V, illustration 9.3) is usually completed in one original and two copies and signed by an officer or person authorized to sign by an officer of the company. Many companies do not complete their own documents and rely on a freight forwarder to complete them. In these situations you must be certain that you have authorized the freight forwarder by giving him power of attorney to sign the export declaration. The freight forwarder must maintain the original of this power of attorney in his usual offices and make it available to customs officials should they request to see it. Should an employee of the exporting firms sign the declaration, he must be certain to include his title as well.

The actual completion of the export declaration is straight forward and uncomplicated. Each item requiring completion is identified by a number. An explanation of each number is found on the reverse side of the declaration (illustration 9.3).

The first information you are requested to supply on the shipper's export declaration (SED) is the complete name and address of the exporter. This should be identical to the name as it appears on the validated export license, if one is required. When completing this information, use only the first five digits of the zip code.

Item 1 (b) of the declaration asks for the *EIN* number. This refers to the exporter identification number. This number is the same as the service employer identification number or in the case of individuals, the social security number.

On item 1 (c) the exporter is required to report if the parties to the transaction are related. If the exporter is a U.S. citizen and the consignee is a foreign company or if the exporter is a U.S. company and the foreign consignee is a foreign national owning 10% or more of the other's enterprise, it must be reported as a related transaction.

Line 2 should contain the date of export if the movement is to be via air. However, if the movement is to be by vessel or by parcel post, this information is not required.

Line 3 calls for the bill of lading or waybill number. On air shipments you should use the air waybill number, on ocean shipments you should use the vessel's bill of lading number.

9.3. Shipper's Export Declaration, Form 7525-V

U.S. DEPARTMENT OF COMMERCE — BUREAU OF THE CENSUS — INTERNATIONAL TRADE ADMINISTRATION

FORM **7525-V** (1-1-88) **SHIPPER'S EXPORT DECLARATION** OMB No. 0607-0018

1a. EXPORTER (Name and address including ZIP code)			
	ZIP CODE	2. DATE OF EXPORTATION	3. BILL OF LADING/AIR WAYBILL NO.
b. EXPORTER'S EIN (IRS) NO.	c. PARTIES TO TRANSACTION ☐ Related ☐ Non-related		
4a. ULTIMATE CONSIGNEE			
b. INTERMEDIATE CONSIGNEE			
5. FORWARDING AGENT			
		6. POINT (STATE) OF ORIGIN OR FTZ NO.	7. COUNTRY OF ULTIMATE DESTINATION
8. LOADING PIER (Vessel only)	9. MODE OF TRANSPORT (Specify)		
10. EXPORTING CARRIER	11. PORT OF EXPORT		
12. PORT OF UNLOADING (Vessel and air only)	13. CONTAINERIZED (Vessel only) ☐ Yes ☐ No		

14. SCHEDULE B DESCRIPTION OF COMMODITIES.
15. MARKS, NOS.. AND KINDS OF PACKAGES *(Use columns 17—19)*

D/F (16)	SCHEDULE B NUMBER (17)	CHECK DIGIT	QUANTITY — SCHEDULE B UNIT(S) (18)	SHIPPING WEIGHT (Kilos) (19)		VALUE (U.S. dollars, omit cents) (Selling price or cost if not sold) (20)

21. VALIDATED LICENSE NO./GENERAL LICENSE SYMBOL   22. ECCN (When required)

23. Duly authorized officer or employee | The exporter authorizes the forwarder named above to act as forwarding agent for export control and customs purposes.

24. I certify that all statements made and all information contained herein are true and correct and that I have read and understand the instructions for preparation of this document, set forth in the "**Correct Way to Fill Out the Shipper's Export Declaration.**" I understand that civil and criminal penalties, including forfeiture and sale, may be imposed for making false or fraudulent statements herein, failing to provide the requested information or for violation of U.S. laws on exportation (13 U.S.C. Sec. 305; 22 U.S.C. Sec. 401; 18 U.S.C. Sec. 1001; 50 U.S.C. App. 2410).

Signature | **Confidential** - For use solely for official purposes authorized by the Secretary of Commerce (13 U.S.C. 301 (g)).

Title | Export shipments are subject to inspection by U.S. Customs Service and/or Office of Export Enforcement.

Date | 25. AUTHENTICATION (When required)

This form may be printed by private parties provided it conforms to the official form. For sale by the Superintendent of Documents, Government Printing Office, Washington, D.C. 20402. and local Customs District Directors. The "**Correct Way to Fill Out the Shipper's Export Declaration**" is available from the Bureau of the Census, Washington, D.C. 20233.

The ultimate consignee's name and address should be placed on line 4 (a). If any intermediate consignees are going to receive the merchandise, this information should be provided on ling 4 (b). If no intermediary is to be used, type "none" in the space allocated. The use of intermediaries is more common than might be thought. There are numerous countries and cities around the world than are landlocked and the only way to ship to them via ocean freight is through a port in another country. For example, if a shipment were consigned to Kabul, Afghanistan the closest ocean port would be in India, so the freight would have to be consigned to an intermediary for ultimate delivery in Kabul.

Line 5 should contain the name and address of the agent of the exporter. This is the freight forwarder who will be responsible for making certain the merchandise is placed on the proper vessel or aircraft.

Line 6 requires the exporter to indicate the point of origin. For the purposes of this document, the point of origin is the state in which the manufacturer is located. The correct way to provide this information is in the form of the two digit postal service abbreviation. If the shipment consists of various goods manufactured in more than one state, then the state, in which the commodity of greatest value was manufactured in should be used. If the merchandise was manufactured in one state but consolidated in another, then use the state in which the consolidation occurred. The reference on the form to an "FTZ number" refers to a free trade zone. Items that depart from free trade zones are assigned numbers and in that situation this number should be used here in lieu of a state.

Line 7 requires the name of the country of ultimate destination. If a validated license is necessary, the name of the country of ultimate destination named in the license must agree with the name of the ultimate country on the export declaration.

Line 8 calls for the loading pier or terminal. You are required to provide the name or the number of the pier in which the merchandise is loaded for shipment abroad. This section of the export declaration should be completed only if the shipment is by vessel. It may be disregarded if the shipment is by any other means of transportation such as air freight.

Line 9 should have the method of transportation used to export the product specified (i.e., ocean freight, air freight, truck, ferry, etc.).

Line 10 asks for the name of the exporting carrier. Specifically the name of the ship, its flag (country of vessel registration), and the pier number. If shipment is to be via air freight, state the name of the airline.

Line 11 should report the U.S. port of exportation. If shipment is to be overland, the U.S. customs port at which the surface carrier crosses the border should be indicated. If the shipment is to be by vessel or air, indicate the U.S. customs port where the goods are loaded on the actual carrier that will take the merchandise out of the country. If the shipment is to be via parcel post, provide the name of the U.S. Post Office from which the merchandise is mailed.

Line 12 should indicate the country and the port from which the freight will be unladen. This line only needs to be completed for vessel and air shipments.

Line 13 asks if the shipment is to be containerized and only applies to shipments via vessel. The freight forwarder will be able to advise the exporter regarding containerization.

Lines 14 through 19 are presented as column, with line 14 making the statement that either schedule B numbers or the description as it appears on the validated export license should be used.

In column 15 the number and type of packages the merchandise is packed in should be described, such as boxes, barrels, or baskets.

Column 16 "D" or "F" should be entered to indicate whether the merchandise is of domestic or foreign origin. It should only be listed as foreign if it departs the United States in the same condition as it entered. If the product has been modified or changed, it should be listed as domestic, The definition of domestic with regards to goods that were originally imported applies only to this export declaration and its use should not be confused with other documents that may be necessary to effect export.

Column 17 requires the schedule B number for the commodity to be entered. *Schedule B numbers* are statistical classifications for commodities that are exported by U.S. manufactures and growers. A list of schedule B numbers may be obtained by writing to the Superintendent of Documents, Government Printing Office, Washington, D.C. or from any of the Department of Commerce's field offices. An illustration of a typical page from the schedule B list is shown as illustration 9.4.

In order to determine the correct schedule B number, consult the table of contents at the front of the list. It is divided into eight sections which are further divided into additional subgroups. Locate the subgroup that seems to apply to the items being exported and then go to the specific page referenced and determine which seven digit number is applicable. If difficulty is encountered in locating an appropriate number, an alphabetical list is also provided. You may search for your item here and then turn to the page that contains a full description of the commodity. Should you feel that your commodity is not among the four thousand items listed, you will nevertheless be required to find one that is acceptable. The government will not accept an export declaration without a schedule B number.

In 1988 the U.S. government planned to introduce a new schedule B nomenclature know as *harmonization*. As of this writing it was not know if or when the legislation would be passed making harmonization law. It is anticipated, however, that sometime in 1988 it will be enacted.

Under harmonization the statistical information gathered by various government agencies will be uniformly collected and reported as an integral part of the whole. In other words, the collected information will be uniform rather than unique, as has been the previous collection.

The new schedule B numbers will consist of eleven digits rather than the seven previously required. For the company new to export, this change

9.4. Typical Page from Schedule B Catalogue

SCHEDULE 7. SPECIFIED PRODUCTS; MISCELLANEOUS AND NONENUMERATED PRODUCTS

(7-4-A)   (7-4-A)

Schedule B number	Commodity description	Unit of quantity	Schedule B number	Commodity description	Unit of quantity
	Furniture, and parts thereof, n.s.p.f.:			Furniture, and parts thereof, n.s.p.f.--Continued Of metal--Continued Furniture designed for office use--Continued	
727.1000	Of unspun fibrous vegetable materials.....................	X			
	Of wood:		727.2740	Other...................	X
	Furniture designed for household use:			Other furniture:	
727.1320	Upholstered..............	X	727.2820	Counters, lockers, racks, display cases, shelves, partitions, and similar fixtures...............	X
727.1340	Cabinet-work designed for permanent kitchen or bathroom installation...	X	727.2840	Other...................	X
727.1380	Other...................	X	727.2900	Furniture parts of metal....	X
727.1600	Furniture designed for office use.................	X		Of materials other than wood or metal:	
	Other furniture:			Furniture designed for household use:	
727.1720	Counters, lockers, racks, display cases, shelves, partitions and similar fixtures...............	X	727.5020	Of plastics..............	X
			727.5040	Other...................	X
727.1740	Other...................	X	727.5060	Other furniture.............	X
727.1800	Furniture parts of wood.....	X	727.5100	Furniture parts of materials other than wood or metal...	X
	Of metal:			Pillows, cushions, mattresses, and similar furnishings, all the foregoing, whether or not fitted with covers and with or without electrical heating elements, fitted with springs, stuffed, or both, or of expanded, foamed, or sponge rubber or plastics:	
727.1900	Furniture designed for household use..............	X			
	Furniture designed for office use:		727.8420	Mattresses....................	X
727.2720	Filing cabinets...........	X	727.8440	Pillows, cushions, and similar furnishings..................	X

will not even be noticed because all that is required is that the company purchase a new list of schedule B numbers and describe its products using this number on its export declarations. For the company that has been exporting for several years the transition to new schedule B numbers will also be relatively simple. The Department of Commerce will make available a concordia in which the old schedule B numbers can be compared to the new numbers. Larger corporations can, of course,. purchase their own copies of the concordia from the government printing office.

In column 18 the net quantity in schedule B units is to be entered. Schedule B units are usually expressed in terms such as each, square feet, lb., ton, gal., and so forth. If units of measure are not necessary for the commodity being shipped, an "X" should be placed in this column.

Column 19 is provided in order to include the gross shipping weight in pounds. This weight is to be provided on a line by line entry for each commodity shipped. This line is only relevant for shipment made by air or by vessel and need not be completed if shipment is via parcel post.

Line 20, which is also in columnar form, should indicate the value of the merchandise at the U.S. point of export. This value should include the cost of all inland freight, insurance, and other charges such as consular legalization fees. This figure should be in whole dollars; omit cents.

Line 21 asks for the validated license number or the general license symbol "G-Dest."

To complete line 22, the *Export Control Commodity Number (ECCN)* should be used. Completion of this request is only necessary for commodities that are subject to the Department of Commerce's export controls. ECCN numbers are listed in the Commodity Control List.

Line 23 should be signed by an employee who is authorized to sign export documents or by the international forwarder as authorized by power of attorney.

On line 24 the signatory of the export declaration certifies "...that all statements made and all information contained herein are true and correct and that I have read and understand the instruction for preparation of this document, set forth in the *Correct Way to Fill Out the Shipper's Export Declaration*. I understand that civil and criminal penalties, including forfeiture and sale, may be imposed for making false or fraudulent statements herein, failing to provide the requested information or for violation of U.S. laws on exportation...."[3]

Complete the form by signing it and indicating the signatory's title and the date.

Disregard line 25.

If additional lines are necessary in order to provide descriptions of all the commodities being shipped on one export declaration, continuation sheets are available.

Export declaration forms and continuation sheets are available from the Superintendent of Documents, U.S. Government Printing Office, Washington, D.C. or from any Department of Commerce field office.

THE CERTIFICATE OF ORIGIN

Various countries have their own certificate of origin forms that must be used when shipping to them. Always check your export manual to be certain you have the correct form. Most forms are readily available from commercial stationers or from the receiving country's consulate. Some countries combine their certificate of origin with consular invoices. Still others require that their consulate legalize the certificate of origin. Legalization is usually required only the Third World countries. It appears to be a way for them to earn a few more U.S. dollars and thus reduce their cost of maintaining consulates in the United States.

Most certificates of origin are simple documents that call for a repetition of the information on the export declaration with the exception that they also will contain a statement that the items being exported are certified as products of the United States of America. An example of a certificate of origin with Chamber of Commerce certification is reproduced for clarification (illustration 9.5).

THE EXPORT LICENSE

Exports from the United States are controlled by the Office of Export Administration through its *Commodity Control List,* also known as CCL. These requirements are published annually by the Department of Commerce and are available from the Superintendent of Documents, U.S. Government Printing Office, Washington, D.C. 20402, or from any Department of Commerce field office.

Most products exported from the United States do not require a validated license, but unless you check the commodity control list you cannot be certain. Therefore, it is highly recommended that prior to attempting export, you procure a copy of this list. The office of Export Administration separates the countries of the world into seven groups identified by alphabetical letters: Q,S,T,V,W,Y,Z. Country group Q is Romania; country group S is Libya; country group T is the Americas; country group V are all countries not included in any other country group (except Canada); country group W consists of Poland and Hungary; country group Y includes Albania, Bulgaria, Czechoslovakia, Estonia, German Democratic Republic, Laos, Latvia, Lithuania, Mongolian People's Republic, U.S.S.R.; Country group Z is comprised of Cuba, Kampuchea, North Korea, Vietnam.

Validated licenses are designated GLV whereas a general license is designated G-Dest. In order to determine if a specific commodity will require a GLV or G-Dest. license, consult the schedule B list. Locate the commodity to be exported and record the first five digits of the seven digit code. Next look up the five digit number on the commodities control list and note the country group code letter for which GLV licenses are required.

9.5. Example of a Typical Certificate of Origin with Chamber of Commerce Certification

CERTIFICATE OF ORIGIN

For general use and for use in the following countries

BRAZIL	IRAN	EGYPT	SURINAM
SWEDEN	UGANDA	YUGOSLAVIA	ZAMBIA

The undersigned <u>John Doe, Export Manager</u>

for <u>American Widgit Manufactureing Co. Ft. Worth, Tx.   76101</u>
(owner or agent)
(Name and Address of Shipper)

that the following merchandise shipped on S/S<u>   American Dream</u>
(Name of Ship)

on <u>12 Dec. 1987</u> consigned to <u>Oy Inco, Pori, Finland</u>
(date)

<u>   </u>are product of the United States of America

Quantity	Marks and Numbers	Weight in Kilos	Description
200 bx.	As addressed 1/200 thru 200/200	40.3/bx. 18.2 net	Widgits– 220v/50 hz

Dated at <u>Ft. Worth</u> on the <u>12th</u> day of <u>December</u> <u>1987</u>

Sworn to before me this <u>12th</u> day of <u>December</u> <u>1987</u>

John Doe
(signature of Owner or Agent)

<u>Fort Worth Chamber of Commerce</u>, a recognized Chamber of Commerce under the laws of the state of <u>Texas</u> <u>   </u>, has examined the manufacturer's invoice and according to the best of its knowledge, find the products named originated in the United States of America.

Supervisor _Kay Smith_

If it is determined that a license will be required, it is necessary to make an application to the Export Administration. This is done on form ITA-622P which is available from the Office of Export Administration, U.S. Department of Commerce, P.O. Box 273, Washington, D.C. 20044.

GLV licenses are for individual shipments or groups of shipments to specific destinations. Licenses have a specific time limit and thus can expire. Also, after a license is received, the transactions that were made under the authority of the license must be noted on the back of the license itself. Holders of validated licenses are advised to keep copies of all documents pertaining to the shipments made under it should the government ever want to review the exporters' actions. Applications for a validated license should be accompanied by supporting documents such as literature, import license, purchase request, and so forth.

When applying for a validated license, be sure to allow at least eight weeks lead time. In fact, for some countries such as the Peoples Republic of China it is advisable to leave as much as ten weeks lead time. When the application is made, enclose a self-addressed stamped post card with the following information written on the reverse side,

Date Received:_____
Case #:_____

Upon the receipt of your request the clerk working on the license will complete the information and provide you with a case number should any questions arise while the application is being processed. Of course it must be noted that not all requests for licenses are granted. In fact, most are not.

If exporting is made under a genera license, it is advisable to have a rubber stamp made up, "G-Dest." in order to stamp the export declaration, rather than repetitively typing the same data.

THE LETTER OF INSTRUCTIONS

There are two letters of instructions used in export. One letter of instructions goes to the exporter's bank and another totally different letter goes to his freight forwarder. The letter to the bank is discussed in Chapter 10, "Collecting Accounts Receivable."

The letter of instructions to your freight forwarder should be sent to him as soon as the shipment leaves you shipping dock. The letter instructs the freight forwarder about what you expect him to do. Letters of instructions generally include the documents necessary for him in order to effect overseas shipment, as well as requests for insurance, the amount of insurance and the method of shipment such as air, or ocean and if the goods are to be consolidated. One of the most important documents you need to include with you letter of instructions is the bill of lading issued for the domestic portion of the trip. This bill of lading should be a straight bill and the goods should be consigned to the freight forwarder. This is not done because the forwarder wants title to your merchandise but, because it will facilitate the rapid transfer of merchandise from the freight terminal to the pier of air terminal. Other documents generally consist of: commercial invoice, certificate of origin, consular invoice, and bank documents. By promptly dispatching the original bill of lading and other documents, you will alert the freight forwarder that the merchandise is on the way. He can then commence booking space on the next vessel or aircraft that leaves the United States immediately after receipt of the merchandise. Failure to dispatch the letter of instructions and the documents can result in delay of the shipment, as well as the accrued storage charges while a new vessel is scheduled to receive your cargo. Most freight forwarders, by the way, have their own letters of instructions they will make available to you if you inquire, Frequently the letter of instructions is combined with the export declaration on the same form. In situations such as this, the combined declaration and letter of instructions are acceptable and the government form 7425-V does not also have to be completed (illustration 9.6).

THE CONSULAR INVOICE

In addition to a commercial invoice, many countries require their own invoice. If the export manual says that consular invoices are required you may call the nearest consulate and obtain the form. Consular invoices vary and the information they require may be different from your commercial invoice. However, whether the information is identical or different, they must be completed or the merchandise will not be allowed into the country. Attention to detail is extremely important, as it is with all documents. Failure to accurately complete the consular invoice will result in delays of the shipment and, perhaps extra costs.

If the consular invoice is in another language there will usually be a letter of instructions in English prepared by the consulate to guide you in the correct completion of the form. If you have any questions regarding the information requested, telephone or write to the consulate and get a clarification. Do not attempt to second guess the form!

Some countries will accept your standard commercial invoice but require that it be legalized. Consular legalization is similar to legalization by your local Chamber of Commerce except it is performed by the consulate. Sometimes countries will even require that their own consular invoice be legalized. Regardless of whichever requirements are demanded by the importing country, you will have to comply if you wish to export.

THE IN-HOUSE ORDER

The secret to handling export orders on the factory or warehouse floor is to make them appear as much like domestic orders as possible. Many individuals are intimidated by the strange sounding names and

9.6. Example of a Combined Export Declaration and Letter of Instructions

SHIPPER'S LETTER OF INSTRUCTIONS

1a. EXPORTER	
	ZIP CODE
b. EXPORTER EIN NO.	**c. PARTIES TO TRANSACTION** ☐ Related ☐ Non-related

⚓ KUEHNE & NAGEL

DOT Authorized International Air Freight Forwarder
World Wide International Freight Forwarders
IATA Agents · Customs Brokers · FMC No. 1162
Over 300 Offices in 60 Countries

KUEHNE & NAGEL, INC.
1240 E. NORTH–WEST HIGHWAY
SUITE 103
GRAPEVINE, TX 76051
TEL: NO. (817) 481–9545
TLX.: NO. 6829163

4a. ULTIMATE CONSIGNEE

b. INTERMEDIATE CONSIGNEE

5. FORWARDING AGENT
KUEHNE & NAGEL, INC.
1240 E. NORTH–WEST HIGHWAY
SUITE 103
GRAPEVINE, TX 76051

6. POINT (STATE) OF ORIGIN AND FTZ NO.   **7. COUNTRY OF ULTIMATE DESTINATION**

8. LOADING PIER/TERMINAL   **9. MODE OF TRANSPORT (Specify)**

☐ PREPAID ☐ COLLECT C.O.D. $ _____

10. EXPORTING CARRIER   **11. PORT OF EXPORT**

☐ AIR ☐ OCEAN ☐ CONSOLIDATE ☐ DIRECT

12. FOREIGN PORT OF UNLOADING   **13. CONTAINERIZED (Vessel only)** ☐ Yes ☐ No

If Shipper has requested insurance as provided for at the left hereof, shipment is insured in the amount indicated (recovery is limited to actual loss) in accordance with the provisions as specified in the Carrier's Tariffs. Insurance is payable to Shipper unless payee is designated in writing by the shipper.

SHIPPER REQUESTS INSURANCE ☐ No ☐ Yes $

MARKS, NOS., AND KINDS OF PKGS. (15)	D/F (16)	SCHEDULE B NUMBER (17)	QUANTITY — SCHEDULE B UNIT(S) (18)	SHIPPING WEIGHT (Pounds) (19)

14. SCHEDULE B DESCRIPTION OF COMMODITIES (Use columns 15—19)

SHIPPER'S REF. NO.   **DATE**

VALUE (U.S. dollars, omit cents) (Selling price or cost if not sold) (20)

Attached   DOCUMENTS
☐ Commercial Invoice
☐ Certificate of Origin
☐ Consular Invoice
☐ Export License
☐ Import License
☐ Bank Documents
☐ Others
☐
☐
☐
☐
☐
☐
☐
☐
☐
☐
☐

21. VALIDATED LICENSE NO./GENERAL LICENSE SYMBOL   **22. ECCN (When required)**

PLEASE SIGN THE FIRST EXPORT DECLARATION IN BOX 23 WITH PEN AND INK.

23. Duly authorized officer or employee — The exporter authorizes the forwarder named above to act as forwarding agent for export control and customs purposes.

24. I certify that all statements made and all information contained herein are true and correct and that I have read and understand the instructions for preparation of this document, set forth in the "Correct Way to Fill Out the Shipper's Export Declaration." I understand that civil and criminal penalties, including forfeiture and sale, may be imposed for making false or fraudulent statements herein, failing to provide the requested information or for violation of U.S. laws on exportation (13 U.S.C. Sec. 305; 22 U.S.C. Sec. 401; 18 U.S.C. Sec. 1001; 50 U.S.C. App. 2410).

Signature

Title

Date

Confidential–For use solely for official purposes authorized by the Secretary of Commerce (13 U.S.C. 301 (g)).
Export shipments are subject to inspection by U.S. Customs Service and/or Office of Export Enforcement.

25. AUTHENTICATION (When required)

NOTE: The Shipper or his Authorized Agent hereby authorizes the above named Company, in his name and on his behalf to prepare any export documents, to sign and accept any documents relating to said shipment and forward this shipment in accordance with the conditions of carriage and the tariffs of the carriers employed. The shipper guarantees payment of all collect charges in the event the consignee refuses payment. Hereunder the sole responsibility of the Company is to use reasonable care in the selection of carriers, forwarders, agents and others to whom it may entrust the shipment. Kuehne & Nagel's Liability is limited to $50.00 per shipment when not otherwise declared & accepted by Kuehne & Nagel in writing.

unpronounceable cities and it is usually more productive to remove all extraneous information from these internal orders. Many companies use a different color paper of their in-house order to distinguish it from their other domestic orders. In this manner they are able to identify export orders from their other orders at a glance. If a product must pass through several different manufacturing operations before completion, manufacturers frequently will create additional copies of the work order and distribute them to the various operations rather than relying on routing one order.

The typical export order begins in the accounting or credit department. This is because no foreign order should begin processing until payment has been arranged to the manufacturer's satisfaction. It is normal not to acknowledge orders until appropriate payment terms have been arranged. Some companies do notify their foreign client upon receipt of their order, but advise them that it will not be placed into production until satisfactory credit arrangements have been made.

If it is usual for an industry to ship overages or shortages, the export manager should verify how his foreign client and the client's government feel about this practice. Usually arrangements can be made to accommodate this type of practice. Like so much having to do with export, however, it is best to verify in advance what will be acceptable so the proper documents can be drawn. With letter of credit transactions this usually means wording the payment sum as "about." When "about" is used in L/C's, a variance of + or - 10% is usually permitted.

Remember that the in-house order is the first document that will be created in the development of an export order; therefore, accuracy is imperative. Usually it is from the in-house order that all other documents will be drawn, so a mistake made on the in-house order will usually result in a mistake on the other documents. You have not lived until you have had to personally retype all the documents necessary to make an overseas shipment!

THE INSURANCE CERTIFICATE

As a means of further pointing out the necessity for paying attention to details, consider the insurance certificate. Although when an exporter insures his cargo he is issued a certificate, many letters of credit demand insurance policies. Therefore, many insurance underwriters have taken to calling their certificates "policies." There are basically two types of insurance certificates (sic: policies): Open Cargo and the Insurance Certificate (or Special Cargo Policy or Special Marine Policy).

The Open Cargo policy is used extensively by exporters because with this type of policy the exporter negotiates in advance of actual shipment the rates he will be charged for all the export shipments he made by sea. The insurance carrier will make available to the exporter Open Cargo insurance certificates preprinted with his name and address. These certificates can easily be completed by the export department on an as needed basis and completely eliminate the necessity of securing rates for each individual shipment.

The difference between the Open Cargo policy and the Certificate is primarily that the Certificate is negotiable, whereas the Open Cargo policy is not. This situation is similar to the manner in which ocean bills of lading are determined as previously mentioned in Chapter 8. The Certificate is usually worded identically to the Open Cargo policy; it primary difference is that the Open Cargo policy is unvalued, whereas the Certificate is valued. The Certificate is issued for a particular shipment on a particular vessel at a particular time. Because it is negotiable, it is transferable by endorsement and delivery.

The Open Cargo insurance policy is limited in its liability. Liability is established by the insurance underwriter and the insured and usually contains clauses naming the conditions under which payment of claims will be made. Insurance can only be for the value of the goods being transported. No conditions on an Open Cargo policy allow the insured to recover more than the value of the goods. This is referenced in the *valuation clause* and is usually the C.I.F. value plus 10%.

Other clauses contained in the policy are *perils:* perils of the sea (usually consisting of loss due to heavy weather, lightning strike, collision, and sea water damage); perils of fire; perils of assailing thieves (which refers to the theft of merchandise through force rather than by clandestine means or pilferage); perils of jettison (the voluntary discarding of merchandise overboard); perils of barratry of the master and mariners (the willful misconduct of the captain and his crew).

In order to cover more situations than those just mentioned, the policy must contain an *All Risk Clause.* Actually, "all risk" is a misnomer because it does not in fact cover all risks, it does, however, usually cover theft, pilferage, nondelivery, fresh water damage, oil damage, sweat damage, contact with other cargo, breakage, and leakage.

Clauses which establish the Extent (or breadth) of coverage are also known as *average terms.* These clauses restrict or broaden the coverage of the perils insured against. Contact a marine insurance underwriter for current available average terms.

There are two clauses that determine the *Duration of Coverage. W to W Clauses* are clauses the cover the merchandise from warehouse to warehouse. Although this clause is self-explanatory, it should be noted that if the ultimate consignee is located within the destination port city, the merchandise must be claimed within fifteen days (thirty days if the ultimate consignee is located outside the port city). W to W clauses must also assume that the normal courses of transit be maintained. MEC clauses are extensions of W to W clauses in that they cover interruption or suspension of transit beyond the control of the assured and by broadening the fifteen or thirty day time limit at destination.

The last clause commonly found in policies are *Exclusion Clauses.* Exclusion clauses eliminate coverage of other specific clauses found in the basic policy. If additional coverage is desired, then additional premium will be required. Many policies in common use today contain exclusion clauses for the Free of Capture & Seizure and the Strikes, Riots, & Civil Commotion clauses. These clauses are generically referred to as War Risk clauses. If the shipper desires to cover risks due to war and civil disorder, he will need a separate policy or endorsement to cover this risk. The inclusion of this endorsement is essential today if cargo is destined for any of the political hot spots such as the southern Mediterranean, Middle East, South Africa, or Sri Lanka.

Some countries will insist that insurance for cargo be placed with an underwriter located in their country. They will usually do this if foreign exchange is scarce. When this occurs, the exporter should get supplemental insurance called *contingent* insurance. This is available by special amendment to Open Cargo policies and only takes effect if the primary underwriter cannot satisfy the claim.

Should it ever be necessary to file a claim for loss or damage, the consignee should immediately notify the nearest underwriter's office. The address and phone numbers of the claims offices are always contained on the insurance certificate. It is also required that the consignee make a claim on the carrier or his local agent. The following documents should then be forwarded to the settling agent of the underwriter:

1. Claimant's invoice of the actual damage
2. Survey report prepared by the insurance agent substantiating the damage
3. Copy of the claim against the carrier with his response
4. Original of insurance certificate properly endorsed by the payee
5. Original or certified copy of the shipper's invoice
6. Original or certified copy of the ocean bill of lading[4]

SUMMARY

The successful export of any item begins with knowing which documents will be needed. Among the best ways to determine which documents will be needed is to refer to a good, current export manual. One such book is the *International Trade Reporter,* published by the Bureau of National Affairs. By consulting this directory prior to preparing export documents, the exporter can be assured he will be using the correct forms and be able to comply with all current regulations.

Among the documents always required in order to export is the commercial invoice. The commercial invoice is usually prepared in triplicate, although additional copies may be required by a few countries. The commercial invoice should give all the details regarding the items being exported such as quantity, description, unit price, total, price, country of origin, country of ultimate destination, shipping marks and package numbers, weight, measurements of the packages, date of exportation, destination control statement, insurance, shipping charges, and the terms. All commercial invoices must be signed by hand.

The description of the items being exported as enumerated on the commercial invoice should be identical to the description used on other documents concerning the shipment. Should discrepancies exist among any of the documents, customs will, at the very least, delay clearance into the country of importation. Discrepancies are what most customs agents are looking for when examining merchandise from overseas. It is in this manner that they locate most contraband and they are generally unsympathetic towards poorly prepared documents. Always use extreme caution in preparing documents and pay attention to the smallest and simplest details.

All exports of commercial merchandise must be accompanied by an export declaration. This is usually on the Department of Commerce's form 7525-V. The export declaration is usually prepared in triplicate, although there are circumstances where only two copies are required, such as shipments to Canada or Puerto Rico. The export declaration must be signed by an authorized person employed by the exporter. If an international freight forwarder is preparing the documents for the exporter, a power of attorney must be provided by the forwarder, and the forwarder is obliged to maintain it in his records.

In order to complete an export declaration, it will be necessary to establish the Commodities Schedule B number. Schedule B numbers are statistical classifications of all merchandise manufactured or agriculturally grown. This classification system is similar to the Standard Industrial Classification (SIC) used domestically by the government to classify all industry. It is important that the exporter determine the correct schedule B number and include it on line 13 of the declaration. Schedule B numbers are published annually and copies may be obtained from the Government Printing Office.

Many other countries require certificate of origin before they will clear the merchandise from customs. There are as many different forms for these certificates as there are countries requiring them. Always try to use the same language to describe contents as is used on the commercial invoice and the export declaration. Certificates of origin may be obtained from the consulate of the country requiring them or some countries do so much business with U.S. manufacturers that they have authorized a commercial printer to prepare their forms. In this latter case, forms may be obtained from a local office supply company or from some commercial printers.

Certificates of origin invariably require the certifying of exports as to their country of origin by the local Chamber of Commerce or in some instances, by the consulate itself. This is called Consular Legalization and there is usually a small fee charged for the service. Allow extra time for transmittal of documents if legalization is required and the consulate is not located in your city.

The U.S. government requires an export license for all merchandise shipped abroad. However, unless the item is of strategic importance to the

United States or its destination is to a country unfriendly towards the United States, only a general license is required. A general license is not a license in the strictest sense because an actual document is not issued or required, only the statement "G-Dest."

In order to determine if an item needs a specific license or can be shipped under G-Dest, it will be necessary to consult the Commodity Control List. If the item to be shipped is required to have a license, it will be necessary to actually acquire a document. Applications for licenses, known as GLV licenses, must be submitted on the Export Administration's form ITA-622P. Applications should include attachments such as descriptive literature and a copy of the original order from the overseas buyer. Processing licenses can take as long as ten weeks, so care should be taken not to commit to shipment and subsequent letter of credit payment until ample time has been allowed for any delays in procuring a license. There is also no guarantee that a license will be issued. If a commodity requires a validated license and the license is granted, then excellent records of the transaction much be kept.

Letters of instruction to the international freight forwarders tell them which documents you have included with products that are being sent to them for shipment overseas and what to do with the documents after shipment has been effected. If the international forwarder picks up the freight from the exporter's shipping dock without the necessity of using a separate transportation company, the letter of instructions should be included with the other documents accompanying the shipment. Instructions should be sent to the forwarder as soon as possible so he may begin to arrange space on a vessel for your merchandise. If the forwarder does not receive the instructions until he actually receives the goods, it may be too late to book space on the next vessel departing for your destination.

An in-house order should be prepared for all overseas orders. This form should attempt to make the export order appear as similar to a domestic order as possible so as to assure its prompt and complete handling. Accuracy is important because the in-house order is usually the first document prepared and it will be from this document that descriptions, weights, measures, and so forth will ultimately be prepared. A mistake on the in-house order may unintentionally repeat itself on all the documents, causing delays and confusion.

There are two types of insurance generally used for shipments abroad. One type, called the Insurance Certificate, is used for specific shipments. If an exporter manufactures products that differ widely from one another, he may find it necessary to insure each shipment separately. This requires the exporter to secure rates and coverage each time a shipment occurs. The exporter who regularly makes similar shipments abroad probably will want to initiate an Open Cargo Policy. With this form of insurance coverage, all international shipments are covered in advance of the actual shipment. The exporter, though, only has to pay for coverage of those shipments actually made.

NOTES

1. International Trade Reporter, *Export Shipping Manual,* No. 1236 (The Bureau of National Affairs, October 25, 1978), pp. 49.1—49.73.

2. *Instructions for the Use of the Shipper's Export Declaration,* Commerce Form 7525-V, U.S. Department of Commerce, Social and Economic Statistics Administration, Bureau of the Census, p. 2.

3. *Shipper's Export Declaration,* U.S. Department of Commerce, Bureau of the Census, International Trade Administration Form 7525-V (3-19-85), (Washington D.C.: U.S. Government Printing Office, Superintendent of Documents, p.1.

4. Gerard R. Richter, *Documentation,* International Trade Handbook (Chicago: The Dartnell Corporation, 1963), pp.177-184.

Chapter 10
Collecting Accounts Receivable

Chapter 10 may be the most important chapter of this book because it deals with how to collect your accounts receivables. In the United States it is a relatively simple matter to create and subsequently collect accounts receivables. However, when dealing abroad with at least two separate governments involved, as well as a buyer and a seller, the remedies for errors or misunderstandings can be laborious at best. Therefore, it is in the seller's best interest to be certain that his foreign accounts receivable are collectable before actual shipment of the merchandise occurs.

In this chapter the five methods of collecting overseas accounts are discussed:

1. Cash in advance or prepayment
2. Letter of Credit
3. Documentary sight draft, documents against payment
4. Documentary time draft, documents against acceptance
5. Open account

Any one or more of these methods, with variations or combinations, may be used by exporters. The choice of collection methods depends on many factors, including creditworthiness of the buyer, the exporter's capital position, the competition, the economic conditions in the buyer's country. Other considerations consist of the size of the order, the importance of the market, and the general trade practices within the country.

THE BILL OF EXCHANGE

Documentary collection is a very popular method of collection in foreign trade because it offers an effective compromise should conflict arise between the buyer's pressure for more lenient terms and the exporter's interest in self-protection.

The term *bill of exchange* and the term *draft* are used interchangeably. A draft is a legal document to the buyer from the seller that orders the buyer to pay a third party a given amount of money at a specified time. Other than selling on open account, it is the medium used in foreign trade to secure payment of funds from the client to the seller. In order to receive payment for merchandise, it is necessary to, draw or draft on the buyer. The draft physically resembles a check or a promissory note but in reality it is a demand for payment. The company making the draft is usually the manufacturer of the merchandise which is refereed to as the drawer and the buyer is called the drawee.

All drafts should show the full name and address of the buyer, the amount and kind of money (U.S. dollars or foreign currency), date, name of payee, signature of the drawer (seller), and an indication of whether the draft is payable at sight, at "X" number of days after sight, or at date of draft. For the protection of all parties, drafts should be in negotiable form, dated, payable "to the order of" the drawer's bank, or to the order of the drawer. If made payable to the order of the drawer, the draft must be endorsed.

There are basically two types of drafts: the *sight* and the *time* draft. The sight draft demands payment "on sight" which realistically means upon presentation. There are several steps involved in a typical export collection using the documentary sight draft. After shipment is completed, the exporter draws a draft on the buyer payable at sight to the exporter's bank for the amount due. Supporting shipping documents are attached to the draft and it is sent to the shipper's bank for collection. The bank endorses the draft as collecting agent for the exporter and sends it, together with the documents, to its correspondent bank in the buyer's country. The draft is then presented to the buyer. After the draft is paid, the correspondent bank sends the funds to the exporter through his bank.

The exporter should instruct his bank to release the documents only against payment. Thus, the buyer will not receive the bills of lading or other documents to clear the shipment until the draft is paid. This enables the shipper to make certain the buyer is unable to take possession of the goods until he is assured of payment. However, this protection can depend on the forms of the bill of lading and the laws and customs of the country of destination.

Documentary time drafts are collected in much the same way as a sight draft except that they allow the buyer a longer time in which to make payment. When the draft is presented to the buyer, he accepts it in writing or by stamping the word *accepted* across the draft, and adding his signature. In doing this, he acknowledges acceptance of the draft as drawn and commits himself to payment of the amount of the draft when it falls due. The controlling documents are released to the buyer upon acceptance of the draft. The exporter does not receive payment until the due date of the draft. However, the buyer's acceptance becomes an obligation of the buyer. The time draft will specify payment within a certain number of days after presentation. For example, if a time draft is for, "90 days after date," payment is due to be made 90 days after the date the draft is issued. On the other hand, if the draft reads, "90 days sight" payment is to be made 90 days after the draft is accepted by the buyer (or his bank). The difference between these two forms of drafts is that in the first example the payment is due 90 days after the date of the draft. The date of the draft will probably be the date the merchandise was shipped and payment is expected and due 90 days later. This is a fixed date in the future. In the second example, though, payment is due on sight 90 days after the draft is presented for payment. The merchandise will probably be in transit already by the time the draft is presented to the buyer (or his bank) and payment is not due until 90 days from that time.

A draft presented without documents attached is called a *Clean Draft* and frequently is used to collect for goods previously shipped on open account, in an attempt to collect on old items, or in special circumstances to provide a form of obligation.

Which form of time draft to us is wholly up to the discretion of firms buying and selling the merchandise. Either form is acceptable, and the one chosen should be left to the discretion of the negotiating parties.

The bill of exchange is documentary because, in addition to the draft itself, several documents are required before transfer of title to the merchandise is granted. The importance of complete and correct documentation is essential to export collections. As in all matters pertaining to export, accuracy is of utmost importance whereas the documentation required will depend on the (1) terms of sale, (2) method of shipment, and (3) legal requirements of the country of destination. In most instances the basic documents will include:

> a draft
> an ocean bill of lading or an air waybill
> a commercial invoice
> an insurance certificate
> U.S. Export Certificate

Depending on the country of ultimate destination, consular invoices or a certificate of origin may also be required. Delay in acceptance and payment is inevitable if the necessary documents are not available to the buyer or if errors cause difficulty in customs clearance. This is particularly true in countries that are not hard currency countries or countries that are currently having exchange and trade controls.

Just because a draft is written and sent to the buyer's bank does not mean it automatically will be paid. Payment will not be made until all the other terms and conditions of the sale are met, at which time the paying bank will rubber stamp the draft with the word *accepted* on its face. The acceptance will also contain the legal name of the drawee and the date the draw was accepted (illustration 10.1).

10.1. Example of a Draft Marked "Accepted"

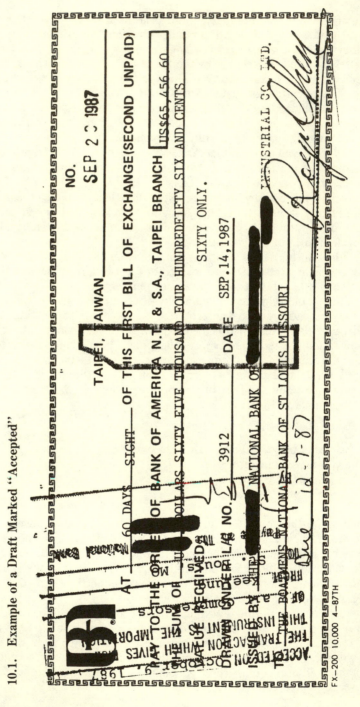

In order for acceptance to occur, it is essential that the draft be properly endorsed. If the draft is made "payable to the order of" the buyer, it will be necessary for him to endorse it either to his bank or in blank. There are several other ways endorsements may be effected, but they are not in common use. Should another method of endorsement be necessary, the buyer's bank will notify him.

Although documentary collections are a common and effective means of collecting payment for exports, the exporter's protection is not always as complete as it may appear in theory. For example, should the buyer refuse to honor the draft for some reason, the shipper would be faced with the problem of disposing of the merchandise in a foreign country. Warehousing or demurrage charges can cause dispute in the case of delayed payment. Protection of the exporter's interests can sometimes be affected or weakened by local laws. The beginning exporter is well-advised to consider all the foregoing items prior to shipment in order to minimize the risk; the documentary draft can be considered a sound and convenient method of collection.

LETTERS OF INSTRUCTION

Letters of instruction and a direct collection letter are the same (illustration 10.2). When preparing instructions and documents for the bank to use in collecting accounts receivable, always use air mail and always make them out in at least one original and three copies. At this point in the export process, the exporter is in a race with the merchandise. It is usual for the documents to reach the client's bank ahead of the goods, so that payment to the exporter's account can be made prior to the actual arrival of the merchandise in the country of destination.

Most international banks offer their clients forms that can be completed and which become the basis of instructions. The purpose of the instructions are to provide a direct collection letter, and to reduce transit time of documentary collections between the exporter, the exporter's freight forwarder, and the overseas collecting bank. It is important to remember that at least two banks will be involved in collecting documentary drafts: the exporter's bank and the importer's bank.

Speed is of the essence especially on air shipments or where documents covering ocean freight must arrive ahead of the cargo. In some ports normal collection procedures are so slow the merchandise reaches its destination ahead of the documents supporting the transaction. By airmailing the drafts, the exporter can minimize the possibility of delayed customs clearance while still having the security of obtaining payment of the drafts before the documents of title are turned over to the buyer.

On shipments via air freight, the exporter may insure delivery of the merchandise to the buyer only after his payment or acceptance of the draft by consigning the merchandise to the foreign collecting bank. In this

10.2. Example of a Letter of Instructions

November 24, 1987

First Interstate Bank Intl.
855 Third Avenue, 4th Floor
New York, NY 10022

ATTN: Export Letter of Credit Department
      Reimbursement Section

IN RE: Overseas Trust Bank's L/C number_____ Our Advice Number 87/E-2122

Gentlemen:

This is in compliance with the instructions contained in the above mentioned Letter of Credit dated September 30, 1987, a copy of which is enclosed. Also enclosed is our sight draft in the amount of U.S. $7,103.98. At maturity please send federal funds to the attention of the undersigned quoting our advice number.

Under separe cover we are forwarding the following documents to Overseas Trust Bank via registered airmail:

    Sight Draft in amount of $7,103.98 in duplicate.
    Commercial Invoice in duplicate
    Three Original Bills of Lading
    non-negotiable Bills of Lading in Quandruplicate

Very truly yours,

JLH/kd
enclosure

cc: Overseas Trust Bank
      160 Gloucester Road
      Hong Kong, Hong Kong

situation the exporter should indicate, "Please note merchandise consigned to yourselves. Release only against payment/acceptance."

Whether the exporter or his freight forwarder prepares the letter of instructions or the exporter's bank completes its own forms is immaterial. What is important is that the following information be provided:

The date.

Address where to airmail the documents. If your buyer has specified a bank, this bank's name should be inserted here. If no bank has been specified, inquire of your bank which correspondent they prefer in the client's country and insert that bank's name here.

Exporter's name and address as the drawer. Any subsequent correspondence as well as the payment will be sent to this address.

Description of item and documents should be handled by assigning each export shipment an internal reference number. This number should be used by the banks in order to determine the complete merchandise description and the documentation, as well as referencing future correspondence and payment.

Date of the Draft should be indicated separately from the date of the letter of instructions even though it probably will be the same.

Tenor as used in international commerce does not mean an adult male voice midway between bass and alto. Rather, it refers to the date the draft is due for payment such as "at sight." Obviously it is important to instruct the bank as to this date.

Amount due on the draft should be indicated in the instructions as well as on the draft itself. Be certain to indicate U.S. $(amount).

The foreign customer's name and address must be provided because this will be different from the name of the bank to which the documents are being airmailed.

The drawee's name and address, if different from the customer's.

General instructions regarding documents and charges should be included. These instructions will specify whether the documents should be delivered against payment on a sight draft or against acceptance on time drafts. Most banks will attempt to collect all banking charges from the drawee. Sometimes, however, the drawee refuses to pay some or all of the collection charges. If the exporter insists the drawee pay all collection charges and has an agreement with the buyer to this effect, instruct the bank "Do not waive charges."

Indicate the documents enclosed. Typically, these enclosures consist of bills of lading (negotiable or nonnegotiable), parcel post receipts, insurance certificates, invoices, consular invoices, packing lists, weight certificates, certificates of origin, and any other documents specific to the transaction.

Advise by cable if the draft is not accepted or if not paid. Failure to indicate this instruction in your letter of instructions may result in further delays should the exporter's bank have any difficulty collecting the draft.

Remit proceeds by cable should be mentioned in the letter of instructions if the exporter wishes to receive his funds as promptly as possible. The exporter should also instruct his bank whether the charges for cabling the funds are to be charged to the drawer or the drawee.

Remit proceeds by airmail is an alternative to cabling the funds. This method is not as fast as cabling, but it is less expensive.

Protest is the term used by the bank to indicate that the exporter wishes it to inform the correspondent bank that the exporter objects to its failure to accept or pay upon submission of the draft. Usually the banks can work out problems regarding nonpayment or acceptance between themselves and the client. Providing the bank with the ability to protest without first notifying the exporter expedites the eventual payment. Usually these problems arise because of inadequate or incorrect documents and can be solved by providing or correcting errors and omissions.

Dollar exchange occasionally can be a problem. The exporter's letter of instructions should inform his bank regarding what action to take should this situation arise. The exporter should be aware that should a dollar shortage exist at the time the draft is presented for payment, the bank will accept foreign currency and purchase dollars at the first date they become available. If there is a loss on the value of the currency, the exporter will be expected to absorb it.

The name and telephone number of the person to contact with questions should be included if different from the person signing the letter of instructions.

The signature of the person authorized by the company to sign documents of this type must be provided.

Many banks' forms contain the draft attached by a perforation to the letter of instructions. This is a convenient way for the exporter to complete his bill of exchange at the same time as his instructions.

Make certain the draft indicates the tenor, the drawee's name and address, and the signature under the company's name of person authorized to sign such legal documents.

The letter of instructions, the draft, and the other documents should be sent to the exporter's freight forwarder with instructions to him to proceed with the shipment as directed and to forward finalized documentation accompanied by original draft via registered airmail to the collecting bank without delay. The first copy of the draft and instructions should be airmailed to the drawer's bank, the second copy to the exporter, and a third and final copy should be retained by the forwarder for his files.

As soon as the exporter's bank receives its copy of the draft and instructions, it will follow up with the collecting bank and notify it of advises and payments received.

CONSIGNMENT

This writer does not recommend shipping products abroad on consignment unless the foreign sales company is well-known to the exporter and the exposure to loss slight. Consignment shipments require the same documentation as regular shipments except for banking instructions and drafts. A typical consignment example will point out the dangers in dealing overseas in this manner.

The American Widget Manufacturing Company ships one thousand small widgets to its agent in London, England with all expenses to their account. Thus, the agent in London receives the goods without any cost on his part. The agent is compensated for his efforts by receiving a 20% commission on all sales of American Widgets. During the first month, the agent sells five hundred small widgits for the equivalent of U.S. $1,000; he remits U.S. $800 to the manufacturer keeping U.S. $200 as his commission. The risk is, of course, that the agent will keep all U.S. $1,000, comfortable in the reality that he has the merchandise at no cost and is separated by over three thousand miles of ocean from the manufacturer. The cost to the manufacturer to recover his expenses would be prohibitively expensive. Of course, on the other hand, should the London agent go into bankruptcy, the American Widget Manufacturing Company can demand the return of its product, because it never was removed from its own inventory.

As a practical rule, consignment shipping should be left to those companies that maintain their own overseas subsidiaries.

COD

In international trade, COD shipments can be a convenient way to transfer small or low value items between one country and another. Most COD shipments are made via parcel post, air freight, or air package express. Basically, these movements are handled almost identically to COD shipments within the United States. Credit risk is minimal because the client does not take possession of the goods until he has paid for them. The only risk is that the carrier will not pay the exporter. In reality this is a very slight possibility because all parcel post shipments are made by the government and most air freight is handled by large domestic carriers or international carriers that frequently are owned, at least in part, by a government.

CASH IN ADVANCE

It may seem odd that anyone would send a foreign manufacturer money in advance after discussing all the things that can go wrong with international dealings, but the reality is that it happens quite regularly.

During the 1970s when Lebanon first began to have serious political problems, this writer was exporting a library card imprinting machine that was in demand by most of the world's libraries. The client in Lebanon wanted to purchase several of these machines but he could not get any letters of credit that were satisfactory to the machine's manufacturer. The problem was that the fighting would come and go and the American banks never knew for certain when a correspondent bank in Lebanon would be open or closed. Of course, later all the banks closed. For a short time the client was able to get letters of credit drawn on French banks, but soon this withered due to a lack of foreign exchange. The only way left for the client to import the card imprinters was to cable the cash (U.S. currency) in advance and trust the exporter. This arrangement worked well until the client was forced to flee the country, at which time all the manufacturer's export activity to Lebanon ceased.

CASH AGAINST DOCUMENTS

A satisfactory alternative to documentary drafts is cash against documents at point of shipment or through a bank in the United States. It is important for the company new to export not to consider cash against documents outside of the United States. Properly done, this is an excellent way to safely be assured of payment without entailing the expenses associated with letters of credit or documentary drafts. These terms are most frequently used when the importer wants to have control over the transit of the merchandise or his government wants to minimize the foreign exchange losses. This is accomplished because the insurance typically used is issued in the destination country and frequently the ship transporting the freight is of that country's flag. An example of how cash against documents usually works will best explain its implementation.

The exporter's client is located in Chile and he and the exporter have already determined the selling price of the commodities he will be purchasing. The client has said he will pay the total cost, cash against documents, F.O.B. New York harbor. The goods are to be accompanied by nonnegotiable bills of lading consigned to his customs house broker in the Chilean port. In addition to these items, the exporter is to provide consular invoices and copies (original airmailed direct) of an application for marine insurance containing the terms and clauses he needs to satisfy his insurance company located in Chile. He will also send an import license which the exporter will surrender to the consulate in exchange for consular invoices when the shipment is ready to be made.

It is important to realize that in this type of transaction the exporter's U.S. bank will be advised of the arrangements being contemplated before any items are actually shipped. The bank contacts the bank in Chile and receives confirmation that payment will be made as soon as it receives the documents enumerated in the client's order. Therefore, there is no real risk because the manufacturer is assured by the American bank that payment will be made upon its receipt of the documents evidencing that shipment has taken place. In this type of arrangement, the U.S. bank would pay the exporter before it actually collects payment from the Chilean bank. This is possible because the American bank debits the Chilean bank's dollar account in the United States. The Chilean's dollar account is called a *nostro account* which is an account that tracks the movement of dollars in United States' correspondent banks.

At the receiving end of the transaction, the client is given the documents by his bank as soon as his account with them is debited of the appropriate amount of pesos needed to purchase U.S. dollar exchange. The client, upon receiving the documents, will forward them to his customs broker who will proceed to clear the goods through customs.

LETTERS OF CREDIT

A letter of credit (L/C) is the written undertaking of a bank, representing a buyer, to honor drafts and other demands for payment upon presentation of documents complying with the letter of credit's specified conditions. Letters of credit are issued by a bank at the request of its customer (usually the importer) and are issued for a specific company (the exporter) which is refered to as the *beneficiary*. L/C's are for a specific amount of money, usually in U.S. currency when opened for American exporters, and they always have a fixed expiration date. Letters of credit may be either revocable or irrevocable.

The novice exporter should shy away from revocable letters of credit because they may be cancelled after the exporter has shipped the merchandise. Should this situation arise, the exporter is confronted with how to dispose of items or pay the additional cost of having them returned to the United States. It is far better to insist that all letter of credit dealings be conducted with irrevocable terms.

One other area of caution should be noted if the letter of credit issued in the exporter's favor is *unconfirmed.* Unconfirmed letters of credit depend on the issuing bank's being able to meet its obligation. This is usually not a problem, but occasionally events conspire that make it impossible for a bank to honor its obligation to its correspondent bank. A war or political uprising may be an example of an event that may keep a bank from honoring its obligation. Or, perhaps the country in which the issuing bank is located will experience a foreign exchange crisis forcing it into default. These possibilities, slight though they may be, can be avoided by insisting that the client open a confirmed irrevocable documentary letter of credit. With a confirmed L/C, the paying bank will be assured that the funds will be paid unless the letter of credit is allowed to expire or unless all the parties agree to its cancellation.

When using letters of credit in international trade, the wise exporter insists that his client not only open an irrevocable confirmed documentary letter of credit, but also that it be drawn on a U.S. bank. Furthermore, the exporter should insist that the foreign bank's American correspondent bank be his bank. When this is done it is called a *straight* credit as opposed to a *negotiated credit.* Straight credits usually contain an *engagement* clause that may read,

> WE HEREBY <u>ENGAGE WITH YOU</u> THAT DRAFTS DRAWN IN COMPLIANCE WITH THE TERMS AND CONDITIONS OF THIS CREDIT WILL BE DULY HONORED UPON PRESENTATION AT REPUBLICBANK DALLAS, N.A., DALLAS, TEXAS, ON OR BEFORE DECEMBER 31, 1983.[1]

If the paying bank is not specified, the foreign issuing bank may issue a negotiation credit that reads,

> WE HEREBY ENGAGE WITH <u>DRAWERS, ENDORSERS, AND BONAFIDE HOLDERS</u> OF DRAFTS DRAWN UNDER AND IN COMPLIANCE WITH THE TERMS AND CONDITIONS OF THIS CREDIT THAT SAME WILL BE DULY HONORED IF NEGOTIATED ON OR BEFORE DECEMBER 31, 1983.[2]

This may sound like a lot of demands being made by the supplier to the customer but, in reality, these are small matters and usually of little concern to the customer. In fact, if the customer has dealt with overseas vendors before he will be more surprised by a lack of demands. Of course, when specifying the bank, the exporter should be assured that his bank is an international bank. Do not attempt to conduct complicated business transactions using a local branch of a big bank or a small local bank. Such banks do not have the staff or expertise to properly handle transactions of this nature.

There are basically four situations that can be defined as risks intrinsic to foreign trade. These are (1) Credit Risk, (2) Exchange Risk, (3) Transfer Risk, (4) Political Risk. Of these risks, the first two can be reduced or eliminated through the use of documentary letters of credit. Among the reasons for the risk reduction is the fact that payment is not made until specified documents are presented. In fact, most letters of credit conform to the International Chamber of Commerce Uniform Customs and Practice for Documentary Credits, (1983 Revision) I.C.C. Publication No. 400, which specifies in article four that "In credit operations all parties concerned deal in documents, and not in goods, services and/or other performances to which the documents may relate."[3] This not so subtle statement should be taken by the exporter to understand that the banks are concerned with the documents supporting the shipment of goods and not with the goods themselves. Banks are institutions typically concerned with the orderly progression of paperwork. When everything is in the proper sequence and everything asked for is provided, the bank in its inimitable wisdom will pay. However, if just one small detail is lacking, payment will not be made without the addition of more documents. When errors or omissions occur it is usually possible to get an amendment that will clear up the problem and as a result, free the merchandise from customs and secure payment from the bank. Amendments are discussed in the section immediately following letters of credit.

In the typical international sales situation, the seller will first receive a request from his potential customer for a pro forma invoice. If the pro forma is satisfactory and its terms call for payment via letter of credit, the manufacturer will learn of this when he receives a letter from a bank that the client has opened a letter of credit for the goods covered in the pro forma. This letter from the bank is called an *advice*. If it is confirmed, the letter will so state (illustration 10.3). If the seller receives an unconfirmed L/C but requires a confirmed L/C, it will be necessary to amend or cause the L/C to be cancelled and a new one opened. In either situation, the original L/C will be provided along with the advising bank's letter detailing how it will handle the transaction for the exporter. If an unconfirmed L/C is received by the bank, the advice will usually be in the form of a letter that contains various statements, any of which will be checked off as applicable to the situation. Illustration 10.4 is an example of such an advice issued by an American Bank. Notice that the bank has assigned the transaction an internal reference number, stating the correspondent bank's L/C number, and indicating the amount of the letter of credit. In addition they have stated that they have enclosed the original L/C and the L/C "...conveys no engagement by us." The bank has also made a special notice that even

10.3. Example of a Confirmed Letter of Credit

INTERNATIONAL DIVISION
Cable address: "TXBNK"
Telex 193185
Tel. 314/425-7810

Correspondent's Irrevocable
L/Credit No.

Advice No.

Beneficiary

Correspondent Bank

Gentlemen:

We are pleased to enclose herewith an irrevocable credit issued in you
favor by   for the account of
for an aggregate amount of $

Drafts must clearly specify the number of this advice and may be presented
at this bank with the original credit, and amendments if any, not later
than

If you are unable to comply with the terms of the credit, please
communicate with your customer promptly with a view to having the
conditions changed.

Please mention the number of this advice in any correspondence with us.

WHEN PRESENTING DOCUMENTS TO US, PLEASE ENCLOSE AN EXTRA SET OF COPIES FOR
OUR FILES.

NOTE: OUR CHARGES WILL BE DEDUCTED FROM THE PROCEEDS OF YOUR DRAWINGS.

EXCEPT SO FAR AS OTHERWISE EXPRESSLY STATED, THIS ADVICE IS SUBJECT TO THE
UNIFORM CUSTOMS AND PRACTICE OF DOCUMENTARY CREDITS INTERNATIONAL CHAMBER
OF COMMERCE BROCHURE NO 400. (1983 REVISION).

WE CONFIRM THIS CREDIT AND THERBY UNDERTAKE THAT ALL DRAFTS DRAWN AND
PRESENTED IN COMPLIANCE WITH THE CREDIT WILL BE DULY HONORED BY US.

10.4. Example of Banker's Advise of Letter of Credit

INTERNATIONAL DIVISION
Cable address: "TXBNK"   Correspondent's Irrevocable
Telex 193185   L/Credit No.
Tel. 314/425-7810

                                         Advice No.
Beneficiary   Correspondent Bank

Gentlemen:

We are pleased to enclose herewith an irrevocable credit issued in you
favor by   for the account of
for an aggregate amount of $

Drafts must clearly specify the number of this advice and may be presented
at this bank with the original credit, and amendments if any, not later
than

If you are unable to comply with the terms of the credit, please
communicate with your customer promptly with a view to having the
conditions changed.

Please mention the number of this advice in any correspondence with us.

WHEN PRESENTING DOCUMENTS TO US, PLEASE ENCLOSE AN EXTRA SET OF COPIES FOR
OUR FILES.

NOTE: OUR CHARGES WILL BE DEDUCTED FROM THE PROCEEDS OF YOUR DRAWINGS.

EXCEPT SO FAR AS OTHERWISE EXPRESSLY STATED, THIS ADVICE IS SUBJECT TO THE
UNIFORM CUSTOMS AND PRACTICE OF DOCUMENTARY CREDITS INTERNATIONAL CHAMBER
OF COMMERCE BROCHURE NO 400. (1983 REVISION).

though the L/C is addressed to the advising bank, the exporter is to consider itself as the beneficiary. The letter in illustration 10.3 represents an actual transaction and it was accepted by the manufacturer even though it is not confirmed. The reason for the acceptance was that the drawee was the Central Bank of Egypt, the equivalent of the Federal Reserve Bank. The exporter's opinion was that any transaction by the oil-rich central bank would not be defaulted.

A facsimile of the actual letter of credit issued by the Central Bank of Egypt can be found in illustration 10.5. By reviewing this L/C the following observations can be made:

> The L/C was originally cabled to a U.S. Bank, therefore this written form acts as a confirmation of the credit and spells out in detail which documents will be needed to complete the transaction.

> The L/C is irrevocable and documentary.

> The L/C is issued in favor of the Ministry of Education in Cairo, Egypt.

> The amount of the credit may not exceed U.S. $2230.78. Presumably the sum may be less than U.S. $2230.78.

> The funds are U.S. dollars.

> The credit is available in the United States which means that both the advising bank and the paying bank (in this case both are the same bank) will be American.

> The L/C will be available to the U.S. exporter until four months from the date that the bank advised the exporter that the L/C is available. In other words, the exporter has four months from the date he is made aware of the order to ship it.

> Payment will be made via sight draft.

> The L/C enumerates which documents must be sent to the bank in order to effect payment. These include an original commercial invoice and six copies certified by the Chamber of Commerce and legalized by the Egyptian consulate. The commercial invoice must be signed by the exporter and contain the following statement, "We certify that this invoice is, in all respects, correct and true, both as regards the prices and the description of the goods referred to therein, and that the country of origin or manufacture of the goods is the U.S.A."

A prepaid airway bill containing the number of the L/C and the value of the goods.

The documents must reflect the information provided on the January 23, 1978, pro forma and must indicate that the amount of the L/C represents the value of the goods CIF Cairo airport and that the insurance premium should be deducted from the amount shown on the pro forma.

The goods are to be shipped on Egyptair, which is the Egyptian flag carrier.

Partial shipments are not allowed.

Transshipment is not allowed, although shipment between cities within the United States is permitted.

Insurance is to be provided by the buyer.

The draft for payment must be marked, "Drawn under Central Bank of Egypt, Cairo Irrevocable Documentary Credit No. 1234/87 dated May 20, 1987."

The original documents are to be posted via registered airmail and the duplicates of the documents by surface mail.

Banking fees will be paid by the issuing bank. This will be done by the U.S. Bank's debiting the Bank of Egypt's account and certifying to them that all the demands of the credit have been satisfied.

Many major international banks maintain accounts in each other's banks from which they can draw funds. Banks that deal in this manner are said to have *depository* relations. If an issuing bank corresponds with a bank with whom it does not have a depository relation, they will still work together but payment will take a little longer because the funds will have to be transferred between them. Frequently this is done by introducing a third bank into the transaction with which the issuing bank does have a depository relation.

In most situations regarding letters of credit, the issuing bank will advise its correspondent bank of the pending transaction by cable. This is important because each cable contains a secret code known only to the banks. This secret code guarantees the legitimacy of the L/C and the issuing bank. If a cable is received by a bank that does not contain the code, the correspondent bank will disregard it. As strange as it may seem, fraudulent letters of credit are fairly common. During 1987 there was a

10.5. Facsimile of a Letter of Credit Drawn on Central Bank of Egypt

THE CENTRAL BANK
P.O Box 35
Cairo, Egypt

REGISTERED

Cable Address: BANKCENTRAL CAIRO
Telex No.1240
Cairo May 20, 1987
REF. 2814/8/2456

TO: The First Bank of New York
P.O. Box 1897
New York, NY 10007

IRREVOCABLE DOCUMENTARY CREDIT NO. 1234/87

Dear Sirs,

We hereby open an irrevocable documentary credit as described hereunder in favor of Ministry of Education for the sum of $2,230/78 say U.S. dollar two thousand eight hundred thirty and cents seventy eight only.

This credit is available in U.S.A. until See N.B.1 below inclusive against the beneficiaries' draft (s) drawn at sight accompanied by the following documents marked (X).

☒   Commercial Invoices (s) in six copies Original of which at least must be certified by the Chamber of Commerce or Industry or other competent authority and legalized by the Egyptian Consulate (if available in the town of origin of the invoice). The invoices must contain the following certification signed by the beneficiaries: "We certify that this invoice is, in all respects, correct and true, both as regards the prices and the description of the goods referred to therein, and the country of origin or manufacture of the goods is U.S.A."

☐   Full set of clean "On board" BILL(S) OF LADING issued or endorsed to the order of the Central Bank of Egypt marked "Notify Ministry of Education" showing "Freight Prepaid" "Freight Payable at Destination" and accompanied by or incorporating a certificate to the effect that the vessel is not owned by an Israeli Company and is not included in the Arab Boycott of Israel List and is not scheduled to call at any Israeli Port during its current voyage.

☒   Air Consignment Notes showing as consignee the Central Bank of Egypt, Cairo for account of the barer and marked! "Freight Prepaid" and bearing the number of this credit and shows the value of the goods.

136

□ Parcel Post Receipt (s) showing as consignee the Central Bank of Egypt, Cairo for account of the buyers and bearing the number of this credit.

□ Certificate of Origin issued by the Chamber of Commerce or Industry evidencing that the goods are of origin.

□ Certificate issued by beneficiaries indicating that the goods are brand new and in conformity with credit.

The documents must evidence the current shipment not later than See N.B.1. Below of the following goods: as per attached proforma invoice No. 1, 2 & 3 dated January 24, 1987.

N.B.1 (4) months from the date of your advising the credit to beneficiaries.

N.B.2. The amount of credit represents the value of the goods CIF Cairo A/F and therefore the insurance premium should be deducted from the invoice, and the amount to be paid to beneficiaries under the credit.

N.B.3. Good are to be dispatched from U.S.A. to Cairo on board Egyptair.

By Air Freight   From   U.S.A.   To Cairo, Egypt

C & F Cairo A/P

PARTIAL SHIPMENTS NOT PERMITTED

TRANS-SHIPMENT NOT ALLOWED (Outside U.S.A.)

INSURANCE IS COVERED LOCALLY BY BUYERS.

Drafts drawn under this credit must be marked "Drawn under Central Bank of Egypt, Cairo, Egypt Irrevocable Documentary Credit No. 1234/87   dated   May 20, 1987"

You are kindly requested to advise the beneficiaries accordingly, without adding your confirmation.

Please forward the original set (s) of documents to us by first registered airmail and duplicates by second airmail.

In reimbursement of all payment and relative charges (if any) under this credit debit our current account with you rash of L/C's being issued by a bogus bank allegedly located in the U.K. This scam can work if the correspondent bank is accustomed to working with international letters of credit. The risk to the exporter is that he may conform with the conditions and ship his merchandise only to find that after he submits his draft to the nonexistent paying bank, that it does not exist and he has either lost his goods or must pay to have them returned. The remainder of the scam occurs after the goods have been abandoned and customs auctions them. Usually by prearrangement with a customs inspector, the culprit is advised when the items are to be auctioned and he purchases them for a fraction of their fair market value.

AMENDMENTS TO LETTERS OF CREDIT

As mentioned previously, the first thing an exporter should do upon being notified that a letter of credit has been opened in his favor is to check it and verify that all the terms and conditions are identical to those previously agreed upon. In most situations this will mean that the terms of the L/C are the same as the terms presented in the pro forma. If discrepancies exist or if there is an error in the L/C itself, the exporter should contact the foreign client and instruct him to cause his bank to issue a letter of amendment to the correspondent bank in the United States. The amendment must be agreeable to all parties, otherwise enforcement will be impossible. As soon as the amendment is issued, the exporter will receive an "Advice of Amendment" from his bank (illustration 10.6).

DISCREPANCIES

Discrepancies occur whenever the documents submitted do not conform with the terms or requirements of the letter of credit. Most discrepancies occur because the beneficiary does not present all the documents called for by the letter of credit or the documents do not strictly conform to the L/C's requirements. Sometimes the beneficiary fails to submit the documents within the time limits stipulated by the letter of credit previously accepted by him.

When discrepancies arise, problems are created for both the exporter and the client. Failure to conform to the terms of the letter of credit can mean that the exporter will not be able to fill the client's order during the period of protection afforded by a L/C or that a delay of payment will occur. From the standpoint of the client, nonconformity can cause expensive delays and complications with customs clearance.

There are five ways discrepancies can be resolved:

1. Correcting errors by the beneficiary or by the issuer of the documents.

2. Requesting buyer to have credit amended by the issuing bank.

3. Instructing negotiating or paying bank to obtain authority to pay or negotiate by telex.

4. Sending documents on approval basis under the credit.

5. Sending documents for collection outside of the letter of credit conditions.[4]

Of these remedies the last two are least desirable for the obvious reason that protection has been lost. These solutions should only be undertaken when the buyer is well-known to the seller and a mutual trust exists.

OTHER SPECIALIZED FORMS OF LETTERS OF CREDIT

Several other forms of letters of credit are available but these are generally used by experienced exporters or exporters who have a specific situation that cannot be handled with irrevocable documentary letters of credit. For example, transferable letters of credit allow the exporter to transfer drawing rights to a third party; back to back letters of credit require the exporter to secure an L/C in order to pay for the goods he shipped against a letter of credit he received; Stand by letters of credit are used frequently in situations where bid bonds or performance bonds are required and other specialized situations where there is concern about the customer of the issuing bank; assignment of letters of credit are used when the exporter may authorize a third party, usually an OEM, to draw a specified amount under the letter of credit.

SUMMARY

Although this chapter specifically deals with collecting accounts receivable, in a larger sense it summarizes the flow of paperwork necessary for commerce to occur between two nations. The sales process begins when correspondence, quotations, pro formas, and contracts change hands between two companies located in two countries. This exchange of information is the catalyst that begins the entire export process outlined in the following flow chart:

Upon the buyer's acceptance of the terms of the pro forma or quotation, he will petition his government for a foreign exchange permit, if one is required.

10.6. Advise of an Amendment

☐ Confirmation of Telex

AMENDMENT TO IRREVOCABLE DOCUMENTARY LETTER OF CREDIT

Date
Advising Bank

Issuing
Bank's Number

Advising
Bank's Number

Applicant

Beneficiary

This amendment is to be considered as part of the abovementioned Irrevocable Documentary Letter of Credit and must be attached thereto.

The abovementioned Irrevocable Documentary Letter of Credit is amended as follows:

☐ Extend latest shipment date to

☐ Extend expiration date to

☐ Increase amount by   making a new total of

☐ Decrease amount by   making a new total of

☐ Other

140

All other terms and conditions remain unchanged.

	Advising bank's notification
Very truly yours,	
Authorized Signatures	Place, date, name and signature of advising bank.

Except so far as otherwise expressly stated, this Irrevocable Documentary Letter of Credit is subject to the "Uniform Customs and Practice for Documentary Credits" as fixed by the International Chamber of Commerce in effect as of the date of issuance hereof.

Upon approval of the application, the buyer is granted an import license and foreign exchange permit.

With the import permit in hand and approval of his government to spend foreign exchange, the buyer will next apply with his bank for a letter of credit if this is the medium to be used to pay for the merchandise. Other options such as open account, cash in advance, cash against documents do not require an application's being filed with the bank.

If a letter of credit is selected, the buyer will be asked to provide the following information:

The type of credit, usually an irrevocable, documentary, confirmed L/C payable at sight and drawn on an American bank.

> The Manner of Issuing, usually an authenticated cable (using a secret code known only to the banks) advised through a United States bank.

The name of the beneficiary, i.e., the seller or the exporter.

The currency, i.e., U.S. dollars.

A description of the merchandise.

The pier or port of loading, i.e., any U.S. port.

The validity of the letter of credit; any term may be specified, but usually sixty days from the date of the L/C's issuance.

The shipping date; the buyer should allow the seller at least forty-five days from the L/C's date of issuance. This date will obviously be predetermined by the information contained in the pro forma and dictated by the manufacturer's lead time.

Partial shipments, usually not allowed.

Transshipment, usually not allowed.

The trading terms; i.e., normally C.I.F., but occasionally C&F, or F.O.B. any U.S. port.

Instructions regarding the payment of banking charges

associated with the opening of all letters of credit, usually to the account of the buyer.[5]

The letter of credit approval.

The letter of credit is cabled to the U.S. advising bank and followed by sending the actual document.

The U.S. bank confirms (or advises) letter of credit and sends it to the seller.

Upon the seller's receipt of the letter of credit, he should verify that all the terms and conditions of the L/C can be met. This is done by performing a check of all the items contained in the L/C:

1. Is the L/C irrevocable?

2. Is the L/C addressed properly?

3. Is the L/C confirmed or unconfirmed?

4. Does the merchandise description agree with the pro forma?

5. What are the shipping terms (i.e., F.O.B. port, C&F, C.I.F., etc.) and do these agree with the pro forma?

6. What are the terms of the draft for payment, i.e., sight or time? If a time draft, who pays the discount charge?

7. What is the latest shipping date? Can this date be met?

8. What is the expiration date? Can this date be met?

9. Is the amount of the L/C sufficient?

10. What are the documents required? Can these documentary requirements be met?

11. Are partial shipments permitted? Not permitted?

12. Is transshipment permitted?

13. Are consular documents required?

14. What is the port of exit? Discharge? Is compliance possible?

15. Are transportation charges to be prepaid or collect? Does this comply with the shipping terms?

16. If insurance documents are not required, is there evidence that the buyer will insure?

17. Are there L/C terms and conditions which need clarification?

18. Do the unit prices agree with pro forma?

19. Is the L/C payable in U.S. dollars or other currency?

20. Comments (is an amendment in order?) [6]

> An acknowledgment and confirmation that the L/C has been sent to the seller is usually sent to the buyer.
>
> The letter of instructions, the original letter of credit, the commercial invoice, and the packing list is sent to the international forwarder.
>
> If a validated export license is required, an application to the Bureau of Foreign Commerce is prepared and posted.
>
> Upon granting of the license application, the actual license is sent to the seller.
>
> If legalization of the documents is required, a request for legalization is sent to the appropriate consulate.
>
> Legalized consular documents are returned to the seller.
>
> The merchandise is sent to the international forwarder.
>
> The forwarder sends the export declaration and export license to U.S. Customs.
>
> U.S. Customs authenticates the declaration.
>
> The merchandise and all necessary documents are transferred to the international carrier at the gateway.

The forwarder books shipment with the international carrier.

The carrier confirms booking and on board information.

The letter of credit, ocean bill of lading (air waybill) and related documents are forwarded to the U.S. bank.

The United States bank pays the seller and mails the documents to the opening bank.

The buyer is notified by means of an arrival notice or telephone call that the letter of credit has been drawn and that the goods are in transit.

The ocean bill of lading (air waybill), consular invoices, and other documents needed for clearance are transferred to the buyers customs broker.

The carrier certificate and copy of the ocean bill of lading (air waybill) and the ship's manifest is given to customs upon arrival.

Upon entry the duties are paid and customs cleared.

The freight is now released and ready for delivery.[7]

NOTES

1. *Letter of Credit Seminar*, RepublicBank Dallas International Department, p. 20.

2. Ibid: p. 20.

3. "National Association of Councils on International Banking," Uniform Customs and Practice for Documentary Credits, Revised, 1983, ICC Publication No. 400.

4. *Letter of Credit Seminar, op. cit.*, p. 54.

5. *Instructions to Buyer for Establishing the Letter of Credit* (Dallas: RepublicBank)

6. *Export Letter of Credit Checklist* (Dallas: RepublicBank)

7. Charles A. Martinez, *Flow of Paperwork on International Shipments* (Houston: Harle Services, Inc.), p.1.

Chapter 11
International
Packing and Shipping

This chapter deals with how to physically package merchandise so it will arrive safely at its destination. Due to the length and method of transport abroad, packing used for domestic shipping is usually inadequate when viewed from the perspective of export.

Of the various methods of shipment, ocean freight is the most demanding but even air freight requires special considerations for some products. Regardless of the mode of transportation selected, the exporter must constantly prepare his shipments to counter problems of breakage, weight, moisture, and pilferage.

AIR FREIGHT

Shipments via air freight and shipments via air express companies can be treated identically and, in general, the packing used for domestic shipments may be satisfactory for international movements. However, the prudent shipper will take extra steps to insure his merchandise reaches its destination intact and he may find it cost effective to use only one type of fiberboard container for all his international shipments, regardless of transportation method selected.

If the commodity being shipped is large and heavy, the exporter is wise to plan on packaging it for air freight as if it were being shipped via ocean freight. The difference between domestic movements and international movements is the duration of the trip and, more importantly, the time the merchandise will be on the ground, possibly unprotected from the elements. Although most smaller items shipped via air freight are taken to warehouses or sheds for storage until customs can clear them, the larger items frequently must be stored outdoors, unprotected from the elements. For this reason it is advisable to plan on the worst case possibilities and package products as if they were being abused. In the next section dealing with ocean freight, the subject of crating will be discussed at length.

Therefore, in this section the discussion mainly centers around small shipments that are packaged in fiberboard containers.

Fiberboard makes an ideal packing material because it is inexpensive and relatively lightweight. Weight is important because freight rates are determined by cube and by weight. It stands to reason that the lighter the package, the less the freight rate will be. Unfortunately, if the package is too lightweight it will not withstand the rigors of international handling. The airports in many parts of the world are not as sophisticated as those in the United States and the equipment used to handle the freight may not be as gentle to the merchandise. For this reason the exporter is advised to never use a corrugated container with a bursting strength of less than 275 pounds per square inch. All fiberboard containers used for export should be selected based on their ability to withstand compression and resistance to puncture. Because all fiberboard containers are designed to be stored "in the flat," the scoring lines that make up the edges of the container are a source of potential weakness. In preparing an overseas shipment, the score lines should be strengthened by adding solid fiberboard corner reinforcements. The flaps of the container should be stapled or strong-glued with waterproof adhesive. To further protect the contents from moisture, the flaps should also be sealed using a plastic packing tape.

Inside the container, waterproof paper should be used to wrap the contents and to form a moisture barrier. Moisture may be the biggest problem confronted in shipments abroad. It is a good idea to purchase fiberboard boxes that have been waterproofed by the manufacturer or to have it done by the actual export packer.

Many airports around the world are overwhelmed with freight and because of this the exporter must take care to be certain that his packages can withstand the weight of other heavier packages being placed on top of them. The best way to guard against damage occurring due to large weights being placed on top (or side or bottom) is to pack the merchandise within the box in such a way that the merchandise supports the sides of the container. If the commodities that make up the contents of the box are such that they do not lend themselves to effectively brace the sides of the container, then the vacant space should be filled with fiberboard bracing. Do not just stuff the empty space with old newspapers or excelsior because this method will do nothing to protect the contents from compression. It may be necessary to have special nesting fillers manufactured in order to meet this need, but if that is the case, then do it! Additional strengthening of the container can be achieved by using a strapping material to wrap the container at right angles, crisscrossing the top and bottom. Do not overpack the container under any circumstances. Putting too much merchandise in a box is as bad as not putting in enough or not properly bracing the interior contents.

Palletizing or unitizing a shipment can provide additional safety if enough boxes can be assembled. Even a thin overwrapping of stretch wrapping will help ward off moisture and help hold the load together.

Lastly, because pilferage is always a problem do not advertise contents on the outside of the container. Use a plain kraft container clearly identifying:

1. The country of origin: Made in the U.S.A.

2. The weight, in pounds and in kilograms.

3. The number of the package and the size of it in inches and centimeters.

4. The handling marks, using internationally accepted pictograms.

5. The cautionary markings ("use no hooks," "flammable") in both English and the language of the country of destination.

6. The port of entry.

7. The marks for hazardous materials.

It is extremely important that all the above markings be legible. Delays or lost cargo will result if these markings are not applied with care. Use a good stencil board or other method of applying these marks. The marking should take into consideration the size of the container being marked. Although typewriter size type may be adequate for a small 30" X 30" box, it will not be adequate for a crate that is several feet in length, height, or width. If the shipment consists of multiple packages, number them consecutively and indicate the total quantity the shipment comprises such as, 1/20, 2/20, and so forth.

Always purchase new containers for your overseas shipments. Old, used boxes cannot be relied on since their strength will have deteriorated from prior use.

OCEAN FREIGHT

Packing merchandise for an ocean journey requires much more care than is necessary for air freight. Ocean freight is handled more roughly, more often, and is exposed to more weather elements than air freight. Therefore, it is important that care be taken in the packing of the goods. Packing for ocean freight consists of the inner packing which may best be described as the standard packaging used to contain the actual article being sold. This package is usually then combined with other similar or identical packages contained in a strong fiberboard box. The package is then either placed in a specially designed metal container or packed in a wooden crate.

Many, but not all, ports of the world can handle ocean freight containers. Containers come in various sizes, but they are always big. If the exporter has a shipment that domestically could be considered a truckload, then he should consider packing his freight into a container (after verifying with his freight forwarder that the port of embarkation and the port of disembarkation can accept containers).

When packing items for containerization, care should be taken that the items occupy as much of the available space as possible. Any empty space must be absorbed by properly bracing and otherwise securing the freight from shifting while the container is being handled. For example, blocks of styrofoam can be cut to fit into small, tight areas between the fiberboard boxes of packing and the roof of the container. For larger voids, sheets of plywood can be vertically placed against the merchandise boxes and cross braced against the container itself. If the merchandise in the container is of irregular shape such as bales or barrels, tension devices such as large rubber bands can be used to secure the items in a tight mass that will help cushion the items during transit and handling.

The greatest risk facing an exporter using ocean freight is moisture damage. Moisture is concomitant with ocean freight. Consider that the average ship's cargo bay is in excess of 100,000 cubic feet and that typically it will have 100 or more pounds of water sloshing around, creating 100% humidity. Should the temperature in the hold change even a little, water vapor can begin to condense. Condensation forms on the underside of the deck and then gravity causes it to fall onto the freight below. The problem of condensation is not limited to cargo exposed in an open hold, but also occurs within the containers themselves. Then again, all freight is not stored in the cargo hold of the ship. Many freight items are stored on the open deck of the ship and the merchandise is thus subjected to the ravages of the weather en route. If below deck storage is required, the exporter's forwarder must request it at the time he is booking the freight on the ship. Add to these transport risks the fact that freight is on and off loaded in all weather conditions and often stored in an open storage yard until customs clearance. If the exporter does not take adequate steps to protect his merchandise, rust, corrosion, stains, mold, mildew, rotting, swelling or warping may occur. It must also be remembered that should damage to merchandise occur in transit, the delays inherent due to the distances involved are expensive and can create ill will with the client. The exporter must take care that he has done everything possible to protect the merchandise from any damages caused by handling or transporting.

Unless the goods being shipped can be treated directly with preservatives, protective packaging will have to be external. The best way to protect items such as paper or wood products and textiles is by employing a waterproof barrier material. This material must not be "water resistant"; it must be "waterproof"! Waterproof barrier materials should be used as a box liner and not attached to the box in any fashion. The seams of the material must be sealed and the opening through which the commodities are added must be sealed with waterproof tape or heat seal closed.

If the items being protected are not in corrugated boxes to begin with, then the waterproof barrier material must be overlapped as it is wrapped around the item, sealed, and then wrapped in a protective material so abrasions caused by handling will not tear or puncture the barrier material.

Metal items should be generously oiled before shipment to reduce the risk of rust or corrosion and then wrapped in waterproof barrier material. Steel and other metals are frequently shipped in sheet form. For these types of commodities, the oiled sheets should be skidded and the entire load barrier wrapped and steel-strapped to the skid. Care should be taken to make certain the skids are constructed to accommodate the forks of the lift truck used in ocean freight. The lift trucks found on most docks are very large and the forks require more clearance than do most domestic fork lift trucks. Exporters should consult with their international forwarder to establish the correct size of skids or pallets that can be handled.

When shipping machinery and machined steel, the exporter should not only oil and use barrier materials, but also provide for adequate ventilation to protect against condensation. Machined edges and surfaces should be "potted" when possible or painted with a preservative. The individual items should then be wrapped further in a grease proof paper. The addition of this paper is to protect the rest of the cargo from oil or inhibitors running off the machinery if the temperature in the hold becomes so great as to cause the material to liquify and run.

Any item that can be damaged by moisture should be protected by adding a desiccant such as silicate gel within the boxes or bundles of goods. The addition of this material will provide a margin of safety that could not be achieved by merely wrapping in barrier material.

Containers and wooden crates provide the exporters with the greatest protection against theft and pilferage because they are difficult to open. However, the cardinal rule of international shipping is never to identify the contents of the container or crate. Easy identification invites theft. There are many ways the creative thief can find to acquire the exporter's merchandise. Several years ago a shoe company was experiencing an unusually high rate of theft at many of the world's docks. Determined to find out why its shoes were subject to such a high rate of theft, the company sent a representative to watch the freight actually being loaded on the ships. The representative discovered that the stevedores loading the shoes, which were wood-cased and skidded, conveniently dropped the cargo from the height of the ship's deck to the dock below. The concussion from a fall of this height caused the crate to brake apart and scatter the contents all over the dock. In the clean up process, numerous pairs of shoes disappeared. The shoe manufacturer thought long and hard about the problem and happened upon a solution he is using to this day; he never ships right and left-handed shoes in the same shipment. The theft problem disappeared as soon as the stevedores discovered that the cargo contained only shoes to fit one foot. In other words, the incentive to drop the cargo in order to get free shoes was eliminated.

A similar situation occurred during the 1970s when *Playboy* magazine was exporting its publications. In the early years, *Playboy* identified the contents of each crate. It did not take the stevedores a New York minute to load and drop a crate, thus exposing *Playboy* to considerable pilferage.

If containerization of the freight is not possible either because the freight does not lend itself to containerization or because the freight is not of suficient quantity, wooden crates should be constructed. A good wooden crate should be assembled from high quality, seasoned lumber and contain no more than 18% moisture. Knots should not be larger than 75% of the width of the lumber and should not be located where they will impinge upon the proper nailing of the crate. Although any nail can be used, cement-coated nails have proven to be best suited for export crating. The cement-coated nail has over 40% more holding strength than a common nail and 100% more strength than a barbed nail.

Entirely enclosed wooden crates are recommended over skeleton-type crates, because greater confidentiality is ensured and protection from the elements can be controlled more effectively. Limit the use of skeletal crates to those items that will not be harmed by the elements and are not usually the subject of theft or pilferage. Items such as punch presses, metal-forming machines, and so forth can be adequately protected in skeletal crates. However, for other items being shipped abroad, construct a closed crate built with a substantial framework and complete with diagonal cross braces and corner braces. The larger the crate, the more likely it will find its way to the very bottom of the ship, where it will be subjected to tremendous weight from other crates' being stacked on top of it. Therefore, be sure the top and the bottom of each crate is built to withstand this additional weight and stress. Construct the tops and bottoms with joists and then support them with cross members, particularly at the ends of the joists where the construction is the weakest. Do not run the vertical plywood sheeting all the way to the bottom deck. Failure to terminate the sheeting fractionally above the bottom of the deck will cause it to be pulled from the frame if the crate is dragged sideways. Similarly, the skids that should form the lower deck of the crate should always be chamfered. If each crate contains only one item, disassemble it as much as possible and try to achieve the lowest center of gravity possible. Do not allow anything within the crate to shift or break loose; use all of the interior space possible and fill out all vacant space with proper bracing to support the load.

As with container shipments, waterproof barrier paper should always separate the crate from its contents. The crate should be ventilated to reduce the likelihood of condensation forming and a desiccant should be added within.

Lastly, if the product being exported is a delicate instrument or of high value, consider using air freight. Even though the cost of air freight is much higher than ocean freight, the handling will be better and the transit time less. Several years ago when this writer was responsible for establishing a manufacturing plant in Japan, he shipped all of the fabricating machinery by air freight. This machinery consisted of heavy items such as modified punch presses and specialty fabricators each weighing several thousands of pounds. Due to the nature of equipment, it was considered worthwhile to ship in this manner because it enabled the firm to get into production quickly and the risk of damage in transit was greatly reduced. The equipment arrived in Japan completely undamaged and was operating several weeks later.

SHIPPING MARKS

The use of shipping marks is unique to export. Shipping marks are required on ocean freight movements and are optional for other modes of transportation. The shipping mark is created by either the exporter or the importer; in either instance it is applied to the outer packing using indelible ink. The mark must be large enough to be conspicuous (2 inches to 3 inches high) and should incorporate a geometric figure such as a circle, diamond, triangle or square. Usually the importer's order number is placed within the geometric figure. Immediately below the figure, the name of the unloading port and the name of the inland city of destination are placed. Below this is placed the number of the crate, usually expressed as a consecutive number of the entire number of crates that make up the shipment, i.e., 1/12, 2/12, 3/12, and so forth. (illustration 11.1). In addition, the crate marking must identify the net, gross, and legal weight of each crate. This information must agree with the information provided on the packing list, the bill of lading, the commercial invoice, and other documents relevant to the shipment.

The use of special marks on cargo shipments enables freight handlers and stevedores to identify cargo without the necessity of knowing the language of the shipper. It is an easy matter for the cargo handlers to put all cargo together that has the same markings and to read the package quantities and know when they have all the items they are supposed to have. The exporter is advised not to incorporate a symbol that describes the contents of his cargo, such as a diamond shape for jewelry. Also, it is good idea if a great deal of exporting from the same manufacturer is passing through the same gateway, to periodically change the markings so the material handlers do not become too familiar with the cargo they are handling. Do not forget to add the legend, "Made in U.S.A."

11.1.   Example of a Properly Marked Ocean Freight Shipping Crate

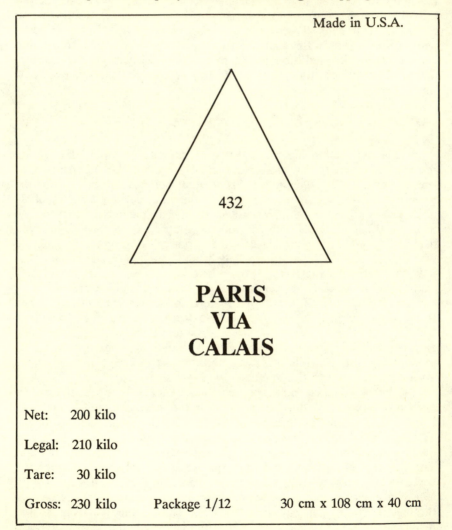

Made in U.S.A.

432

**PARIS
VIA
CALAIS**

Net:	200 kilo		
Legal:	210 kilo		
Tare:	30 kilo		
Gross:	230 kilo	Package 1/12	30 cm x 108 cm x 40 cm

PARCEL POST

Packing for shipment via parcel post overseas is little different from packing for domestic parcel post. The important idea to keep in mind is that restrictions vary from country to country. Always consult your International Mail manual before preparing a shipment of merchandise going abroad. There are several items, however, that are universally prohibited. These include:

1. Potentially harmful or dangerous items or substances

2. Gas or liquid under pressure (including aerosol containers) with specific exceptions

3. Explosives

4. Flammable materials that are liquid, having a flash point below 100° F and flammable solids that may under conditions incident to transportation cause fires through friction, absorption, or spontaneous chemical changes; matches and oxidizing materials

5. Weapons

6. Substances that give off a "bad" odor

7. Animals, plants, or other perishable products

8. Food and other perishable items which cannot reasonably be expected to reach destination without spoiling[1]

SUMMARY

The most important element in packing for export is to protect the shipment from moisture. Freight is frequently left on the docks or out of doors awaiting custom's clearance. In ocean movements, the exposure to condensation is great and on-deck cargo is subjected to continual salt spray.

In order to avoid theft and pilferage never identify the contents of a shipping container on its exterior. Containers and wooden crates provide the most secure packing. Because international shipments are generally over a greater distance than domestic shipments, extra care must be taken to protect the merchandise from damages that occur from handling or transit.

The outer packing required for ocean freight must be constructed durably enough to withstand the weight of several other crates being stacked on top. Cross-bracing of empty spaces left in containers or crates is imperative in order to avoid damage caused by shifting loads during handling and transit. The material handling equipment used on the docks is larger than is generally used for domestic handling. Therefore, the exporter must build his skids to accommodate the larger forks of the lift trucks. All methods of loading freight on board a ship may be used, so the exporter must anticipate loading via lift truck, net, or crane. The international freight forwarder can assist the exporter by providing answers to specific questions regarding loading, storage, and packing.

All ocean freight must be identified with a geometric figure with the destination in 2-to-3 inch lettering indicated below the figure. This marking (as well as all external markings) should be done in indelible ink so it can withstand moisture. The markings must include the legend "Made in the U.S. A." The gross weight, net weight, legal weight, tare, and number of each box must be marked.

If ocean freight is going to be interlined in the United States, it is advisable to staple a tag to the crate indicating the consignee at the gateway. The consignee will usually be the forwarder. Because the tag probably will not be removed prior to loading aboard ship, it is a good idea not to include the exporter's name and address on the tag so that material handlers cannot determine the contents of the crate and pilfer it.

NOTE

1. *International Mail*, Publication 42, Transmittal Letter 83, *U.S. Postal Service*, (Washington D.C.: U.S. Government Printing Office, January 2, 1976), § 323-323.142.

PART III
MARKETING ABROAD

Chapter 12
The Need for Foreign Language Sales Literature

This chapter discusses the necessity of producing sales literature in the languages of the countries to which export merchandise is being shipped. The need for advertising agencies, whether foreign or domestic, is addressed. Translations and conversion of American literature for foreign markets are also discussed.

SALES LITERATURE FOR THE BEGINNING EXPORTER

Many years ago an unknown sage made the observation that "You can't sell from an empty cart." This observation aptly describes the situation confronting the exporter. His prospect must know what he is buying before he will purchase it. Most people have visited an expensive French restaurant where the menu is printed only in French. Many of the restaurant's clientele cannot read any or all of the items on the menu so the maitre d' usually must translate: *fois gras* becomes goose liver, entrecôte becomes steak, and *pommes frites* become French fries. Imagine how difficult it is to attempt to interest a prospect in the advantages of ABC Valve Company's model 31 super hydrol faucet without being able to extol its virtues in a language the client can understand. Without language it is very hard to communicate, and it is absolutely essential to communicate in order to sell.

Few products can sell themselves without an explanation of their benefits and usually a comparison with the competitor's product. Even as simple an item as tea is difficult if not impossible to sell solely on the basis of a picture or the word. First, the word *tea* is not universal. Much of the world does not have a clue what tea is. For all of Asia to understand, it must be called *cha*. Even if a picture of a cup of tea is used to describe it, the client may be confused as to whether the cup or the tea itself is the product. If the client is sharp enough to deduce that the product is indeed tea, he still will not know what kind of tea it is, or if it is any better or different from any other tea he could purchase.

The exporter who attempts to sell his product abroad but refuses to produce descriptive literature in the foreign country's native language(s) will find it very difficult to achieve credible results. A subtle but equally vexing problem in selling to another country that uses the same basic language as Americans are semantic differences. The words may be the same, but frequently the meanings are different. For example, if the exporter is interested in selling trucks in England, he should refer to them as "lorries"; flashlights are "electric torches"; ladies hosiery are "tights"; napkins are "serviettes"; and rubber knee boots are "wellingtons."

The beginning exporter is often overwhelmed by the need to provide literature and other selling aids in a multitude of foreign languages. This need not be the case. Although it is extremely important to provide this literature, it does not have to be all done at once nor does it have to be expensive. How extensive a marketing program must be will certainly depend on the goals of the company and the availability of budget to support them. The nature of the products being offered also will bear directly upon the cost and need for literature. Because most products manufactured or services offered are specific as opposed to general, this chapter dwells primarily on the myriad products that make up the bulk of American manufactured goods: items such as printed circuit boards, screws, nuts, bolts, springs, headlights, brakes, and so forth; the nonglamorous ordinary kind of products that American manufacturers are turning out daily. We do not consider items such as wheat, coal, iron, steel, vegetables, or automobiles.

The American manufacturer who has a successful product in the United States and believes it can be sold abroad must be prepared to produce sales literature or have it created in a language the potential audience will understand. Once the form of distribution has been selected, and the representative or agent selected, the manufacturer must begin to heed his suggestions regarding methods for marketing the product. The manufacturer must take the advice of his representative seriously. Failure to take him seriously should cast serious doubt on the selection itself. Why would a company select an agent or representative to market its products without respecting his judgment regarding how to sell them?

A good way to start the process of marketing is for the manufacturer and the representative to discuss how similar products are already being marketed in the targeted country. If print advertising is an accepted means then it should be considered, even if it is not an accepted means in the United States. If the product is highly technical, then the directions for its use must be in a language that the ultimate customer can understand. Priorities must be established in order to conserve available cash and to spend it wisely. In most cases it will make no sense to create a high-priced advertising program until basic descriptive literature is first created. Many small representatives will take it upon themselves to create their own literature. This is an inexpensive way to begin, but it will usually lack the quality the manufacturer may want to project. It may also contain errors of which the manufacturer is ignorant because he may not understand the language in which the literature is prepared. As a compromise it is suggested that the manufacturer and his representative examine all the manufacturer's existing literature and reach a consensus as to which are the most important. These are the pieces that should be selected for duplication in the language of the representative's country.

Among the least expensive ways to actualize this is for the manufacturer to provide the representative with the actual photographs used in the literature. The manufacturer should be certain to inform the representative of the number of the screen used to print the photographs. In order for printers to copy a photograph, they must first rephotograph it through a screen. By doing this the photograph becomes a series of dots that are printable. Because of the varying degrees of grey in (black and white) photographs, it is impossible to print them. They must first be changed into a medium that can be printed in either black or white. The use of a screen accomplishes this.

The type face used in the U.S. literature should also be provided so the representative can duplicate it abroad. The type of paper used and the finish of the paper should also be made available to the representative for duplication. The identical type of paper used may be difficult to obtain abroad, but at least the representative will be able to go to a paper merchant and attempt to reproduce the paper. If colored inks are used to produce the literature, the representative should be given the name of the ink used or, if that is not possible, the "Panatone" number of the color. If line drawings are used in the literature, the representative should be provided originals consisting of black ink on white paper. Line drawings, by the way, are less expensive to print than photographs because halftones do not have to be made.

If the American literature consists of printing all the way to the edge of the paper itself, this is called *bleed edge* printing. Bleed edge printing is more expensive than printing that contains a margin of the color of the paper around the copy. Perhaps it would be a good compromise in the first pieces of literature produced to eliminate the bleed edge and save the extra cost (illustration 12.1). As long as the manufacturer and the representative agree that the piece will not suffer, it is perfectly acceptable to economize in this manner.

The translation will not occupy the same amount of space as the original language so an accommodation of text may have to be considered. For example, text in French requires more space than in English. It may be necessary to set the text in smaller type in order to say the same thing in French as in English. Some languages such as Arabic and Chinese are not printed reading top to bottom and left to right, so it will be necessary to accommodate the graphics in different positions than in English language literature.

Weber Modell 40 Automatik Etiketten-Drucker

Kompakt
Preiswert
Leicht nachzufüllen
Leicht aufzustellen
Leicht zu bedienen

Etiketten-Längen von 16mm bis 86mm
Etiketten-Breiten von 51 bis 102mm

Weber

Weber Modell 40 ist die jüngste Neuentwicklung im Programm der Etiketten-Schnelldrucker. Diese preiswerte, kompakte Druckmaschine ist genau das Richtige, um Ihre Etiketten-Produktion leistungsfähiger und wirtschaftlicher zu machen. Außerdem ist sie besonders leicht, damit Sie Ihre Etiketten überall dort herstellen können, wo sie gebraucht werden. Modell 40 wurde „auf menschlich" konstruiert, um alle Bedienungsaspekte so einfach wie nur möglich zu machen.

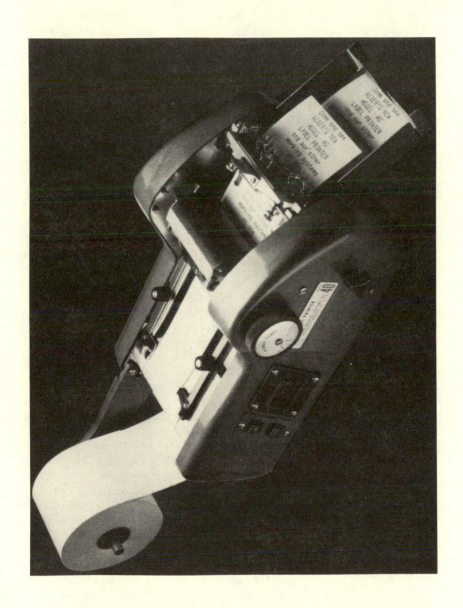

Some of the photographs used in American literature may contain English text. Unless the lack of the native language in the photograph is critical, it is suggested that the foreign representative can accommodate this exception. There is nothing that can be done about this except to shoot new pictures.

Another area that becomes difficult to handle in printing foreign language versions of literature is the use of reverses. A reverse occurs when words are created by printing a solid background, causing the outlines of the words to appear. In other words, the words themselves are usually the color of the paper and the background is the color of the ink. If reverses are going to be used, entirely new negatives must be prepared (illustration 12.2).

If reply cards are going to be incorporated into the literature, consider not perforating the card as it would be in American literature. Instead, use a little picture of a scissor to instruct the reader to cut the reply card from the literature. It is expensive and difficult to find printers capable of doing the perforations if they do not run the entire width or length of the page.

For countries with more than one language such as Canada, it may be possible to print one piece of literature in two languages (illustration 12.3). However, do not confuse the reader by providing row upon row of text explaining technical features. Certainly at one time or another everyone has been confused by multi-language literature designed to serve several markets. Camera and watch instructions from Japanese companies are usually a prime example of how not to create readable literature.

When preparing literature for consumption in another country, do not make a mistake by believing that just because the language is the same in two different countries, no modifications are necessary. The French that is acceptable in Quebec may not be acceptable in France or Belgium. Literature that is prepared for the French Canadian market should not be used in France. It is acceptable to use literature that is prepared for France in Canada, but usually it is not acceptable for Belgium. To mistakenly prepare literature this way will subject the exporter to ridicule from his distributors or representatives, as well as his clients. If it is the only literature available, it will probably be used but it always puts the representative in the position of having to explain the unusual turn of a phrase or grammatical usage rather than reinforcing his sales effort. Furthermore, your representatives will probably want to have their name or logo on the literature. They may even go so far as to suggest that the exporter's name or logo be deleted. Do not agree to this. Should the exporter agree to delete his name on the literature, he may be contracting beyond the terms of the original agreement with the representative. Also, it is in the exporter's best interest to maintain a high profile in the event it should ever become necessary to terminate the manufacturer-agent relationship. By all means allow the representative to have his name included along with the exporter's name on the literature because it will help his customers locate the representative should service or reorders be required.

12.2. Example of Reverse Printing

Comptoir-Services présente Weber

Weber

Machine Modèle 80 à faire les étiquettes

100
8 lbs.
STEREO
NOYER
AMPLIFIER KIT
WEBER MARKING SYSTEMS, INC.
ARLINGTON HEIGHTS, ILLINOIS 60005

12.3. Example of a Catalogue Prepared in Two Languages

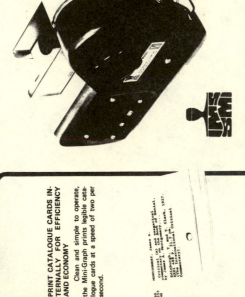

Some companies prepare literature, including their logo, for their representatives in the native language. Subsequently, they prepare identical literature for areas in which sales occur without representation. For example, an exporter may have a representative in Spain for whom he agrees to provide negatives for preparation of literature in Spanish, including the representative's name and trading style. However, the representative must also provide the exporter with Spanish text, so he may prepare his own literature for use in South America. In this example it would be far better for the exporter to prepare a separate piece for each country in South America but the cost and the volume of sales may not permit such a sizable investment. The best compromise is to prepare a universal piece using proper Castilian-style language. Castilian is considered the mother tongue just as Parisian is the mother tongue of French. The creation of a universal piece of literature would not have been as successful had the primary representative been located in Venezuela rather than Spain.

Another good, inexpensive source of foreign literature is the exporter's advertisements (illustration 12.4). Advertisements that are obsolete in America may be exactly what is needed in other countries. The level of sophistication in other countries may not be as great as it is in the United States. Consequently, literature and advertisements that are a few years old may still be very applicable abroad. Because the exporter has already amortized the cost of these pieces, the actual cost to provide the negatives and artwork is minimized. Some domestic advertisements can also be turned into brochures by printing additional information, or perhaps, by adding a mailing card on the reverse side of the piece. For example, in illustration 12.5 an American advertisement that was two pages wide has been translated into German and the representative's name and logo added. This piece was folded in the middle and on the backside, which then became the front page; the representative listed the trade shows at which he would be exhibiting during the year. On the backside he listed the other products and services he offered. This was a very successful piece of literature because it was used as a space advertisement, a brochure, a handout at trade fairs, and as a reply card to create a lead file. All this was accomplished at very low cost to both the manufacturer and to the representative.

A word of caution regarding translations is in order; although the best way to translate product information into another language is to rely on the actual representative in the country, one must be aware that all persons do not use perfect grammar. Although very few foreigners spell as poorly as Americans, they do make mistakes and it is in the exporter's best interest to avoid this. Therefore, all translations provided by foreign representatives should be checked by another party, preferably an academic. For a nominal fee, a language professor at a local university will proofread copy. It is best if this is done in the target country, but if not practical, consult a local U.S. university. After corrections have been made by the academic, resubmit the copy to the representative and grant him the opportunity to give final approval to the copy. This final approval is necessary in order to be assured the academic did not change an idiom that is critical to understanding the product.

A number of years ago an American company was exporting devices used to address cartons. The device was called a "handprinter" in English. The French academician called this device a "tampon" which was incorrect. A tampon is a rubber stamp. The correct word provided by the dealer was *imprimeur*. Had the exporter accepted the academician's selection, the dealer in France would not have been able to use the literature and all the cost associated with printing would have been lost. This example is a good illustration of why the local representative must have the last word in approval of foreign text.

The creation of foreign language literature is not limited to advertising copy. It should also include all technical bulletins and product training manuals. As mentioned earlier, it is important for the beginning exporter to try to do business with representatives or agents who are fluent in English. One of the reasons for this stipulation is that it will be necessary to translate all the technical data into the representative's native language. If the distribution network is only a single individual, no translation may be made because he will simply read the literature and then place the material in his library for future reference. However, if the organization is larger, it will be necessary to translate the data and distribute it to salesmen and technical representatives. In this situation it is essential that the importing organization be able to provide adequate translations.

One of the fears many exporters share is that often they have no way of knowing if the material they send abroad is actually being used to train sales persons and technical personnel. At first the representative is willing to send copies of the translated text to the exporter, but as the volume grows this chore becomes more onerous and the representative may begin to feel resentment toward the exporter. This resentment is caused by the importer's beginning to believe that the exporter is exerting too much control over him. He may begin to perceive that the exporter does not trust him, which is a personal affront, or that his judgment of what is relevant is being questioned, which is a professional affront. Obviously this is a situation that should be avoided. The exporter must walk a thin line and not be over-zealous regarding how the representative markets his products. Many times the flow of information is one sided: from the exporter to the importer. An exchange of relevant information must be nurtured from the beginning.

A good method of developing good communications between seller and purchaser is to decide early in the commercial relationship who will pay for advertising, literature, training aids, manuals, bulletins, and so forth. Some exporters take the position that after they sell their product, any costs involved with its marketing are to the account of the importer. Others consider it their obligation to provide all materials at no charge to the importer. Still others compromise and establish rules regarding who will be responsible for paying for specific items. Of these approaches, the last is the most flexible and equitable.

A good method for developing a marketing program is on a country by country basis. Determine through discussions with each purchaser what his needs will be during the first few years. Typically, the agent or representative will want copies of everything the exporter has in the way of sales literature and technical data. He will spend a great deal of time reviewing this material and developing a marketing plan that he feels will work. Frequently what the representative would like to do and what he can afford to do are quite different. Naturally, the representative will not articulate this to the exporter because he does not want the exporter to think that he made a mistake in selecting him to represent the products abroad. Therefore, the exporter may not penetrate the market as fast as he would like. When the exporter and the representative have different opinions of what is needed in terms of sales literature and other selling aids, it is in everyone's best interest to compromise and jointly develop a marketing program that is equitable to all parties.

It is a given that most companies will not agree to send U.S. dollars to another country to pay for marketing expense. This is also likely to be the first request the foreign representative will make. It should not become an arguable point. What should develop is an agreement whereby both parties agree to share an equitable percentage of the costs for marketing the products through the creation of foreign language literature. One such equitable arrangement might be for the exporter to provide the photographs, line drawings, text, and the representative provide the translations and the printing. Some companies agree to extend additional discounts on their products as a means of freeing up capital for the representative to pay for the printing of literature. Typically this is not a good idea. After a time the representative tends to forget that the additional discount is for marketing expenses and begins to think of it as additional profit. If an arrangement of this type must be considered, it should have a definite time limit on it so the representative is continually reminded why he has the discount. There is also the possibility that the representative will not perform the expected marketing and in fact will use the additional discount as extra profit.

Frequently the representative will agree that the arrangement for splitting the production costs of literature is fine as far as it goes, but does not help him with out of pocket expenses such as postage for direct mail. If the exporter wants to offer assistance for this type of marketing, he should determine the amount of assistance he is willing to give and predicate it upon the results he expects to achieve. For example, if a representative wants to mail ten thousand pieces of direct mail, the exporter should only agree to compensate him for the postage and allied costs in proportion to the amount of business the mailing generates. If one hundred orders are received due to leads generated by the mailing and the representative can document them, then a cash payment or rebate may be in order. If the

12.4. Example of a Reprinted Advertisement in German

12.4 (continued)

Das wirtschaftliche Denken bei der Gestaltung der Endverpackung und der Versandabwicklung erfordert moderne, leistungsfähige und hochqualifizierte Systeme für Adressierung, Produkt- und Inhaltskennzeichnung.

Ganz gleich wie die Problemstellung aussieht, Versandadressierung nach neuen Maßstäben, Inhaltsetiketten für die Endverpackung oder aussagefähige mehrteilige Anhänger mit der Doppelfunktion der Auszeichnung und der Warenflußkontrolle, Weber Marking zeigt eine ausgewogene Lösung für jeden Anwendungsbereich. Für jeden Produktionsbetrieb bietet das Weber-System entscheidende Vorteile, die in der Gestaltung des Arbeitsablaufes Ausdruck finden.

Der Weber-Fachberater analysiert das zur Diskussion stehende Einsatzgebiet und demonstriert praxisnahe die Systemlösung aus der Weber-Perspektive. Hierbei kann aus der Vielfalt des Angebotes die wirtschaftlichste Druckmethode ausgesucht werden; das trifft gleichzeitig auch für das Farbensortiment und das weitere Zubehörprogramm zu. Aus der breitgefächerten Papierpalette lassen sich auch die Aufkleber und Anhänger bestimmen, sowohl in puncto Farbe, Format, Klebstoff oder Vordruck, Perforation oder Numerierung, die den gewünschten Organisationseffekt auslösen.

Fordern Sie bitte die Fachberatung an! Auch übersenden wir Ihnen gerne als Vorabinformation unsere ausführlichen Kataloge "Direktmarkierung mit System" oder "Sofort-Etiketten mit Weber Marking."

Deutliche und markante Direktmarkierungen der Endverpackungen, auf weite Distanz gut lesbar.

Etikettendruck nach Bedarf für die Adressierung und Inhaltskennzeichnung – nur drei Handgriffe

Weber®

Firmengruppe
BLUHM

Honnefer Strasse 41
Postfach 28
5463 UNKEL/Rhein
Telefon: (0 22 24) 7 13 49 + 4582
Telex: 0 885 228 bluhm

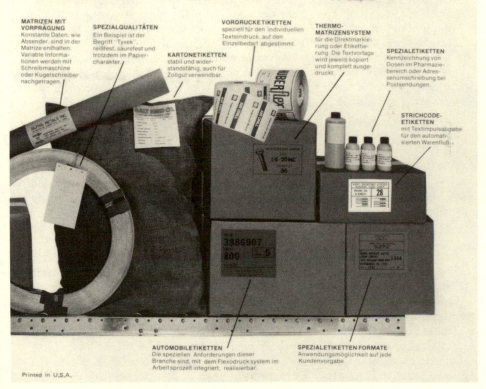

MATRIZEN MIT VORPRÄGUNG
Konstante Daten, wie Absender, sind in der Matrize enthalten. Variable Informationen werden mit Schreibmaschine oder Kugelschreiber nachgetragen.

SPEZIALQUALITÄTEN
Ein Beispiel ist der Begriff "Tyvek", reißfest, säurefest und trotzdem im Papiercharakter.

KARTONETIKETTEN
stabil und widerstandsfähig, auch für Zollgut verwendbar.

VORDRUCKETIKETTEN
speziell für den individuellen Texteindruck, auf den Einzelbedarf abgestimmt.

THERMO-MATRIZENSYSTEM
für die Direktmarkierung oder Etikettierung. Die Textvorlage wird jeweils kopiert und komplett ausgedruckt.

SPEZIALETIKETTEN
Kennzeichnung von Dosen im Pharmaziebereich oder Adressenumschreibung bei Postsendungen.

STRICHCODE-ETIKETTEN
mit Textimpulsabgabe für den automatisierten Warenfluß.

AUTOMOBILETIKETTEN
Die spezielen Anforderungen dieser Branche sind, mit dem Flexodruck system im Arbeitsprozeß integriert, realisierbar.

SPEZIALETIKETTEN FORMATE
Anwendungsmöglichkeit auf jede Kundenvorgabe.

purpose of marketing is to create awareness or image for the representative, than it is appropriate that he pay all the costs associated with it.

Occasionally the exporter will be confronted with a situation where the representative wants some of his discount in the form of cash paid to a bank account in the United States or even a third country. Many of the countries the exporter will be dealing with have currency restrictions. Several years ago France had such strict regulations that it was nearly impossible for French representatives to journey out of their own country on business. When one is engaged in international trade, a certain amount of international travel is essential and the funds to pay for this travel must be available. Situations such as these often force foreign businessmen to find ways to make funds available to themselves abroad. One such way this may be done is for the exporter to charge the representative more for his products than he does for a domestic dealer: just a few percentage points. These extra points are then deposited in an American bank account for the representative to use when he travels to the United States to visit the exporter.

For example, the exporter markets his products in the United States through a network of distributors who purchase his product 50% off the list price of U.S. $100. The American distributor therefore is paying U.S. $50 net for the product. The foreign representative agrees to purchase the same product for 48% or U.S. $52 with an additional 2% or US $2 to be deposited in a U.S. bank. The disadvantage to the representative for this is that he will be working with a smaller margin than his American counterparts and with a strong dollar he may be forced to overprice his product for the market. The advantage to the representative is that he can shelter income and have it available for traveling expenses.[1]

THE ROLE OF ADVERTISING AGENCIES

The beginning exporter typically does not have a relationship with one of the multi-national advertising agencies of the world. More typically he will be dealing with a smaller agency that specializes in his industry or geographical location. If the exporter has a satisfactory relationship with his agency, then there probably will be no reason to change just because he has decided to export his product. The domestic agency can help the exporter by providing the same services it did before exporting commenced. After all, the exporter is going to rely on the foreign representative to provide translations and actual printing. The only difference now is that instead of the agency sending its films to the printer, it will be providing a second set of them to the exporter for mailing to foreign representatives for printing in another country. The exporter may want to caution the agency not to create anything in the future that contains reverses or uses bleed edges. He may want to stress the international flavor of his business by including photographic references to the international segment of the business or by listing the foreign representatives similar to the way he lists his domestic

12.5. Example of a Foreign Agent's Adaptation of an American Advertisement (the cover of Illustration 12.4)

Ideenpaket
für die
Warenflußkennzeichnung

Messepräsentation 1978

Europack, Weis/Österreich
vom 12. 4. – 15. 4. 1978
Halle 31,
Stand Nr. 3100

Transport 78, München
vom 17. 10. – 21. 10. 1978

Hannover-Messe 78
vom 19. 4. – 27. 4. 1978
Halle 18 Cebit-West,
Stand Nr. 606 a

ORGATECHNIK Köln 1978
vom 24. 10. – 29. 10. 1978

Interpack 78, Düsseldorf
vom 8. 6. – 14. 6. 1978
US-Gemeinschaftsstand
Halle 10, Stand Nr. 10035/3
und Freigelände, Stand Nr. 33

Ratio 78, Friedrichshafen
vom 8. 11. – 12. 11. 1978

Eine Eintrittskarte haben wir für Sie reserviert.
Die Antwortkarte erbitten wir rechtzeitig zurück.

Firmengruppe

BLUHM

Berlin, Hamburg,
Hannover, Dortmund,
Düsseldorf, Bonn,
Frankfurt, Karlsruhe,
Stuttgart, Nürnberg,
München,
Linz/Donau, Wien

Zentrale:
5463 UNKEL/Rhein
Honnefer Straße 41
Postfach 28
Telefon: (0 22 24) 7 13 49
Telex: 0 885 228 bluhm

☐ Kostenlose Eintrittskarte für Messe ....

☐ Fachberatung im Werk

☐ Spezialkatalog

Sachgebiet ....

Firmengruppe Bluhm

Postfach 28

5463 Unkel/Rhein

Absender: ....

Name: ....

Firma: ....

Position: ....

Straße: ....

Ort: ....

distributors. More than likely, many other American companies already purchase from him, and he may want them to know that his products are now available to them abroad, as well. Basically the role of the advertising agency does not need to be changed until much later when the exporter actually becomes an international business producing its own foreign language literature and foreign marketing programs.

When the exporter becomes this large, he will need the services of a large international agency with its representatives in many countries. Large agencies are expensive and like all large service companies, the quality of work usually depends upon the actual individuals doing the work. It is entirely possible to have an excellent working relationship in Europe and a terrible one in Asia all within the same firm. For this reason, many large international marketers use several agencies throughout the world. They have learned that different agencies have varying levels of expertise within specific markets.

SUMMARY

It is difficult if not impossible to attract a client's interest into a product if the client does not understand what benefits he can derive from it. For this reason it is important that the exporter understand that literature and technical data must accompany the product and that the intended beneficiary of the product must be able to read and comprehend it.

The preparation of literature and technical data must begin with translations of the material initially created for the domestic market. The exporter working in concert with the foreign representative must convert this existing material into acceptable foreign literature. In order to expedite this process, the exporter should provide the film negatives of any advertisements or literature scheduled to be rewritten in a foreign language. He should also provide the text, the type, line drawings, the weight of the paper used, and the color and manufacturer of the ink used to print it. Reverses should be avoided.

The exporter should rely on the representative to provide translations of the text into the language of the targeted country. The translations should be checked by an academician for accuracy, with any questions resolved by the representative. Literature and technical items such as instructions should not be prepared as universal pieces. Too many languages on the same sheet of paper only confuse the reader. If a single language is going to be used to serve several markets, make certain the idioms of the language are acceptable in all the countries that will be receiving the literature.

Payment for advertising and marketing materials is traditionally shared by the exporter and the representative. Actual cash payments by the manufacturer (exporter) to the representative are rare. Usually the manufacturer will provide all the materials necessary to produce the literature, whereas the foreign representative will pay for the actual production of the materials. The cost of sending artwork and mechanicals abroad is less than the cost of sending the actual marketing material itself. Usually there is no duty assessed on mechanicals although there is duty on the advertising materials themselves. Obviously the freight is less for mechanicals. If additional direct compensation for marketing costs is going to be incurred on behalf of the representative by the exporter, it will usually be subordinated to the actual benefit derived. In other words, the exporter will only pay additional costs if actual orders attributable to the marketing are realized.

Some representatives will request that the exporter charge them a small premium over the actual cost of the products and deposit the difference in a bank for them. This is a commonly accepted practice in many countries as a means for the representative to have available cash when it is necessary for him to travel out of the country (see note).

The role of large multi-national advertising agencies is important to major companies who have diverse interests overseas. These agencies are expensive and usually geared to global thinking. Most of these agencies are not capable of handling a small exporter with a limited budget.

Small domestic agencies can work well with the beginning exporter. The needs of the exporter are not very different from his domestic needs except that additional copies of film negatives and line drawings will be required. The agency should be instructed to avoid reverses and bleed edge printing. All advertising material should state, "Printed in the USA."

NOTE

1. The author neither approves nor condemns this procedure because it may be illegal in the representative's country and place the exporter in a questionable posistion. Always seek legal advice before entering into the type of arrangement mentioned.

Chapter 13
Manufacturing Your Products for Foreign Markets

Other than commodity items, most products destined for overseas will need to be modified or reengineered in order to comply with foreign governments' safety requirements or with generally accepted specifications unique to each market. This chapter deals with the variances the exporter can anticipate and hopefully will help him modify his product to make it acceptable for foreign consumption.

The metric system of measurement, the voltage and amperage differences around the world are mentioned, and the major governmental codes are examined. The economies of making engineering changes in the United States versus abroad are studied.

METRICS AND OTHER SYSTEMS OF MEASUREMENT

In the United States the common system of measurement is the "inch-boot" system, also know as the "British Imperial" system. Under this system it is necessary to multiply by sixteen if one wants to convert pounds to ounces and to multiply by twelve if one wants to convert feet into inches. This system of measurement is cumbersome, but the population has been brought up using it and has decided that it is too inconvenient to change to an easier system. In 1975 the United States established the Metric Conversion Act, which was intended to ease the population into use of the metric system. The metric system was established under Napoleon in 1791 and is based on the meter, which is equal to one ten-millionth of the distance between the earth's equator and the North Pole. The reason the metric system is so easy to use in everyday situations is that it is based on units of ten, rather than twelve or sixteen. Therefore, all that is necessary to convert from one unit to another is to divide or multiply by ten. For example one meter equals 100 centimeters which equals .001 kilometer.

Today virtually every country in the world except the United States and Burma use the metric system. Even in the United States many companies use the metric system for some of their products. In order for companies to sell their products universally, it is necessary to scale them metrically. For example, the automobile industry has converted to metrics, as have the pharmaceutical and medical industries. However, the bulk of America still goes along thinking in feet and Fahrenheit which for everyday situations may be satisfactory. However, for international situations, it will be necessary to think metrically (illustration 13.1).

Other countries may also have additional systems of measurement, but these are rarely used in international trade. There are, however, a few terms that seem to turn up occasionally. For example, in the U.K. weight may be expressed in "stone" (one stone is equal to 14 pounds), or hundred weight (Cwt.), which is equal to 112 pounds. In Japan one "Shaku" equals 11.93 inches, and in China a "Tael" is .22 pounds.

For most exporters it will be necessary to provide product in metric sizes rather than in the sizes produced for domestic consumption. Failure to do this will only result in lost sales and create animosity between the exporter and his representatives. If the item being exported is not metric, it will be necessary for the manufacturer to provide measuring equipment and tools that are generally not available anywhere else except in the United States. Likewise, he will have to provide his representatives with adequate small parts such as nuts and bolts threaded to American standards. This is always a cause of friction because in most cases the best representatives will

13.1. Metric Conversion Table

Metric Equivalents of U.S. Weights and Measures

Dry Measure
1 pint = .550599 liter
1 quart = 1.101197
1 peck = 8.80958 liters
1 bushel = .35238 hectoliter

Avoirdupois Measure
1 ounce = 28.349527 grams
1 pound = .453592 kilogram
1 short ton = .90718 metric ton
1 long ton = 1.01604 metric ton

Liquid Measure
1 pint = .473167 liter
1 quart = .946332 liter
1 gallon = 3.785329 liters

Square Measure
1 sq. inch = 6.4516 sq. cent.
1 sq. ft. = 9.2903 sq. decimtr.
1 sq. yd. = .836131 sq. meter
1 acre = .40469 hectare

Long Measure
1 inch = 2.54 centimeters
1 yard = .914401 meter
1 mile = 1.609347 kilometers

Cubic Measure
1 cu. inch = 16.3872 cu. cent.
1 cu. ft. = .028317 cu. meter
1 cu. yd. = .76456 cu. meter

Source: *International Trade Handbook*, The Dartnel Corporation, p. 1254.

succumb to Murphy's law and they will lack the one screw that is needed to fix a critical machine in one of their customer's offices. When (not if) these situations occur, the enterprising serviceman will usually re-tap the screw hole and change it to metric thread. After this happens several times, it will no longer be clear which machine has which thread and where that thread is!

In some countries the government has established certain standards that call for metric sizes and if the equipment being exported cannot conform to the standard, it will not be salable. Several years ago it was necessary for an American company that manufactured label printing machines to change them to metric because the railroads in Europe mandated that all labels used to address cartons had to conform to specific metric sizes. Because this manufacturer's machines produced labels using the inch-boot system, it was necessary for them to re-tool and build a separate machine for sale abroad. Had the manufacturer not done this, it would no longer have been capable of marketing its product in Europe.

In the United States it is usual for some industries to sell and package their products in multiples of twelve. In the rest of the world these types of items are sold and packaged in multiples of ten. Although it is not critical to sell and package in metric units, it does evidence an attitude on behalf of the exporter that he is willing to be flexible and adaptive to his client's needs.

STANDARDS

Many nations of the world have established varying standards for product safety and performance. In some instances compliance is mandatory and in others it is voluntary. Of those countries that have established standards, most are industrialized nations while only a few of the lesser-developed nations have formalized standards.

Whether a country has established standards or not is of little consequence when the exporter is attempting to market his products in a country that does not have easy compatibility with his product's characteristics. A great many nations of the world, for example, operate on 220 volt 50 Hertz electrical current. If the exporter manufactures equipment that will only operate at 110 volt 60 Hertz, he will obviously have difficulty selling his products. One method some exporting manufacturers have developed to overcome this problem is to ship their machines without any motors. They rely on their agents to provide the motors from a local source. If satisfactory motors are available, this is not an unreasonable solution, however many times quality motors are not available. The exporter contemplating this alternative should be cognizant that the ultimate purchaser of his product will not take into consideration that the product purchased was locally jerry-rigged in order to make it operative and he may hold the manufacturer responsible for his perception of quality. Machines that use fractional horsepower motors are particularly susceptible to inferior local quality or scarcity in small markets. Even if acceptable motors are found locally, the wiring of the machine will probably be considered inadequate by clients. In the best of situations the exporter who incorporates electrical motors in his products should concentrate on selling only in those markets that offer a large enough potential to justify engineering his product to conform with local standards; he should then maintain an inventory of machines and spare parts to service those markets.

Another area of constant concern for the exporter of electrical appliances is the cord used to plug in the device itself. Even if the motor will properly operate with the local electricity, the plug at the end of the cord may not fit any outlets! The three prong plug used in the United States will not come close to fitting an outlet in Europe. In fact, the plug used in the U.K. is quite different from the one used in West Germany. Likewise, the fuses used on electrical apparatuses usually are different from those used in the United States. Even if the device is 220 volt, the fuses will not be satisfactory for use in Europe and other parts of the world because the cycling of the current is different. In the United States even though 220 volt current is common, 50 Hertz is not. Motors operated at 50 Hertz will burn out prematurely and operate at higher speed than on 60 Hertz.

If the expected volume of foreign sales does not justify the engineering and fabrication of electrical apparatus to conform with market requirements, then the exporter should carefully work with his representatives in the foreign markets to develop machines that can be adapted satisfactorily to local conditions. The exporter should rely on the representative to locate potential local sources of items that will have to be substituted to meet local requirements. These items should be sent to the manufacturer of the original equipment in the United States for thorough testing. No product should be substituted without the manufacturer's approval. Typically, local adaptations will include motors, wiring harnesses, fuses, electrical cords and plugs.

Even shipment of electrical apparatus to Canada requires compliance with their local regulations. Canada has a very strict testing procedure for a great many items and before they may be allowed across their border, they must comply with Canadian standards. Certification of electrical apparatus must be performed by the Canadian Standards Association (CSA). For complete information on CSA, the interested exporter may write to:

Canadian Standards Association
178 Rexdale Blvd.
Rexdale, Ontario, Canada M9W1R3

When it comes to standards, the West Germans have established one of the most comprehensive systems in the free world. At present there are around fifteen thousand standards established and in use covering everything from electrical apparatus to the casters on an office chair (it must be equipped with brakes). These standards are know as DIN. Most persons have loaded a camera with film and they may have noticed two different possible settings mentioned on the film itself: ASA and DIN. In the United States the ASA setting is always used. However, the reference to DIN is for the benefit of those persons operating German cameras that have film speeds calibrated by *Deutsches Institut fuer Normung e.V.*, more commonly know as DIN. The DIN standards are voluntary, but the exporter would be wise to consider them compulsory because they are widely accepted, not only in the Federal Republic, but also by most of Europe. Of the fifteen thousand or so standards, approximately three thousand are available in English and can be obtained by writing:

> Beuth-Vertrieb G.m.b.H.
> 1000 Berlin 30
> Burggraferstr. 4-7
> Federal Republic of Germany

Ask for "DIN--English Translations of German Standards."

If sales are anticipated to the German government itself or agencies of the government, it is not unusual to find that DIN compliance has been written into the specifications. Needless to say, the government of the Federal Republic will only entertain quotations that comply with DIN standards.

In Japan several agencies are responsible for setting standards and safety requirements. The principal agency, however, is the Japan Industrial Standards Committee (JIS) which is an agency of the Ministry of International Trade and Industry (MITI). Operating under the Electric Appliance Control Law, electrical apparatus used by consumers is divided into two classes. Class A goods require prior approval before it will be allowed into Japan. Some of the items covered under this classification include transformers for radios, stereo sets, electric heat appliances for craft-work and handicraft work, electric work tools, toys employing electric heat, toys employing electric light, electronic toys, game equipment, automatic vending machines.

Class B goods are only required to meet Japanese technical standards and include items such as video recorders and electronic watches. These standards are published and available by writing to the

> Japanese Standards Association
> 1-24 Akasaka, Minato-ku
> Tokyo, Japan

Any products that are new to Japan must first be tested by government-designated laboratories prior to importation into Japan. These tests can be time consuming and expensive. Testing and approval are not limited only to electrical apparatus but also mandated for all agricultural and chemical products. The rules for agricultural products' acceptance are determined by

Japan Agriculture Standards (JAS). Likewise, standards have been established to control emissions of industrial nitrous oxides into the atmosphere. Automotive emissions and automotive safety standards have been in effect in Japan since 1978.

Most countries' standards programs have also established labeling requirements for identifying contents and other technical data important to the operation or service of the equipment. Many countries have laws prescribing that contents must be measured metrically and that electrical hazards must be identified (usually by incorporating a diagram of a thunderbolt). Drugs and cosmetics are typically quite carefully monitored and labeling requirements usually include accurate statements regarding the contents in terms of weight and measure, as well as an accurate statement regarding the intended use and a statement of precaution should a drug be habit forming, poisonous or otherwise injurious to the public.

Food products are almost always required to meet standards in packaging, marking and labeling, ingredients identification and serving instructions, and so forth. Instructions, marking and directions in almost all situations must be in the native language(s) of the importing country.

No exporter should attempt to develop a product for export without the assistance and the guidance of a local representative. The laws and rules of the various governments and agencies are too diverse and subject to tradition and custom to be tackled without local assistance from someone who wants to share in the benefits that will be derived by the product's successful importation.

SUMMARY

When manufacturing a product for export, it is important to recognize the need to convert sizes and specifications from the British inch-boot system of measurement to the continental metric system. Although other measuring systems abound, the metric system is a universal standard. Many countries require the specific labeling of products in metric dimensions, as well as in their native languages. Failure to abide by these rules may be grounds for denying entry of the products into the foreign market.

The vast majority of industrialized nations has established safety and performance standards for products. Manufacturers eager to export their products must be certain the products conform with each country's standards in order to be assured access to the marketplace. In most instances, compliance will mean that electrical apparatuses must meet minimum standards established either by the government or by testing agencies that are traditionally viewed as providing a minimum standard of safety or performance.

The United States' major trading partners have established procedures with which exporters must comply in order to sell products in their countries. These are either government-sponsored or private agencies such as the United States own Underwriter's Laboratories. Foreign markets have various standards with very little continuity among markets. It is, therefore, important that the exporter verify each country's standard requirements prior to exporting. For example, if a manufacturer of an electrical product receives a request for a pro forma from Belgium, among the first things he should do even before attempting to provide the pro forma, is to verify that the equipment will operate in Belgium. Although Belgium has no formal standards program, there is room for considerable confusion regarding what kind of electrical appliances will operate in the country. In Belgium the following electrical current is available: A.C. 50 Hertz, 110/220, 130/220, 220/240,115/220, 200/300, 127/220, 110/190 volts. If the exporter only manufactures his equipment in 110/220, 60 Hertz characteristics, he must inform the prospect of this and await the prospect's decision regarding whether he still wants the machine. Maybe he will want it without the motor. If so, certainly the price the manufacturer will quote on the pro forma will be less than if the motor had been included. Perhaps the manufacturer makes several models of machines that will conform with the prospect's request. However, before he can complete the pro-forma, he must still determine which electrical characteristics will be required for the actual location where the equipment will be situated. Even after the type motor has been determined, the exporter will still have to ask what kind of plug he should place on the electric cord in order to be able to plug the machine in. Additionally, it is very difficult to find U.S. manufacturers of plugs for use outside of the United States. Most plugs must be imported into the United States and then re-exported with the machine.

Cosmetics, pharmaceuticals, and food products usually must conform to standards established regarding unit of measure, contents, and instructions for use. A good export manual, such as the BNA International Trade Reporter, can give the exporter an overview of what each country's requirements are with regard to standards and labeling. For more detailed information, the exporter must depend on his representative in the country of import to seek out the necessary approvals.

Chapter 14
Servicing Products Overseas

If an exporter manufactures a product for sale overseas, at one time or another he will be called upon by his foreign agent to provide training, testing, or service for the product. This chapter delves into the various methods by which American companies can fill this need.

CONTRACTS

When an exporter first begins to market his products abroad, he is likely to find that he is ignorant of the differences in commonly accepted trading practices within the country to which he is exporting. These differences can lead to confusion and misunderstandings, to say nothing of the expense in attempting to litigate over vast distances. In an effort to take some of the sting out of dealing overseas, the International Chamber of Commerce has published international rules for the interpretation of trade terms. These rules were first presented in 1936 and later revised in 1953, using the acronym *Incoterms*. Incoterms deal primarily with the three areas of difficulty most companies encounter. They are:

1. Uncertainty as to which country's law of what country will be applicable to their contracts.

2. Difficulties arising from inadequate information.

3. Difficulties arising from diversity in interpretation.[1]

In 1955 the International Chamber of Commerce published a pamphlet demonstrating how the ten most commonly used clauses in international trade were interpreted by eighteen nations.

The ICC adopted the principal that a contract price settled on the basis of Incoterms 1953 would provide for minimum liabilities on the part of the seller. Thus, parties to a transaction willing to provide for greater liabilities than those in this set of rules must specify the additional liabilities. For example, if a buyer insists upon protection against wharf risk, the contract should then specify "Incoterms 1953, plus wharf risk insurance."[2]

In those situations where there is no clear ruling contained in the Incoterms, the matter is to be settled by the custom of the port or the trade. Every effort has been made by the ICC to limit these situations, but it has proven impossible to eliminate them altogether. In situations where specific clauses have been inserted by either the buyer or the seller in the contract, they will take preference over Incoterms, as represented in the quotation about wharf risk insurance.

The rules established by the Incoterms generally deal with those terms described in chapter 7 and include Ex-(factory, warehouse, foundry, works), F.O.B., FAS, C&F, C.I.F. The exporter must be extremely careful when contracting under the terms C&F or C.I.F. and not vary or customize the terms with additions or specifics such as, "... CIF Cleared and Customs Duty Paid...."[3] or entirely unanticipated results may occur in the interpretation of the contract.

In both common law and civil law countries, the consent of both parties (buyer and seller) is required to create a contract. Contracts can consist of one or more documents and oral changes or modifications usually cannot be enforced. The exporter must be cautious that in his correspondence with his representatives he does not create what could be construed as a contract in his client's country. Likewise he must exercise caution in his advertising claims. What passes for hard sell or gimmickry may be considered fraud in civil law countries. The prudent exporter always seeks legal counsel prior to entering into agreements with representatives in foreign countries. The legal counsel should be selected based on their experience in the foreign country and their experience in working with similar companies in the same or allied industries. After all, if the advice of the attorneys turns out to be incorrect, it is not the law firm or the individual attorney who will have to settle the account! Because all countries do not adjudicate in the same manner as the United States, the exporter is advised not to make assumptions. Most assumptions are based on experience, and unless experience has been gained dealing in other countries with their unique judicial systems, it is best not to assume anything. Question everything that is of substance and that may be subject to legal interpretation at a future date. Most disputes between contracting parties occur because each party has a different perception of the contract's intent, not because of the words themselves.

Contracts in civil law countries differ in many respects from those in common law countries. For example, in the United States it is common for a contract to be accepted with modifications. However, in a civil law country such acceptance is perceived as a counter offer. The effective date of a contract can also become an issue when two different systems of law are involved. In the United States, it is usual for the contract documents to become effective the moment they are placed in the mails. For this reason, most legal documents are sent via registered or certified mail, return receipt requested. In civil law countries, however, the contract is not valid until the reply to the offer is actually received by the originator. Similar differences may occur regarding offerings at certain prices. In fact, an advertised product at a specific price can be presumed to be an offer and the seller is obligated to provide the product at that cost. In the United States, the same offer may be rescinded up to and until such time when it is actually accepted by the purchaser. The advice to the exporter here is that he should not advertise open-end prices, nor should he allow his representative to do so. Advertisements should contain a definite time limit or the product may have to be provided at the advertised price even years after the ad campaign has been terminated.

In the United States, if one of the parties violates the terms of the agreement, the other party has every right to consider the agreement dead and he also has the right to discontinue performance. But in many civil law countries, he may not discontinue his performance until a court formally rescinds the contract. Failure to know this can cause the exporter to be placed in the uncomfortable position of having to continue to abide by the terms of an agreement while the other party disregards it.

The reader may have been momentarily puzzled by the need to legalize documents in the section dealing with documentation. This puzzlement may have been due to the fact that the actual act of legalizing amounts to no more than having a notary public sign and seal the documents. In the United States, the notary in the office is usually a secretary who has paid the state a small fee and has been given the right to notarize documents. The only prerequisite is usually that the person applying for the notary public has not been convicted of a felony. In many other countries, however, the position of notary is quite different. Usually the notary will be a degreed lawyer with many years of experience who is respected within his community. This person will meticulously maintain ledgers of all the documents to which he has affixed his signature and although he does not represent either party to the transaction, he will actually do the drafting of the agreements brought before him. Usually he is consulted only on major matters such as drafting articles of incorporation or real estate contracts. Contracts that are prepared in such a manner are said to be *protocolized*. Protocolized contracts are not usually necessary for contracts having to do only with personal property. If a contract must be entered into that requires protocolizing, the exporter should have his own attorney present during the drafting.

It is usual for a contract in the United States to be supported by some form of *consideration* in which a promise is given in return for another promise from the other party. This is not necessarily the case in civil law countries. Civil law countries seek *causa* rather than consideration. Causa is the reason or the motivation behind the contract. A similar distinction exists between the concept of acts of God and *force majeure*.

The differences among legal systems also extend to the area of warranties. Almost all countries recognize expressed warranties but some also recognize implied warranties. A warranty is an agreement by which a party assures another party of the quality or usefulness of an item for which title has passed. Many countries go beyond the written expression of warranty and state that a warranty also implies that the object of the warranty must be free of any latent defects, whether the seller knows of them or not. For example, food products are perceived to have an implied warranty that they are fit for human consumption; a motor oil is assumed to be harmless to an automobile's engine.

Naturally, whenever there is trade among people from different countries with different legal systems, the cost of adjudication is very expensive. In an effort to reduce the cost to all parties involved in disputes, most private disputes are arbitrated rather than litigated. Statutes vary widely among countries regarding handling of disputes, but in those situations where questions regarding the quality of goods, time of title change, place of title change, and matters of custom are disputed, arbitration is preferable to litigation. Contracts should, therefore, be drafted containing an arbitration clause that specifies which kinds of disputes will be settled by arbitration and where the arbitration will take place. The clause should also specify the quantity of arbitrators and their selection process.

Anytime a product is sold, servicing may well be required at some future time. It is in the exporter's best interest to make certain that warranty problems are promptly handled and that other service incidental to the product's use is expeditiously performed.

SERVICE

The exporter of a product abroad must be aware that he has responsibilities to provide service and training similar to what he would provide for a domestic sale. Naturally, the logistics of service and training abroad require more expense and thought than domestic transactions. Language skills and time become prime considerations that every manufacturer confronts when he offers his product overseas. Although these considerations are troublesome, they are not insurmountable, and can be effectively handled by recognizing the potential problems and developing a plan to overcome them. One of the prime ways exporters have traditionally responded to service and training requirements has been to conduct regularly scheduled in-plant training sessions for their foreign representatives. By providing training within the United States, the manufacturer has all the necessary aids at his disposal. This practice also removes the problems of time normally associated with traveling great distances. However, it does not alleviate the problems associated with language. As stated previously, the exporter is advised wherever possible to attempt to retain foreign nationals as representatives who are fluent in the English language. When this is not possible, it will be necessary for translation and interpretation to be provided. Usually it is to the exporter's advantage to attempt training with only one foreign language group at a time. By addressing only one foreign language at a time, an informality is possible that is generally conducive to creating dialogue between the trainers and the trainees. Should it be necessary to train in more than one language at a time, then the use of simultaneous interpretation will be necessary. Equipment such as head sets and microphones is generally available in most cities. As a general rule, it is easier to provide competent interpretation abroad than it is in the United States. This is because most foreign nations are used to dealing in other languages, whereas in the United States it is rarely necessary. The best source of interpreters in the United States is the United Nations. Many of the interpreters used there can arrange their schedules to accommodate short private services if ample notice is given.

If the exporter has never dealt with simultaneous translation, he should arrange time before the venue to talk with the interpreters and make certain they have an understanding of any items, phrases, idioms, or trade terms that are likely to be discussed in the actual training sessions. It is helpful to the interpreters to have copies of literature before them that deal with the subjects that are likely to come up in the training sessions. A review of the literature also affords them the opportunity to make notes on specific terms with which they are not personally familiar, and which they will want to research before the meeting.

The exporter should not be intimidated if it is determined that simultaneous interpretation is necessary. The interpreters with whom this writer has worked have all gone out of their way to provide a meaningful service to their employer, and have provided a high level of interpretation. The ease of training and communication among staff with different cultural and ethnic histories is reason enough to consider this type of arrangement as opposed to attempting to muddle through using sign language and drawings to communicate ideas. The cost of the interpretation services is money well spent, because it will enable the exporter to train staff quickly. This assures him of a high level of expertise much sooner than would be possible with more amateurish efforts.

Certainly, training in the United States is more costly than training in the foreign country. Usually training in the United States entails transportation costs for several persons, room, board, and entertainment costs that would usually be required for only one person abroad. However, the recipient of the training is richly rewarded by being able to train in the United States because it enables him to create personal relationships with the exporter's domestic staff and affords him the opportunity to work with the persons who are actually producing the product he is expected to sell and service in his own country. One cannot exaggerate the value gained by face-to-face contact among domestic and foreign personnel. If a problem should arise abroad that the representative is unable to answer, it is very easy in this day and age for him to simply pick up the telephone and talk with the person in America who can answer his question accurately and quickly. If the foreign national is only exposed to one person in his dealings with the exporter, then it stands to reason that this is the only person he can call for help. Usually, the person with whom the foreign national is most familiar is the sales manager or a person who has been hired especially to interface between the foreign sales organization and domestic management. This person typically is not fluent with all technical issues, so frequently it will be necessary for him to field the representative's questions and relate the answer to him at a later time. There is a risk that the information will not be complete, necessitating additional calls for clarification. This problem, coupled with the reality of distance and time zone changes, can make a simple problem very complex and time-consuming. The best foreign sales organizations are those that have access to all the technical people in the exporter's organization.

Many first-time exporters find it expeditious to only train the principal of the foreign enterprise and then rely on him to train his staff. This can be very effective, but it depends on the willingness and the level of experience the foreign representative possesses. In order for this approach to service training to work, the foreign organization must be relatively small. Larger companies are generally too specialized to be able to rely on the representative to provide the training. For example, it is difficult to imagine that when Xerox and Rank combined in Europe the actual persons negotiating the agreements were the same persons to be trained in the service of the equipment. Obviously the training methods are relative to the size of the organization being trained.

SUMMARY

Although servicing American products abroad is similar to servicing domestic products within the United States, the cost and time involved is substantially greater. American exporters of manufactured goods should be aware of the Incoterms published by the International Chamber of Commerce in Paris. They should always use accepted terms when contracting for international services such as cartage and insurance.

International trade is hampered by the differences in legal systems among governments. For example, all English-speaking countries use a system of common law whereas France and much of Latin America use civil law. Inadvertent violation of one another's laws can be minimized by adherance to the proper use of Incoterms and by seeking counsel from qualified international law firms on contract issues. Contracts between parties where the parties have different legal systems should contain clauses stipulating that specific disputes will be settled by arbitration rather than by litigation.

Product and service training is essential to the success of any manufactured product sold abroad. Service training may be done in the United States or abroad, though it is usually less expensive to do it abroad. However, service training in the United States generates benefits that are frequently not possible in the field. Training in the United States places the foreign representatives in close contact with the exporter's technical people, and they subsequently learn the quickest way to find answers to their questions after returning to their own countries.

If it is necessary to use interpreters, the exporter should be careful to make certain they receive instructions on the use of specific terms unique to their industry. Interpreters are usually more available abroad than they are in the United States.

NOTES

1. *International Trade Handbook*, op. cit., p. 1093.

2. Warren J. Keegan, *Multinational Marketing Management* (Englewood Cliffs, New Jersey, Prentice-Hall, Inc.,1974), p. 408.

3. *International Trade Handbook*, op. cit., p.1095.

Chapter 15
Traveling the Territory

How often should the exporter travel abroad to visit with his representatives? What about jet lag? Will foreign holidays interrupt travel plans? How can samples be taken on a trip? How should one pack for a major sojourn abroad? These and other questions are discussed in this chapter.

HOW OFTEN SHOULD THE TERRITORY BE TRAVELED?

Traveling abroad on business is usually one of the greatest experiences in the American businessman's career. Exposure to other cultures and ideas will always contribute to the businessman's acumen and make him more knowledgeable than his peers who have not had the opportunity to share in the broadening experience that only foreign travel affords. Travel by and of itself is broadening, but traveling with foreign business associates is even more intellectually widening. The local representatives will know of many places to visit that are not on most tourist itineraries and visits to their homes provide insights that one cannot get from the window of a moving bus. The rapport and interaction among people that normally accompanies the development of foreign markets contributes to developing the executive who travels the territory into a better manager. Certainly, the exporter who know his foreign markets from close personal experience has more awareness of the competition and new developments that may affect the marketing of his product than he could have if he remained in domestic markets.

The exporter must carefully determine how often it will be necessary to travel and visit his representatives. His major concern should be to visit often enough so the level of interest in his product is maintained by the foreign representative, but not so often that his trips become a burden to himself and to his host. Most trips are so costly that it is wise to plan them long in advance; they should form a circle. It is too expensive for most businesses to allow an executive to go to only one place and return. Certainly there will be situations where it will be necessary to make one-stop trips, but these should be carefully monitored to make sure they do not become the norm. It is typical to plan a trip to Europe, a trip to Latin America, a trip to Asia, a trip to the Middle East and Africa, and a trip to Australia and New Zealand. For a company that has representatives in Europe, for example, a typical itinerary would have the exporter leaving his home town and traveling to one of the major European gateways such as London, Paris, or Amsterdam. The trip should be circular so that the travel encompasses the entire marketing area.

If the exporter is represented in the major European cities, his travel itinerary might be as follows:

Depart New York on a Saturday; arrive London Heathrow airport Sunday morning. Hotel booking will not be available for occupancy until afternoon so the traveller should be certain to carry personal grooming items such as comb, brush, razor, and so forth. separately from his baggage so he can clean up prior to landing in London. By arriving on a Sunday, the exporter has a full day to attempt to adjust to the time change before he must begin doing business on Monday. The exporter should decline the generous offer of his representative to meet him at the airport on his arrival. He should plan on having the time to himself to make the seven to nine hour time adjustment. If the exporter does allow the representative to meet him, he will be forced to discuss business when he is tired and he may well regret some of his decisions the next day. It is best to leave business until properly rested. Spend the day sightseeing or just relaxing.

The exporter should plan on two or three days in each city for business discussions and problem-solving before moving on to the other cities.

Keeping the circular route in mind, the exporter might elect to travel in the following order: London, Copenhagen, Helsinki, Stockholm, Oslo, Amsterdam, Brussels, Paris, Frankfort, Vienna, Milan, Rome, and return to New York. A trip encompassing all these cities would require over a month to complete.

Most experienced overseas travelers do not like to be away from home more than one month at a time. Therefore, the novice traveler should not plan as aggressive a trip as to cover all the European cities at one time. Split the trip into two separate trips, a month or two apart. A good way to do this is to travel northern Europe during one trip and southern Europe during a second trip.

Plan on spending the weekends in cities where maximum comfort will prevail. Do not plan, unless you cannot help it, to spend a weekend in a small town in a country where you do not speak the language and cannot have the laundry done. Stick to the larger cities where the hotels will be staffed with people who do speak your language and where you can have your laundry done. Laundry is an important consideration in traveling abroad. It usually requires two days to get it completed, so the exporter must know in advance where he will be.

Typical travelers usually pack for five day intervals between laundry stops. Once a person has lugged baggage through airports and train stations, he will appreciate packing as efficiently as possible and not carry more than is necessary. Purchase of souvenirs for the family should be made during the last stop or mailed home.

Because of the distances involved in traveling, Pacific trips tend to be longer than ones to Europe. However, the same logic used to plan the European itinerary applies to the Orient. Pack for five days and plan on using the weekends for laundry and rest. A typical Eastern business trip should evolve similar to the example below:

Depart San Francisco International airport on a Friday or Saturday. Flying time between San Francisco and Tokyo is approximately ten to eleven hours. Depending on the starting point of the journey, travel time can consume as much as seventeen or eighteen hours. This is a very long and arduous trip, so adequate time must be allowed for rest and acclimatization to the prevailing time and date.

From Tokyo, the typical commercial traveler will go to Hong Kong and on to Singapore, Khula Lumpur, or Bangkok. From these final destinations, the return trip is so long many exporters will include Australia and New Zealand in their itineraries so as not have to make a separate trip later. The flight from San Francisco to Tokyo is about the same length as the trip from Bangkok to Sydney. A return trip from Auckland to San Francisco is about eighteen hours with a stop in American Samoa or similar intermediary point. Breathing the dry air in a commercial airline for so long taxes even the strongest traveler, and he is advised not to imbibe too much alcohol because that will only further his dehydration.

When planning trips abroad, the exporter should be cognizant of the variability of the airlines and how their scheduling can affect the itinerary. Many cities are not served daily and an extra day here or there may be required in order to make the necessary connections. Furthermore, many cities are geographically located in areas where long international flights transit through them at some of the worst hours imaginable. Travel in and out of the Middle East is a prime example. Flights from Europe to Asia transit through cities such as Teheran, Amman, and Damascus in the middle of the night. Coupled with the usual delays this area is famous for, it is not unusual to have to catch a flight at 2:00 or 3:00 in the morning.

For most businessmen, there is not too much business in areas adjacent to the Middle East so they will normally be connecting between cities such as Athens, Rome, and Bangkok, or Tokyo. This can be especially frustrating if one must vacate his hotel room at 10:00 in the morning and catch a flight that does not leave until 2:00 or 3:00 the following morning. Experienced travelers to the Middle East will frequently book their rooms for an extra day in order to sleep for a couple of hours before their scheduled departure.

Most Americans are used to traveling from city to city using the commercial airlines and this is certainly the best way to travel internationally, except in those areas of the world where there is a great deal of commerce accomplished in a small area. Rail transportation is often the vehicle of choice in Europe and Japan. The time it would normally take to fly between Paris and Brussels, for example, can be more comfortably and less expensively served by taking the Trans European Express (TEE). European and Japanese rail services are excellent and the prudent world traveler will avail himself of these methods of transport whenever convenient.

Because most of the commercial airlines in Europe are controlled and run by their various governments the rates are not as competitive as in the United States. Cost should always be a consideration when traveling modest distances.

International travel can be further complicated by the work habits of the population of the area being visited. For Example, it is hard to accomplish much in Europe, during July or August. Entire countries virtually shut down for vacations. France and Italy are great examples of countries whose commerce is on hold during these two months. Not only is it difficult to secure appointments, but accommodations are very difficult to obtain because the hotels and restaurants book up fast. The frustration of traveling on business in Europe during the summer can be offset by planning business trips during the rest of the year. Caution should be taken during Easter because each country seems to celebrate this holiday during different times and for different durations. The exporter should always verify that travel plans are acceptable with all the persons on whom he will be calling during his trips. Once the traveler is abroad, it is too expensive to return for a day or a week just because an error in judgment was made or research was inadequate.

Other countries also have holidays on which they completely close down. In the Middle East one does not want to find himself in a Moslem country during Ramadan or similar holidays because during these occasions the commercial life of the indigenous population stops, making it difficult to impossible to conduct business with the local population. Most international airlines prepare a list of holidays for the countries they service. A telephone call to them will be enough for the exporter to determine if a planned trip can be taken without incident. Even the business days of the week are not universal. Again, the Middle East works on Sunday, taking

Friday and Saturday off. Knowing this can influence the days on which the international businessman plans his arrivals and departures from a particular region.

JET LAG

A great deal has been written about jet lag and certainly everyone is aware of it. However, it is a serious problem that must be addressed. Not everyone responds to jet lag to the same degree, although everyone does experience some discomfort when journeying over great distances. Every person has a biological clock governed by his everyday life-style. When a person begins to travel over great distances very rapidly, the body does not have adequate time to adjust to these changes naturally. Primordial man's travel was limited by how far he could go on foot in one twenty-four hour period. Later, man could travel by horseback and even automobile. Throughout this time, it was unlikely man would go through a different time zone in one day that would seriously challenge his body's biological clock. With the advent of the airplane, however, it suddenly became possible for man to travel through not only one, but several time zones in less than twenty-four hours.

The average traveler who goes to Europe from the mid-west will have to adjust to seven time zone changes of one hour each. Suddenly the body finds itself eating dinner when it should have been asleep several hours ago. Likewise, the body must digest its food at times that are unusual to it. If the traveler is forty years old, his body has become accustomed to one schedule for forty years and it must now adapt to a seven hour difference. This experience may be unpleasant.

The longer the traveler can stay in one time zone, the less problem he will have with the effects of jet lag. In addition, there are several things he can do to ease the discomfort, the most important of which is to *never* conduct business on the day of arrival overseas. After a six or seven hour flight and a six or seven hour time change, one's body and mind are not as sharp as they will be after a few hours sleep and a good meal. With the Concorde it is possible to be teased into thinking that jet lag will be minimized because of the speed with which one is delivered to the Continent. In some instances the lag is delayed, but it is never eliminated. It takes time for the body to adapt to its new environment.

Wherever possible, the traveler should attempt to make accommodations in an hotel that can provide the services that will ease him into the new environment. Amenities should include twenty-four hour room service, laundry, and food service that is not foreign to the traveler's palate. The hotel should also have beds in their rooms. This may seem silly until one or more nights must be spent in a traditional Japanese hotel where the guests sleep on futons and rest their heads on ceramic pillows. Even in Europe it is possible to book a room with a bed that may seem foreign to the American businessman. In some German hotels the beds adjust similarly to hospital beds. If the traveler is tired or a little slow-witted, he may not realize that the bed is adjustable and may spend the night sleeping in a semireclining posture.

It may also come as a shock to the person uninitiated in foreign travel that all bathrooms are not created equal. In many parts of the world, the bathroom is not only down the hall, but it consists of nothing more than a hole in the floor with a shower cord that must be pulled in order to flush it. One is cautioned to stand aside while he pulls the cord to avoid being drenched. Native experiences are a great perk one gains from foreign travel, but they should not be experienced until the body has had adequate time to adjust to the onslaught of new senses and time.

Several years ago while this writer was establishing a manufacturing facility for his company in Tokyo, it was necessary to fly in an associate from America to work with the sales force. This individual was about thirty years old at the time and this was his first trip abroad, except for some minor journeys to the Caribbean on pleasure. Upon his arrival in Japan he was booked into a small hotel that offered American services and was close to the Ginza so he could entertain himself in the evenings. The day after his arrival in Japan, he was invited to go to lunch with the Japanese partner and asked what type of food he would like. This young man wanted to impress his host so he told him he would like to sample some native food. He was cautioned that his dietary tract probably had not had enough time to adjust to something as drastic as a native Japanese diet. The associate persevered, however, and was taken to an authentic Japanese restaurant.

This restaurant was so native that the trainer was the first Occidental to ever visit it, although it had been in Tokyo for over three hundred years! The restaurant had an aquarium in its front window with several carp swimming in it. Because the carp in Japan are more like the large gold fish that are found in the United States the associate commented on their beauty. Acting as an interpreter, the partner inquired if there was any one fish that he thought was particularly nice. The trainer responded and pointed to one of them. With this the proprietor took out a net and collected the fish. He slit open the fish's belly and placed the fish on a plate before the trainer. It must have only been a few seconds, but it seemed like minutes before the look of astonishment appeared on the trainer's face. At this point, false pride caused him to consent to eating it, which he did! One hour later he was totally incapacitated. It was necessary to locate a doctor to treat him and five days elapsed before he was capable of conducting the training he was sent to Japan to perform. Some of the suffering was caused, no doubt, by the mere thought of what he had eaten, but a large part was also due to the bacteria in the fish that his system was not used to accommodating, in addition to the very real time change. The purpose of this real-life story is to point out that pride should never be allowed to take the place of good judgment. The hosts for the international businessman are aware of the differences in culture, habit, and diet and they will not be annoyed if the guest declines certain items.

Above all else, the greatest attribute a businessman can have abroad is flexibility. He must be flexible enough to accept and *enjoy* differences between life styles and cultural heritage. Inflexible persons will inevitably be poor ambassadors for their companies and their complaints will cause friction. Inflexible persons would be well-advised to remain at home, inside their comfort zone.

HOW TO PACK FOR FOREIGN TRAVEL

Accompanying the businessman throughout his trip will be his luggage. Other than business matters, luggage will become his greatest concern. Therefore, it is important to carefully plan on what will be needed and to leave out what is not absolutely necessary. If a specific item of clothing such as a swimming suit might be needed, don't take it. One can always be purchased if it is needed and the traveler will not be burdened carrying it through a half dozen countries where it is unnecessary. The same advice applies to other non essential items such as travel clocks, several different colors of shoes, radios, more than one cologne, and so forth. For example, the traveler should not take one brown suit and one blue or black suit. Take colors that are complementary. If two suits of totally different colors are taken, it will be necessary to carry different color socks and ties. If two suits are from the same spectrum, then only one color of socks and ties need be selected. Never carry more than two suits. Only one suit can be worn at one time and with two of them, the traveler will probably never have to wear the same suit twice in front of the same client. Only take white shirts for the same reason--theywill go with everything. Take one or two casual shirts and slacks for weekends and informal occasions. Most foreign businessmen are formal so it is not necessary to take along sport coats; they only contribute to the weight of the baggage that must be carried from terminal to terminal and taxi to taxi.

Also stay away from electrical gadgets for shaving and hair drying. The adapters necessary to fit all the outlets of the world could not possibly be included in the kits. The traveler who carries these will quickly learn that inevitably he seems to have the wrong adapter. Instead, shave with a safety razor and do not take a lot of blades along. Items such as blades are readily available virtually everywhere. If a hair dryer is essential, purchase one abroad rather than in the United States. By doing this the traveler will be assured of having one that will work in the country being visited. The devices manufactured in the United States for use abroad usually do not have the proper amperage necessary for the equipment to operate at peak performance. If the traveler stays at the better hotels in the major cities of the world, he will likely find out two currents are available in hotel rooms: 110/60 hertz and 220/50 hertz. Many electrical luxury items are also available today that operate from batteries, thus eliminating the problems inherent with different electrical standards.

Experienced travelers try to avoid changing planes en route because this is the single largest cause of lost luggage. While in many parts of the world one can usually find something to wear while he waits for his luggage to be found, in some destinations, such as the Orient, it is not that easy. A strapping six-foot-tall American will have difficulty finding trousers and shirts to fit him anywhere in the East. Even in Hong Kong usually two or three days are needed in order to custom-make clothes. The loss of luggage can be minimized if the traveler includes a tie, pair of socks, and a change of underwear in his attache case.

CARRYING SAMPLES OR ADVERTISING MATERIALS

Carrying samples or advertising materials is not advisable. No matter how this subject is viewed, it is a hassle. Many, if not most, countries assess duty and taxes on samples and advertising materials. It is not a problem if the exporter has only one or two pieces of advertising materials with him. But if he tries to take in an appreciable quantity, he will be delayed at customs and will have to pay duty. This is a particularly vexing problem when the exporter deems it necessary to show a sample(s) of a new product or a product enhancement to his representatives. If the exporter is going to hand-carry demonstration equipment that is destined for a trade show, or if he is going to take the sample from one country to another, the only way expeditiously to transport such items is with an *ATA Carnet*.

Carnets are issued by the U.S. Council for International Business. The Council has convenient offices throughout the United States with headquarters located in New York City. An application fee for the carnet, an insurance bond, certified check, or L/C equal to 40% of the value of the goods must be posted. This fee guarantees that duty will be assessed if the merchandise not re-exported. Upon return of the merchandise to the United States, the carnet is returned to the Council for International Business and the bond or L/C is then cancelled. Although most carnets are valid for twelve months, the security may not be returned for up to thirty months due to the time it may take to process any claims that may be brought against the Council in connection with the carnet.

Carnets are similar to passports, except that instead of stamping an arrival indicia in the document, the customs inspector removes a voucher. When the goods leave the country, another voucher is removed, proving that they did not remain in the country. The exporter who plans to bring substantial amounts of merchandise into a country under a carnet is advised to go to the airport the day before departure to make the necessary arrangements with U.S. customs for the technical documentation that must be provided *prior* to departure. If the exporter is only carrying one item, he may be able to clear these formalities the day of departure. He is still at risk that clearance will not be accomplished in a timely manner.

The exporter should pack the merchandise in such a manner that the customs officials can easily open and reclose the containers without the necessity of repacking. All countries of the world do not honor carnets; only those countries that subscribe to the carnet agreement allow transiting goods. A partial list of those countries follows:

> Australia, Austria, Belgium, Bulgaria, Canada, Cyprus, Czechoslovakia, Denmark, Finland, France, Gibraltar, Greece, Hong Kong, Hungary, Iceland, Ireland, Israel, Italy, Ivory Coast, Japan, Mauritius, The Netherlands, New Zealand, Norway, Poland, Portugal, Rumania, Senegal, Singapore, Sri Lanka, South Africa, South Korea, Spain, Sweden, Switzerland, Turkey, United Kingdom, United States, West Germany, and Yugoslavia.

Because this list will change periodically, the exporter should secure a new list prior to any journies where the use of a carnet is contemplated.

PASSPORT CONTROL

The exporter new to foreign travel has no doubt heard horror stories about clearing customs and immigration. Some of these stories are true, but for the most part they are fall-backs to the precomputer days. Customs clearance in the United States is still more time-consuming and difficult than in much of the world, but it has improved greatly during the last decade. No longer do surly agents insist on going through every bag with a fine tooth comb. Now the inspection usually encompasses only one or two bags per passenger, though returning U.S. citizens may be subjected to some form of personal search of their luggage.

For the rest of the world, the entry process is usually much simpler. Europe and many other parts of the world use the green door/red door system of entry. After luggage is claimed from the baggage carousel, the traveler is confronted with customs agents and beyond them is the set of red and green doors. If the deplaning passenger has nothing to declare, then he should walk past the customs inspectors and go through the set of green doors into the terminal itself. If the traveler does have an item(s) to declare, he should go to the customs inspector in front of the red doors and make arrangements to pay the duty assessed.

Before embarking on a trip abroad, the exporter should verify which countries require visas and make the necessary application well in advance of the trip. In order to obtain a passport, a birth certificate must be presented to the passport office as proof that the applicant is of U.S. birth. Naturalized citizens must present the original certificate of naturalization. If a person has had a name change such as through marriage or divorce, he must produce a certified document of name change. Two 2 X 2 inch photographs are also required.

If visas are required for any part of the trip, the country's consulate must be contacted and application made. There is usually a small fee for this service and processing visa applications by mail is usually permissible.

Before applying for any visas, the traveler should be certain to have his passport in hand because it will be necessary for the visa to be rubber stamped into the passport itself. Visas have a definite time limit for which they are valid. If repeated trips are anticipated, it will be necessary to stay current on the visas so the traveler does not inadvertently travel with an expired document.

If the traveler has acquired something that is of foreign manufacture and is concerned that upon returning to the United States he will be assessed duty, he should visit customs *before* departing with the item. Customs will issue a certificate of registration that should be retained and presented upon the traveler's return to the United States. It is a good idea to have watches, jewelry, and cameras registered in order to avoid arguments and delays upon returning. The traveler who acquires a product abroad that is subject to duty and tries to fool the customs agent into believing it was actually acquired in the United States should be aware that for many popular items, such as Japanese cameras, the serial numbers will be different from those acquired in the United States.

The World Health Organization prints a yellow form in which the traveler can have his doctor enter his record of innoculations. This is a convenient form for the traveler on which to record his shots. It also provides space for notations such as eye glass prescription and prescription drugs that may have to be refilled during the course of the journey. However, the prudent traveler should always attempt to take enough of his medication to last the duration of the trip, because it is occasionally difficult to find prescription drugs in other countries. The record of prescriptions should be considered only as a hedge in case luggage is lost. If the prescription is critical, then a small supply should be carried directly on the person.

The exporter who has not traveled extensively may be pleased to find out that he does not have to clear customs and immigration each time he stops in a country to change planes. Passengers who are transiting through a country are escorted to a transit lounge where they can wait until their next scheduled departure. Transit lounges vary throughout the world, but most offer comfortable surroundings with food and beverage service.

FOREIGN EXCHANGE

Foreign exchange is the term used to describe the act of exchanging the currency of one country for the currency of another. When one takes U.S. dollars and exchanges them for pounds sterling, he is said to have purchased foreign exchange. The purchase or sale of foreign exchange while traveling is usually only for the purpose of paying expenses. Expenses such as hotel rooms, taxis, restaurants, and so forth, are billed in the local currency. However, in a pinch most major establishments in foreign countries will accept dollars in payment for services. In these situations the rate of exchange is always to the advantage of the proprietor.

The best place to buy and sell exchange is a bank. However, banks are not always open and there is always the problem of getting from the airport to the bank without local currency. In order to overcome this problem, exchange should be purchased either before the flight departs, or at one of the convenient exchanges available at most airports. Ideally currency should be purchased in the country where it will be used. It should also be sold in the country in which it was acquired if at all possible, because a more favorable rate will be provided than one can normally receive in a third country. Usually it does not make sense to save leftover foreign currency until the next trip, since rates fluctuate so much it is always a gamble as to whether it will be worth more or less next time.

Some credit cards are accepted abroad and have somewhat reduced the dependency on cash. Credit card transactions, however, are billed in the currency of the country in which the charge occurred and the rate of exchange that the user of the card is charged is determined solely by the credit card company. These types of transactions are among the most expensive.

If a great deal of time is going to be spent in one country and there will be a recurring need for local currency, it may be advisable to arrange for a letter of credit to be opened at a local bank in the traveler's name. Just as a commercial L/C can be used to purchase merchandise, so an individual can open an L/C in his own name. All that is required is that the traveler deposit the appropriate amount of U.S. dollars in an account in the United States and have that bank correspond with another bank in the city and country being visited. In these situations, the L/C is similar to having an ordinary account in the bank. The traveler can draw on the L/C whenever he needs funds.

TERRORISM

Acts of terrorism can happen at any time and in any place. There are, however, some places that are more likely to be targets of terrorism than others. Airports and airplanes are always likely targets. Some specific airlines are more frequently targeted by extremists than others. Airlines and airport authorities generally do a very credible job of providing security to ensure passenger safety, but some do it better than others. The traveler should always try to limit his exposure to situations that could become violent. If time must be spent at the airport, try to limit the amount of time spent in front of ticket counters. Avoid large congregations of people in terminal restaurants. If possible, join several different airlines' executive clubs where time may be spent in relative safety because access to the facilities is limited and usually off the beaten track. Some carriers have very extensive routes and clubs in many cities. Consider Pan American's Clipper Club, American Airlines Admirals Club, or clubs of foreign carriers such as Swiss Air, Air France, Lufthansa, and British Airways. The idea is not to congregate in public places for long periods.

Many foreign airports have better security than is found in the United States. Frequently passengers about to board a flight may find their luggage set out next to their plane. The idea is that each passenger must identify his luggage before boarding the plane. Any luggage not claimed by a passenger will be left behind. Some airports have military police guarding the actual aircraft, as well as all the access roads into the airport property.

If the traveler finds himself in the middle of a demonstration, he should make every effort to extricate himself promptly so he is not accidentally assumed to be a participant and arrested, or worse, by the police. Avoid restaurants that are popular tourist spots. Many times extremists have bombed restaurants that have a reputation for catering to tourists.

Because the United States has such a large presence abroad, Americans are frequent targets of terrorism. The best protection an American has is to not be easily available to terrorists. This not only means that tourist gathering spots should be avoided and time in airport terminals limited, but it also means that one should not dress in such a manner that anyone looking at him would immediately identify him as an American. The exporter should make an effort to blend in with the indigenous population. In other words, if the local dress is slacks, sandals, and open shirts, dress in the same manner. The traveler should not draw attention to himself by being the only person in a group wearing a three-piece suit.

If he finds himself in a terrorist situation, he should make every effort to melt into his surroundings. He should not attract attention to himself. If a foreign language is known, try using it when addressed, rather than English. If English is the only language known or if it is the only foreign language known by the terrorist, avoid using words that are not common. Do not try to impress them with your English language skills. Because many of the terrorist acts are committed by persons of Middle Eastern extraction, avoid carrying personal items in your hand baggage that may offend them and give them a reason to beat or kill you. Specifically do not carry copies of literature that contain photographs of naked women.

Terrorism is a real threat and the traveler who is caught up in a hijacking probably has a better chance of survival than one who is kidnapped off the street. If many people are involved, it is in the governments' and airlines' best interest to attempt to peacefully resolve the conflict. If an American businessman is kidnapped and held for ransom, the U.S. government can not do very much to come to his aid. The sovereignty of the nation in which the kidnapping occurred and cooperation with the local authorities must be considered. No nation wants terrorism or kidnapping to occur within its borders, but sovereign nations also do not welcome interference from foreign governments; therefore, the victim is usually in some type of purgatory until negotiations can begin. In situations where the motive of the kidnapping is ransom rather than some philosophical principal, the victim's company is in the best position to negotiate his freedom. Before departing on company business, the exporter should extract an understanding as to what will happen if he should be kidnapped or held hostage. Will his pay be continued? Who will negotiate for his freedom? How much ransom will be paid? Will his job be maintained for him in his absence? Will the company arrange to help his spouse through the difficulty if he is kidnapped or held hostage? Items such as these may seem small, but the knowledge of what steps are being taken on behalf of victim can provide the only consolation and diminish the feelings of abandonment.

SUMMARY

Traveling abroad is a wonderful experience that enables the traveler to grow in experience and intellect because he is exposed to different cultures and business practices that, hopefully, will enable him to increase sales and profitability for his employer.

Because traveling is expensive, trips should be planned in order to maximize the return on investment of the travel dollar. Trips should be planned so a circle is completed whenever possible, preventing the traveler's dead-heading back to the United States. Dead-heading is costly in terms of time and flight fees. Trips of five weeks or longer are tiring and should be avoided whenever possible. Packing should include five of each basic article of clothing and laundry should be planned for each weekend.

The best travel times for businessmen are in the spring or fall. During these times tourism is at its lowest and accommodations are easier to arrange. Avoid national holidays if possible. If travel is unavoidable during major holidays, plan on spending the time waiting for the holiday's end in a major city or resort where comfortable accommodations can be found. Stay in hotels where English is readily spoken and where there are enough distractions to keep yourself interested while waiting to conduct business after the holiday.

Demonstration equipment, samples, professional tools and many other items that are not of a consumable nature may be taken into and out of countries without having to pay taxes or duties if the traveler obtains an ATA carnet from the U.S. Council for International Business before departure. The Council is affiliated with the International Chamber of Commerce and, together with approximately forty other affiliates, offers this easy and inexpensive way to transport items from one country to another. A deposit equal to 40% of the retail value of each item for which a carnet is applied must be made with the council. In addition, there is a small fee charged for the service. This fee varies from U.S. $60 for items valued at under U.S. $500 to U.S. $150 for items valued at U.S. $15 thousand or more.[1]

The least expensive place to purchase foreign exchange is the bank. However, because banks are not always convenient to the traveler, he should purchase his exchange at the airport or depot of arrival. The rate of exchange, although important, should not be the only concern of the traveler wanting to purchase local currencies. The service fee charged in order to make the transaction should also be considered. These fees will vary widely, with hotels generally charging more than banks or foreign exchanges. The traveler should make certain he exchanges enough money at his point of destination in order to pay for taxis, tips, and other incidental costs inherent to getting to his hotel or appointment.

While traveling abroad, the businessman should avoid large public gathering spots as much as is practical. Terrorism is a fact of life and it can occur at any time and in any place. However, airport lobbies, nightclubs, hotels, restaurants, and so forth. frequented by foreign persons, especially Americans, are more dangerous than other less conspicuous spots. The American businessman should always avoid public demonstrations so as not to be targeted either by the demonstrators themselves or to be inadvertently injured by the authorities attempting to bring the demonstration under control. Inflammatory statements in public can create a confrontational situation in some societies. The traveler must always use sound judgment and be careful not to make inflammatory statements. Except in the private company of his associates, the businessman should not make any statements that could offend the local government or factions that may be opposed to the current government. The traveler must always remember that he is a guest in the country and that all countries do not afford him the same freedoms he enjoys in the United States.

Prior to leaving on trips overseas, the executive should have an understanding or an agreement with his employer as to how each will react if the executive is kidnapped or hijacked. The incapacitated executive should not have to worry about the well-being of his family while he is in captivity and he should have some prior arranged means of communicating his physical and mental condition to his family and employer. Being the victim of a terrorist act is akin to being a prisoner of war, and the same techniques that sustain prisoners should be employed by the captive executive.

NOTE

1. *Application Procedure for ATA Carnets*, (New York: U.S. Council for International Business), New York, p.2.

Chapter 16
Foreign Patent and
Trademark Protection

Foreign patent and trademark protection generally includes all industrial property rights abroad. The exporter can protect his rights to patent and trademarks only by filing for them on a country by country basis. The United States is a signatory to about ninety international agreements that, when considered together, encompass the total protection; there is no comprehensive international patent nor trademark system. However, the treaties (some of which are referred to as conventions) are honored by approximately eighty countries, including Communist countries such as the U.S.S.R.

Of the treaties in force around the world, the most important ones are The International Convention of the Protection of Industrial Property, the Patent Cooperation Treaty, the European Patent Convention, and the Madrid Agreement for the International Registration of Marks.

The International Union for the Protection of Industrial Property (commonly called the Paris Convention) contains the broadest provisions for protection of industrial patents and trademarks. The all important Rule of National Treatment states that all member nations have agreed to grant the same rights to foreign applicants from other member nations as they do to their own nationals. However, because each nation establishes its own laws, the rules may vary from one country to another. This means that an applicant in one country may not receive the same rights as he might receive in a second country, even though both nations are signatories to the same agreement.

RIGHT OF PRIORITY

The Right of Priority is an important concept set forth in the Paris Convention that enables a patent applicant in a member country to file patent applications in other member countries within one year of the home country's filing date and thereby claim the home country filing date as the filing date for each foreign patent application. If the Convention did not contain this provision, the owner of a U.S. patent would be likely to find himself in the position of not being able to apply for a patent in a member country at all. The laws of many foreign countries prohibit the grant of a patent if there has been disclosure of the invention anywhere in the world prior to the filing of the patent application. By claiming the U.S. filing date for the foreign patent applications, any disclosure occurring after the U.S. filing date does not bar the granting of the foreign patents. Thus, a U.S. applicant has twelve months in which to file for the foreign applications and claim the U.S. filing date. Should the applicant wait longer than this period, he may obtain foreign patents that will ultimately be invalid or he may have to incur great expense to prove that the invention was not disclosed anywhere prior to the actual filing dates of the foreign applications.

The period of priority for trademarks is six months. By claiming the U.S. trademark application date for foreign trademark applications, the applicant gains priority over anyone who has filed for trademark protection in a given foreign country after the applicant's U.S. filing but before the actual date of application filing.

Under the Patent Cooperation Treaty of which there are some twenty-eight signatories, the patent application is made to all the member countries at one time. Therefore, it is not necessary to file eighty applications in eighty countries.

PRINCIPAL OF INDEPENDENCE

Since patents and trademarks are awarded by individual countries, it is reasonable to expect each country to independently enforce its own provisions regarding expiration and validity. The principal of independence means that the lapse or revocation of a patent in one country does not affect its validity in another country. Of course, it also follows that each country's laws must be followed regardless of the laws of another country. Many countries' laws regarding patents and trademarks stipulate that in order for a patent or a trademark to be valid, it must be in use for a specific period of time. These rules are known as Compulsory Working Provisions. Under the convention, the signatories have agreed not to invalidate a patent or a trademark unless it has not been in use for four years from the date of the filing or three years from the date of issuance.

The procedure to be followed in seeking an international patent usually begins at the U.S. Patent and Trademark Office. Applications, however, can be sent to several other receiving locations among them the African Intellectual Property Organization, the European Patent Office, and the World Intellectual Property Organization. After submission of the patent application and the filing of the necessary documents, the application lays dormant for twenty months during which time the Patent Office searches for prior art. At the conclusion of the search, the office sends its results directly to the applicant. This generally takes about nine months from the date of filing. After the applicant is advised of the results of the search, he can elect to continue with his international filing for a patent. It is then up to the individual countries to decide whether or not to issue a patent to the applicant. This phase of the procedure usually takes up to eighteen months.

TRADEMARKS

Many companies consider their trademark one of their most important and valuable assets. Therefore, it stands to reason that they will want international protection of the mark wherever possible.

Companies that have trademarks registered in the United States cannot automatically have their trademarks registered in a foreign country. Although the United States has signed agreements with approximately ninety-five countries, these agreements only protect the bearer from discrimination by the foreign governments. Under all the treaty agreements, U.S. trademark owners are guaranteed to be treated equally with national trademark owners. Thus, it is necessary for companies that wish to register their marks in other countries to file applications on a country by country basis.

A revision to the original International Convention for the Protection of Industrial Property, known as the Paris Convention, made it possible for applicants for trademarks in member countries not to demonstrate that the mark has a prior home country. This revision also had the effect of strengthening prior law regarding registering of service marks as well as marks for merchandise.

As mentioned earlier, the United States is not a signatory to any international agreements that would facilitate an international filing for a trademark. There are, however, several international agreements, though not signed by the United States, that will accommodate centralized filing. The major international agreement is known as the Madrid Arrangement.

In order for the owner of a mark to register it in one of the approximately twenty-four countries that are signatories of the treaty, he must be domiciled in one of them. A company is considered to be domiciled if it has a branch office or a subsidiary. The risk to companies that have such arrangements is, of course, that they may lose control of the mark in those markets where application is made under the terms of this treaty. For example, if an American company has a minority position in a joint venture domiciled in a member country and it files under that company's auspices and then later disassociates itself from the venture, it could lose control of the mark. The incentive for filing under the umbrella of the Madrid Arrangement is that the cost for filing is substantially reduced. Instead of paying for filing fees in each country, it is only necessary to file once and pay one fee.

The period of registration is identical for all countries at twenty years, with renewal for additional twenty year periods. In order to utilize filing under the Madrid Arrangement, a single international application is made to the central bureau of the Intellectual Property Organization located in Geneva, Switzerland. When the central bureau receives an application along with instructions as to which countries applications should be filed, it will publish the information in an international journal and forward copies to the countries in which registration is sought. Each country has the right to judge the application in the same manner it would judge application from its own nationals. Therefore, it is possible that an application could be accepted in one country while denied in another. However, if the application is denied, the denial must occur within one year from the date of publication in the journal. There is one other caveat that could affect registration; if the home country cancels the registration, other countries may also cancel it. However, if the home country cancels the registration after it has been in effect for five years or longer, then the other countries cannot cancel it on the grounds of the home country's cancellation.

Another treaty with more limited signataries than Madrid was negotiated in 1973 and became effective in 1980. This treaty is know as the Trademark Registration Treaty (TRT). The TRT has five members: Congo, Gabon, Togo, Upper Volta, and the U.S.S.R. The United States has signed, but until current trademark law can be amended to base registration on intent, it cannot ratify the treaty. The advantage to an American firm seeking registration under the treaty is that unlike the Madrid Arrangement, the TRT does not require a prior home registration. Otherwise, the procedure for filing is similar to the Madrid Arrangement. Filing remains with the World Intellectual Property Organization in Geneva. The company interested in filing trademarks utilizing the TRT should be aware that in most countries it is not necessary for the applicant to present evidence that the mark(s) has been in use before application. In the common law countries, the applicant must demonstrate use or intended use. However, most countries have civil law systems and in these instances, the first applicant to apply at the registration office with a mark is granted it. There are instances where individuals or companies have deliberately sought trademarks registered in the United States by U.S. companies and registered them in their own country. By doing this, they are in a position to blackmail the originator of the mark to negotiate a license fee if he wants to use the mark in their country. Some persons seeking specific American lines to represent have gone to the registration office and registered a trademark in order to force the original owner of the mark to appoint them as his representative.

There are other regional patent and trademark agreements that the exporter will want to query his patent attorney about before embarking on an extensive registration procedure. Some of the regional agreements include the European Patent Convention (EPC), the EEC Trademark Convention, and the African and Malagasy Industrial Property Office. In addition, various bilateral agreements exist between former British

Commonwealth countries that can benefit American companies with offices in one or more of the member nations.

TRADEMARK AND INFRINGEMENT PROBLEMS

Trademarks around the world are classified according to goods and services. In fact, the United States and about sixty other countries ascribe to the Arrangement of Nice Concerning the International Classification of Goods and Services to Which Trade Marks Apply. With this arrangement, merchandise is divided into thirty-four classes, whereas services are classified in seven. Matters pertaining to trademarks should always be discussed with competent legal counsel in order to determine the exact legal requirements in each country being considered for trademark registration. Problems concerning trademarks are usually not insurmountable unless the trademark being sought is considered generic. When one considers the quantity of countries and numerous languages in the world, it will be no surprise that questions regarding generic names would arise. There is an old story that has circulated in export circles for years that at one time a city in Japan renamed itself USA, pronounced "yousa". The story continues that all items manufactured in this city could be said to have been "made in USA." This author does not know if there is any truth to the story, but it does illustrate how some persons or companies may try to take advantage of a generic term and gain exclusivity to it in their own markets.

Primarily it is up to the owners of trademarks and patents to police the use of their industrial property within the United States and as well as outside of it. Should the owner of a registered trademark or patent abroad learn that it is being used by someone else, then it is up to the owner and his counsel to take the necessary steps to cause the infraction to cease. Stopping the infringement will be up to the local government and its local laws. There is realistically little the U.S. government can do to help the owner protect his rights abroad, because it has no jurisdiction. The Commerce Department cannot become involved in disputes between two American firms competing abroad. The owner of the mark or patent is, therefore, requested not to attempt to involve the Commerce Department in such disputes. However, the Commerce Department will make some attempts on behalf of American firms if the infringement is against a foreign firm. In order to receive the most assistance available, the owner of the mark or patent should attempt to provide as much information regarding the infringement as possible. This information should include a copy of the American firm's U.S. patent or trademark, foreign registration, samples of the mark or item infringing in its original packaging. A sample of the American product should also be enclosed so a comparison may be made. If a U.S. patent or mark has been litigated and upheld, a photocopy of the judgment should also be included. If the name and address of the foreign imitator is known, it should also be provided. In other words, the owner of the mark or patent should provide as much information as possible so the commercial attaché in the embassy can make a strong case on behalf of the American owner. Results from the Commerce Department seem to vary in relation to how strong the bonds and relations are between the United States and the country in which the infraction is said to occur.

Many of the complaints typical to infringements involve unsophisticated and easily copied items, although most complaints regarding marks result from untimely registrations.

With regard to the misuse of generic terms, there are a few things the government can do to attempt to stop the infraction. It is very important that no foreign person or firm gain exclusivity to generic American terms. If such a situation were to be tolerated, it conceivably could prohibit applicable goods from being imported into the country, make it impossible to use common names in marketing and advertising, and also make the company that does in fact import a generic product subject to an infringement suit in the local courts. If the U.S. government learns of infringements of generic terms, it will usually alert the U.S. embassy in the country in which the infraction occurs and attempt to persuade the local government to cancel the mark.

JOINT VENTURES AND LICENSING ABROAD

Many American companies choose to license their technology abroad rather than to export actual product. This decision is usually based on the reality that licensing does not require as large a capital investment as many foreign marketing programs. Also, licensing generally will create a quicker return in actual currency than exporting, and occasionally it is a means of circumventing another country's import restrictions.

As good as the reasons are for considering a foreign licensing program, there is a down side, as well. Every time a license agreement is concluded, the possibility of creating a competitor exists. Human nature seems to dictate that once technology is understood, greed steps in and pressure is applied to either renegotiate the agreement or terminate it and go into direct competition with the licensor. The control the licensor has over the license regarding quality and marketing frequently grows into resentment. When this occurs, the damage to the licensor's trademarks and reputation may permanently affect his market position. Lastly, licensing is no doubt less profitable to the licensor than direct market sales.

The most common items to be licensed consist of industrial property such as patented products, know-how, architectural and engineering designs, as well as items covered by copyright.

Foreign licensing agreements generally consist of the following clauses:

1. The Territory: one country or several countries that are usually adjacent to each other or where unique bonds exist such as between

Great Britain and its Commonwealth nations.

2. The Rights: generally limited to patents, trademarks, know-how, and/or copyrights.

3. Future Rights: usually stipulate that the licensor will not grant rights to another person or company at a lower royalty rate than is being charged the licensee.

4. The Agreements Tenure: licensing agreements that usually are limited to the life of a patent. Other rights such as know-how, copyrights, and trade secrets are for a fixed period that varies greatly.

5. Marketing and Management Assistance: usually a part of the agreement and provided by the licensor. There may be additional fees charged for this service or they may be included in the basic agreement.

6. Maintenance of Quality: several countries such as the United Kingdom have *registered user* requirements. These requirements stipulate that certain minimum quality standards must be maintained or the government has the right to force maintenance. Even without the heavy hand of the law on the shoulder of the licensor, it is to his advantage to ensure that quality standards are maintained in order for his reputation not to be impugned.

7. Non-technical Services: such as management assistance, technical assistance, purchasing assistance, and marketing assistance may be included in the agreement or they may be dealt with in a separate agreement between the parties.

8. Fees: licensing agreements contain clauses that stipulate the royalty to be paid. Royalties are frequently based on the net selling price. That is the price charged the consumer less any discounts, returns, taxes, etc. Typical licensing agreements range from 5% to 6% of the net selling price.

9. Payment: always a major consideration of the licensing agreement. Usually the first fee is a lump sum based on the expected sales volume during the first year the agreement is in force. Future payments are then made on a quarterly or annual basis. The licensor generally insists on the right to audit the licensee's books and verify that the amount of royalty being remitted is correct. Some countries have currency

restrictions; for this reason most agreements contain a clause that requires the licensee to deposit the equivalent of U.S. funds in local currency with a fiduciary, such as a bank.

10. Jurisdiction: usually the United States except where local law prevails and requires litigation be conducted in the local country. Due to the high cost of international litigation, most agreements contain clauses stipulating that should disputes arise they will be settled by arbitration rather than litigation. Arbitration typically is conducted by the American Arbitration Association or the International Chamber of Commerce.United States; export control laws must be respected, therefore most agreements contain clauses guaranteeing this right.

11. Termination: because all agreements eventually come to an end, it is incumbent on the licensor to stipulate the conditions that can result in termination of the agreement.

Agreements usually contain other clauses that are of special interest to the parties to the agreement. It is essential that all agreements be concluded under the watchful eye of competent international attorneys familiar with international patent and trademark law. Most firms specialize in one or several countries, and the neophyte to licensing is wise to search out a firm to represent his interests that has experience in the countries in which he is interested in establishing licensing agreements.

Most companies enter into joint ventures because each party to the venture has something to gain and something to contribute. Frequently, it is the American company that has the technology or product while the foreign partner has the distribution. Joint ventures generally do not cost as much as going it alone in a foreign country, so the prospect of enhanced distribution coupled with the lower capital requirement can prove very attractive. Companies will occasionally enter into a joint venture in order to protect themselves from some distant and unknowable future expropriation. In addition, some governments will not allow wholly owned foreign companies. Governments that take this position generally do so in order to encourage their local companies to grow and thus help to expand the local economy.

Joint ventures must be organized under the local laws of the country in which they are formed and in which they will do business. In most common law countries, the corporate structures are familiar and related to United States' forms of companies. In the civil law countries, however, there are a few differences. The largest size companies are referred to as being formally structured and will usually be identified as *société anonyme* or *sociedad anonima*. These forms are similar to American public corporations and the terms société anonyme or sociedad anonima are similar, at least in concept, to incorporated or limited.

The smaller corporations in civil law countries are referred to as informal and they are similar to American privately held corporations. These firms are known as *société à résponsibilité limitée* or *sociedad de responsabilidad limitada*. The informal company is usually subject to lower taxes than the formal company, and the laws regulating the transfer of ownership are less stringent in the informal organization.

TAX CONSIDERATIONS

With today's tax burdens, it is no wonder corporations continually seek ways to limit their social costs. Many foreign countries, unlike the United States, do not tax income earned from outside their borders. American companies that are either wholly owned or joint ventures are usually eligible to receive tax credits for the tax they must pay in their host country. This is necessary in order to avoid double taxation. In other words, if the United States were to tax the income an American firm earned in England and the English government were to tax it as well, the firm would be paying a double tax to the United States and to England.

If the host country's tax is equal or greater than the U.S. tax, no U.S. tax will be due on that income. However, if the foreign tax is lower, the United States will levy a tax on that portion of income that exceeds the local tax. Anyone considering forming a joint venture with foreign partners should be certain to consult with a large American accounting firm with offices in the country in which the venture is contemplated. The expert advice of accountants is invaluable and their experience in dealing with international tax issues should not be ignored. The Internal Revenue Code sections 861-863 detail how the income from foreign corporations should be treated in light of United States' position regarding worldwide income.

Because most joint ventures evolve out of a desire to share in one another's strengths, capital is frequently not the basis on which the venture is founded. Rather, it is patents, know-how, or trade secrets. When this is the case, the U.S. government may view the transaction as subject to a capital gains tax rather than as ordinary income. In order to qualify for the lower capital gains rate, however, essentially all rights to the patent, know-how, or trade secret must be transferred. Interestingly enough, the transfer of title in certain countries with tax dividends at a lower rate than royalties can result in lower taxes for the entity and the U.S. partner. Care must be taken regarding the amount of ownership the American company has in the joint venture. If less than 80% of the venture is owned by the American firm and a transfer of patents, know-how, or trade secrets is made in exchange for stock, the transaction may be taxed by the United States as ordinary income. On the other hand, if the foreign venture is 80% or more owned by the American firm, the transaction may avoid taxes entirely. This action is detailed under section 367 of the U.S. tax code and is similar to section 351, which applies to domestic corporations.

Needless to say, noncash transactions are more complicated than cash transactions, so the importance of sound advice from both accountants and lawyers is an absolute necessity!

The last important area any American company should consider before entering into joint venture agreements or licensing agreements is that the U.S. government has strict laws and regulations regarding the transfer of technology. As a general rule, there will be no problems in exporting technology if the exporter does it under a general license. However, if a validated license is required, prior approval of the transfer should be sought.

SUMMARY

Patents, trademarks, know-how, and trade secrets are carried on most companies' balance sheets as assets. It stands to reason that in international trade they will likewise have great value. In order to protect these assets, it is essential that the owner of them, with advice of counsel, diligently register them abroad and then staunchly monitor their use.

Patents and trademarks are protected abroad through various treaties signed by the United States and other governments. The primary treaties are:

The International Convention of the Protection of Industrial Property.
The Patent Cooperation Treaty.
The European Patent Convention.
The Madrid Agreement for the International Registration of Marks.

These treaties give American companies the same rights that local companies have under each country's own domestic law. Thus, signatories of these treaties promise not to discriminate against foreign products in their own markets because they are unique.

In civil law countries, the first person to register a trademark is usually awarded it. This can work against the American company who owns a strong trademark because failure to register the mark can forever block its use in a country. It also opens American companies up to a form of blackmail in which a foreign owner of an American mark is forced to pay a fee in order to use it or to appoint the owner as his exclusive representative in the country where the abuse occurred.

Should disputes arise concerning infringement of patents or misuse of trademarks, it is up to the owner of the patent or the trademark to attempt to remedy the situation through the local courts. Realistically, there is little the U.S. government can do to interfere in the domestic jurisprudence of another country. Through the Department of Commerce, however, documented cases of patent infringements and trademark violations can be brought to the attention of the foreign government through U.S. embassies. The degree of success in assisting the American victim is usually limited by the degree of friendliness and goodwill demonstrated by each nation. In situations where the abuse is blatant and generic in nature, the best case the American government can often make to influence the foreign government is to no longer allow the foreign government's companies access to American markets. In other words, the U.S. government may establish duties for a particular item that will make it prohibitively expensive in the United States or they may simply prohibit importation. This may be a way for the government to "get even," but it is little solace to the exporter who is trying to market his product abroad.

Foreign licensing agreements are frequently made because the investment required is less than direct participation in the market. Joint ventures are frequently made for the same reasons as licensing agreements, except that with joint ventures, both parties stand to benefit from one another's expertise. Tax considerations should be reviewed prior to entering into joint ventures and competent legal counsel sought. Technology licensing and technology transferred under joint venture agreements must be approved by the U.S. government before exportation will be allowed.

NOTES

The author gratefully acknowledges the assistence of Mr. Ronald V. Thurman of the law firm Hubbard, Thurman, Turner & Tucker in the preparation of this chapter.

From Vincent Travaglini, "Protection of Industrial Property Rights Abroad," *Foreign Business Practices*, U.S. Department of Commerce, International Trade Administration, Superintendent of documents (Washington, D.C.: U.S. Government Printing Office), pp. 30-34.

From Joseph M. Lightman, *Foreign Patent Protection: Treaties and National Laws*, U.S. Department of Commerce, International Trade Administration, Superintendent of documents (Washington D.C.: U.S. Government Printing Office), pp. 35-36, 58-64.

From Vincent D. Travaglini, *Foreign Licensing and Joint Venture Arrangements*, U.S. Department of Commerce, International Trade Administration, Superintendent of documents (Washington D.C.: U.S. Government Printing Office), pp. 58-64.

Chapter 17
Foreign Trade Fairs

Trade shows are more important in foreign countries than they generally are in the United States. This chapter will discuss their relative importance, the different types of trade fairs, and the appropriate way to staff them.

THE IMPORTANCE OF TRADE FAIRS

Although trade shows in the United States continue to grow in size and quantity, their relative importance to the market is diminishing. Most of the growth witnessed in the U.S. trade show calendar is due to increasingly specialized activity. After World War II, trade shows developed, becoming a major method for manufacturers to demonstrate their products to the public. Beginning with state and county fairs, the concept was expanded until it grew into annual shows in major cities throughout the United States. With the advent of inexpensive and frequent air transportation, the convention became an American institution.

As society grew and technological advances were made, it became inevitable that trade fairs would become more and more specialized. The age of specialization created many more companies manufacturing and marketing look-alike products than in previous years. This growth in quantity of products on the market began to squeeze the space available to hold such events. In response to the diminishing dates available for shows and the overwhelming size, many U.S. associations and trade organizations began to establish regional shows and shows that were limited as to the industries invited to participate.

With television and later with video recorders, the need to have hands on personal demonstrations to large audiences was diminished. Add to this the explosion of trade publications directed at very specific market segments, and it is easy to understand why trade shows have lost some of their former glitter in this country.

However, in Europe and the rest of the world the trade fair is still a major event at which manufacturers can demonstrate their wares. In many, if not most, countries television as a medium is controlled by the government and in these states public advertising is generally limited. Thus, one very large avenue of marketing open to American sellers is closed to native or American firms operating in their countries.

Another consideration exporters have to make when determining how to market their products abroad is the availability of print media. The size of foreign markets, for the most part, is smaller than in the United States. Even in those countries, such as China, that offer potentially larger markets than the United States, the disposable income is much lower. In countries where the average standard of living is much lower than in the West, unless the exporter has a product that is considered essential, his market potential is small. For these reasons, foreign markets do not have the proliferation of specialized media through which to market products. Therefore, the trade fair must still occupy a central portion of the domestic manufacturers and exporter's marketing budgets. Trade fairs are widely attended in most parts of the world. It is at trade fairs that new products are unveiled and enhancements touted.

The degree of specialization found in American trade shows is not evident in most foreign shows. Whereas in the United States there is a show dedicated to packaging machines and material handling equipment, a similar show abroad would probably include metal-fabricating machinery. In Third World countries, there is virtually no specialization and trade shows are often open to the general public. At these types of shows, it is imperative that the exporter keep an open mind because his staff will be inundated with questions from the general public and it will sometimes be difficult to separate the serious prospect from the curious individual. Many trade fairs in the less developed countries take on the air of a carnival, which is hard for the American exporter to adjust to unless he is flexible and recognizes that this is how marketing is done in some countries.

The largest and the most important trade fair in the world is the Hanover Fair held each year in Hanover, West Germany. Originally this show was held in Leipzig, but when the country was partitioned after World War II, the sponsors needed a new location. East Germany still holds a Leipzig Fair, but compared to Hanover it is poorly attended. For those who are interested in marketing in East Europe, the Leipzig Fair should be considered. However, Hanover is the major European show attended by thousands from all over the Continent and the world. The logistics of Hanover are staggering because it is so expansive. Lodging is provided by private residents since the hotels are generally booked years in advance. Exhibit space is hard to come by and expensive. The fair is divided into various pavilions specializing in specific industries. For example, if an exporter manufactures tractors, he would be in the agricultural implements pavilion. If he manufactured computer software, he would be in the computer pavilion. Although Hanover is open to the public, the fair is so large that most attendees only visit those pavilions that contain items that are of interest to them. The general public that attends Hanover as a lark usually visits pavilions that are less technical and generally geared toward the consumer, like stereo, TV, housewares, and so forth.

Many companies new to export will forego exhibiting at Hanover the first few years and become established in some of the more specialized regional fairs throughout the world. This is a sound strategy because it enables the exporter to test the market to determine acceptance of his product. It also enables him to slowly adjust to receiving orders from abroad and to respond to the increased sales themselves. In the primary developed markets of the world, there are many trade fairs specialized to some degree or another. If the exporter is in a major field such as automotive, he will not have any difficulty locating several trade fairs dedicated just to his area of expertise.

STAFFING

How the exporter will staff his exposition is, of course, dependent on many factors including the size of the booth, the attendance anticipated, and the quantity of equipment exhibited. Many exporters depend on their local representatives to provide staffing for the trade shows. Local staffing is advantageous because they will be familiar with the local market conditions and acquainted with customs and business practices for their country. Also, language is not a problem if the booths are staffed with natives. For major shows, a person attached to the export staff or an experienced domestic salesman or technician functioning in an advisory capacity frequently will also attend. It is helpful for the person responsible for developing the export markets to attend as many major shows as is practical, because this is one of the best ways to gain insight into the various markets around the world. The exhibition booth is a great place to analyze the local representative's sales force and learn their strengths and weaknesses. It is usually not necessary to even know the language in order to make these evaluations. Much can be learned from body language and gestures. Voice inflection is another good way to detect stress or misunderstanding and should it be observed in either the seller or the prospect, it is beneficial to query the salesman about situations that did not generate the anticipated response. The primary purpose of exhibiting in foreign fairs is to acquire sales leads from qualified prospects that can be evaluated daily. For example, if the trade fair produces prospects from a country's major manufacturer of metal- fabricated products and the exporter has a similar customer in the United States, it is an opportune moment to teach the prospect about the application in the United States. By doing this, the exporter is training his representative in the product's application and giving him additional knowledge so he can close the sale later during a personal sales call.

Generally speaking, the best sales results will come from participation in local trade fairs where the booth is sponsored by the local company representing the exporter. This will give the appearance of permanence and make it easy for local prospects to communicate with their peers. Sometimes this is not possible, and in these cases it is best to participate in those shows that have pavilions sponsored by the U.S. Department of Commerce. However, it should be realized that participation in most of these pavilions will not generate many sales leads, because there is no local representation. For that matter, how could the exporter expect to service an account several thousands of miles away without some kind of presence in the market? Therefore, participation in U.S. sponsored events should be limited to those events that will generate interest in companies to import and market the exporter's products.

The larger regional trade fairs will create leads from countries not serviced by the local representation. Many foreign nationals attend major regional shows in an attempt to determine what is new in their industry. They may see the exporter's product, like it, and inquire about it. The local representative will generally forward these sales leads to the export department in the United States for follow-up. Unfortunately, this process is usually quite slow and the lead is stone cold by the time the representative in the third country is advised of the prospect's interest. It is helpful if the inquiries can be forwarded directly to the third country representative or at least telexed to the United States immediately after they are collected at the trade fair. In reality, this is hard to police because the sponsor of the show usually wants to cover his own leads first and only as a courtesy will he forward "out of country" leads to the exporter.

The beginning exporter should contact his Department of Commerce representative for a list of trade shows, and with department guidance, select those shows that he determines may be beneficial. The more experienced exporter can contact the consulates or embassies of countries where he is interested in establishing commercial relations and secure a list of trade fairs. It is usually necessary to commit to space a year in advance of the actual show, so it is important to plan ahead. Local industry associations are another source of information about foreign shows available to members. Lastly, it is often helpful to the exporter to make a trip abroad to visit some of the major shows to get a feel for the market and to make personal contact with potential importers of his products or services. This last suggestion is expensive, but it is probably the best way to seek out qualified representatives in the large, established markets. It certainly is not cost efficient in the less-developed markets and thus not recommended.

SUMMARY

Very few of the world's markets are as large or as developed as those of the United States. Due to this lack of market size, other countries have not developed the degree of product specialization prevalent in the United States. This lack of specialization limits the exporter's available media marketing tools.

Because few countries have specialized journals, magazines, or commercial television, the trade fair remains an important aspect of any foreign marketing program. The more developed the country, the more specialized its trade fairs have become, though few have grown to be as specialized as those in the United States. In the lesser-developed nations, the fairs are so unspecialized that they are usually open to the general public.

Foreign trade fairs should be staffed with nationals who represent the exporter. Attendance by the exporter is helpful in order to answer questions and to provide knowledge about domestic applications for his product.

Attendance by American exporters in U.S. sponsored pavilions is beneficial if the exporter does not have representation already in place. Participation in these shows can help the exporter locate local distributors or representatives for his products.

Chapter 18
Foreign Political Considerations

As long as man has been trading across borders, he has been subject to its inherent risks. Although communications and education have greatly reduced the risks of trading, the risks are still substantial in certain areas. The person new to export must be cautious about where and how he markets his products. Not only is there risk in fluctuations and availability of currencies, but serious political risks can exist as well. During the 1950s and 1960s there were few, if any, persons who had anything but enthusiasm over the prospects of doing business in Iran and in Lebanon. Today everyone knows that it is next to impossible to do any business with the current regimes. The annals of history are filled with examples where political upheavals have interrupted foreign commerce. In this chapter, foreign political risks are discussed, as well as the U.S. position regarding boycotts and antidiversion laws. A review of antitrust laws and FDA and EPA regulations is also included.

THE ANTIDIVERSION CLAUSE

U.S. export control regulations require all exporters to state on their declarations, commercial invoices, and bills of lading a destination statement. This statement serves to inform all foreign persons coming in contact with the shipment as to which countries the item may be re-exported. The verbiage for destination control statements follows:

A. For both validated and general license shipments:

"These commodities licensed by the United States for ultimate destination: (name of country). Diversion contrary to United States law prohibited."

"These commodities licensed by the United States for ultimate destination in _____ and for distribution or resale in _____. Diversion contrary to United States Law prohibited.

B. For general license shipments only:

"United States law prohibits distribution of these commodities to Cuba, the Soviet bloc, Communist China, North Korea, Macao, Hong Kong or Communist-controlled areas of Viet-Nam and Laos, unless otherwise authorized by the United States."[1]

The U.S. government is quite serious about abuses of exporters and their distributors, agents, representatives, licensees, and partners regarding diversion of American technology. At the time of this writing, Toshiba Machine Company of Japan had been found guilty of shipping American technology to a company in Norway which subsequently sold the technology to the Soviets. This technology concerned a method of manufacturing propellers for submarines that enables them to run more quietly than conventional propellers. The quieter the propellers, the more difficult it is to locate and identify the submarine. The U.S. government was so angry over Toshiba's breach of security that the Congress forbade them from selling any of their products in the United States for several years. In Japan this breech of security and the resultant U.S. action was viewed with such embarrassment that the president and the chairman of the giant company resigned in disgrace. As of this writing, it is unknown what the final effect will be on the future of Toshiba, but it will certainly suffer from not being able to compete in the American market.

Prior to the invention and popular use of personal computers, the government had a relatively easy job of keeping track of American technology. Transfers of technology occupied the time of many Ian Flemming type spies who lived a double life garnering secrets from the United States and then whisking them away either through embassy diplomatic pouches or by meeting foreign submarines off the coast of desolate islands. To be sure, some of this hocus-pocus still lingers, but today it is a simple matter to hook up one end of a computer in the United States to a modem and transfer the technology over telephone lines (or satellite transmissions) to a person with a similar modem in another country. This type of espionage is difficult to stop. In addition, it is necessary that all apprehended offenders be severely prosecuted.

On occasion even the innocent exporter may be unjustifiably punished if he is doing business with a foreign company that is determined to have diverted technology to an unfriendly country. The American exporter can also be prosecuted and fined; he will be censured and unable to continue to export. The exporter is, therefore, cautioned to know with whom he is dealing and what his representation is doing with the technology or products he supplies. Some of the typical conduits for illegal technology occur in states that border the Soviet bloc nations such as Finland and Austria.

ANTIBOYCOTT REGULATIONS

The Export Adminstration Act of 1979 is a fine example of a document with teeth in it! This act states that:

It is the policy of the United States - -

> (A) to oppose restrictive trade practices or boycotts fostered or imposed by foreign countries against other countries friendly to the United States or against any United States person;
>
> (B)...to refuse to take actions, including furnishing information or entering into or implementing agreements, which have the effect of furthering or supporting the restrictive trade practices or boycotts fostered or imposed by any foreign country against a country friendly to the United States or against any United States person;[2]

This law does not apply only to countries that conduct commerce with an American company, but also with any country that is friendly toward the United States. In other words, an exporter can find himself in trouble if he provides any information to another country that has a boycott or trade restriction against another country friendly to the United States. In reality this law is designed to discourage Arab nations from discriminating against the state of Israel. If an exporter agrees not to transship through Israel as a condition of sale, he is effectively complying with the trade restriction and as such is liable to action initiated by the U.S. government.

The government hopes to be able to bring economic pressure to bear on countries that refuse to do business with American allies by not allowing American companies to supply them with goods or services.

Enforcement of this act is delegated by the president to any department or agency that is presidentially appointed with the advice and consent of the Senate. These departments or agencies have the authority to

> ...make such investigations and obtain such information from, require such reports or the keeping of such records by, make such inspection of the books, records, and other writings, premises, or property of, and take the sworn testimony of, any person. In addition, such officers or employees may administer oaths or affirmations, and may by subpoena require any person to appear and testify or to appear and produce books, records, and other writings, or both....[3]

Section 12 of the act (previously quoted) provides the government with the means to locate any information it deems important in order to prosecute its case against the American exporter who is suspected of complying with restrictive trade practices or boycotts. Certainly, there are not many companies that want the government pouring over their books and records. There is nothing in this act that says information gleaned will be provided by the Internal Revenue Service, but the possibility should be enough reason to deter any American businessman from straying from the straight and narrow. As a father inducement to compliance, the act establishes severe penalties for firms or persons found guilty of complying with restrictive trade practices and/or boycotts. Specifically,

> ...whoever knowingly violates any provision of this Act or any regulation, order, or license issued thereunder shall be fined not more than five times the value of the exports involved or $50,000, which ever is greater, or imprisoned not more the 5 years, or both....

> The head of any department or agency exercising any functions under this Act or any officer or employee of such department or agency specifically designated by the head thereof, may impose a civil penalty not to exceed $10,000 for each violation of this Act . . . either in addition to or in lieu of any other liability or penalty which may be imposed.[4]

In addition to these heavy company and personal fines and possible imprisonment, the act provides the government the authority to force the offender to stop exporting. The act provides that export activity may not be allowed for as long as one year after the satisfactory payment of any assessed fines. Clearly this is a law that the government wants its businesses to understand. Furthermore the government will not compromise. As if to underscore the point, the act states: "No person shall be excused from complying with any requirements under this section because of his privilege against self-incrimination...."[5]

This act is so broadly written that American persons or companies must be extremely careful not to be led into thinking that because they hold a minority position in a foreign company, they can skirt this law. If the U.S. government wants to prosecute a person or company because of a transaction that violates the act, it will find a way to do so. The best advice for Americans dealing abroad is under no circumstances to tolerate or even to consider any action that could even remotely be construed as diversionary or discriminatory.

Most novice exporters get in trouble with this act when they accept a letter of credit that contains some requirements that the United States deems as restriction of trade. Illustration 18.1 is an example of typical conditions placed on some business transactions by boycotting countries. The illustration is of an actual rider or supplement to a confirmed irrevocable L/C drawn on Rafidain Bank in Baghdad and offered through their correspondent bank, Bankers Trust Co. of New York. It is correct and permissible for the bank to forward the L/C to the beneficiary, but it is absolutely against the law for the beneficiary to accept the L/C because it discriminates against a country that is friendly toward the United States. Had the supplement only required the beneficiary to include a certificate of origin stating that the goods being sold were manufactured in the United States, there would not have been a problem. However, in this example, they have singled out Israel and that makes acceptance of the L/C illegal.

In this case of the Iraqi bank letter of credit, the beneficiary is charged with the responsibility of reporting the discriminatory condition to the Commerce Department. However all events having to do with discrimination, diversion, boycott, and black listing are not reportable due to the overwhelming quantity of paperwork that would ensue. Each exporter is advised to procure a copy of the act that contains numerous examples of reportable and nonreportable offenses. Each time a situation occurs that is suspect, the exporter should consult the act and determine if he should report it. If he is in doubt, he can call the Commerce Department and inquire.

In addition to the restrictive trade practices and boycott restrictions, the Export Administration Act was created in order to stop companies and persons from willfully exporting anything that is restricted due to national security or due to foreign policy purposes. This act is taken very seriously by the U.S. government and it was this act that Toshiba, as mentioned earlier, was accused of violating. Specifically the Act states:

> Whoever willfully exports anything contrary to any provision of the Act or any regulation, order, or license issued under the Act, with the knowledge that such exports will be used for the benefit of any country to which exports are restricted for nationals security or foreign policy purposes except in the case of individual, shall be fined not more than five times the value of the exports involved or $1,000,000, whichever is greater; and in the case of an individual, shall be fined not more the $250,000, or imprisoned not more than 10 years, or both. Any person who is issued a validated license under this Act for the export of any goods or technology to a controlled country and who, with the knowledge that such export is being used by such controlled country for military or intelligence gathering purposes contrary to the conditions under which the license was issued, willfully fails to report such use to the Secretary of Defense, except in the case of an individual, shall be fined not more than five times the value of the exports involved or $1,000,000 whichever is greater; and in the case of an

individual, shall be fined not more than $250,000, or imprisoned not more than five years, or both.[6]

The exporter is advised that the excuse of "just working for someone" is not an acceptable excuse for violating the act. If an employee of a company is told to perform some action that the individual knows to be illegal, he is subject to prosecution under the Export Administration Act and subject to the fines and imprisonment mentioned. This is one situation where just doing your job can cost the individual his job, his income, and his freedom!

Part 387.13 of the act sets forth the requirements for record keeping. The exporter is required to keep all export control documents including memoranda, notes, correspondence, contracts, invitations to bid, books of account, financial records, restrictive trade practice or boycott documents and reports and other written materials for two years. The exporter is advised, however, to maintain his records for at least five years, because the statute of limitations on criminal activity is five years, as is the limitation for administrative compliance.

If an individual working for a company believes his company is violating the Act, he should report it to the Office of Export Enforcement in Washington, D.C.

The purpose of the Export Administration Act and its amendments through 1985 is to protect the nation and its assets from foreign threats to its security and its citizens from discriminatory trading. Although the act can be terribly punitive, the exporter has nothing to fear if he conducts his business in accordance with U.S. laws and tenants of personal integrity.

ANTITRUST LAWS AND CARTELS

At first consideration, the exporter may believe that because he is conducting his business outside of the United States his foreign transactions will not be subject to antitrust laws. This is erroneous, however, because American antitrust statutes include foreign as well as domestic commerce. In fact, companies engaged in international trade must take into consideration not only U.S. antitrust law, but also similar laws enacted in each of the countries in which they will conduct business. In 1958 the Treaty of Rome was signed into existence and the European signatories established what has come to be know as the "Common Market." Articles 85 and 86 of the treaty detail which type of company agreements and undertakings will be viewed as unfair trade practices and will not be tolerated. This was a major undertaking for the European community because up until this time, much of the commerce of each nation was in the hands of a few exceptionally large companies and associations of companies called cartels. These large conglomerates controlled a great deal of trade and were able to force legitimate competitors from the marketplace. However, even with the firm hand of the EEC intervening in commerce, its view of restrictive trade is somewhat different from that of the United

States. Therefore, any American company contemplating an association with not only a European company, but any foreign company, should consult with a legal firm specializing in matters of this type.

The mere size of a business is not universally viewed as reason enough to consider it to be trade restrictive. Indeed, the perception of how much commerce a company controls is very subjective, with the government of each country deciding at what point market share becomes detrimental to general well being. True monopolies are restrictive to trade and American businessmen abroad should always maintain a concept of free enterprise in their dealings abroad. Opportunities to review competitors' price lists, however innocent, should be scrupulously avoided. The simple act of reviewing the list could be grounds for restriction of trade claims. Similarly, contracts between the largest manufacturer in a particular industry and a supplier of raw materials should be structured in such a manner that other manufacturers do not have to purchase their raw materials from the competition. It is as much a restriction of trade to control the source of material as it is to fix the selling price of a product.

Fixing a price does not only mean that an industry consorts and agrees to sell at one price. Price fixing can encompass minimum pricing as well, because such pricing tends to lower all competitors' prices to the lowest possible. In some areas of the United States, building contractors are reputed to have an understanding regarding which company will get construction contracts. Because most cities only have a few contractors who can bid on substantial jobs, such contractors frequently know the order of rotation of one another's last jobs. Through this means they intentionally price themselves above the next scheduled recipient of the construction bid. This effectively guarantees the winning bidder a comfortable profit margin: this practice is illegal. Likewise, it could occur in international dealings and it is just as illegal. Just because certain industries cross international borders,they are not exempted from the rules of good conduct and free trade.

Patents are another area where one needs to tread softly, because the granting of a patent in and of itself provides a monopoly; the owner of a patent should take steps to be careful that his licensing agreements do not run longer than the patent itself. Otherwise, it could be construed as a restraint of trade.

Businessmen must be cautious not to establish a minimum price for an item nor should they limit sales territories, although the latter may be judged reasonable depending on the local government involved. International businessmen are more likely to trip over a local law than they are in their home country simply because they are not as familiar with local laws and because there are so many countries in which they may be doing business. Suffice it to say, however, that the conditions of sale, terms, discounts based on quantities, and segmentation of markets should be avoided at all cost. The same rules should apply on the supply side of any arrangements such as with purchase contracts or dealing with boycotts that restrict production.

The exporter or the international businessman who has many varied dealings around the world should always carefully consider the following situations only after competent legal advice has been secured:

1. exclusive production contracts with subsidiaries
2. exchanging patents on an exclusive basis
   market division agreements
3. know-how or trade processes
4. licensing contracts with subsidiary corporations
5. licensing agreements with other foreign companies[7]

PRODUCT LIABILITY

During the last decade, there has been a steady increase in the quantity of product liability cases brought to court. Juries around the United States have demonstrated a propensity for making larger and larger awards to persons injured due to product shortcomings or defect. The rest of the world has also witnessed an increase in product liability suits and settlements. For the American exporter, the future with regards to product liability appears to be a gathering storm on the horizon of international litigation.

Any international litigation is horribly expensive and the determination of jurisdiction can be difficult. Imagine, for example, an American manufacturer who produces a product in Texas, exports it through an independent agent in New York who sells it to an importer in France, who resells it to a department store chain with several locations, who finally sells it to an individual who is injured as a result of a product defect. Who is responsible for damages? Who has jurisdiction over the case? And how can the courts be assured that the proper defendants have been legally notified of the suit? These are typical problems that must be sorted out in any international law suit. Another problem can occur even if liability is determined; if the defendant has no assets or is indifferent about doing further business in the market, there may be no way to enforce a judgment.

The world economic community is working on ways to improve the ability of the various courts to answer three questions regarding:

1. How to determine who is responsible for damages?
2. Which court will have jurisdiction in product liability cases?
3. How can defendants be properly notified of an action that
   is taken against them?

It appears from the cooperation among nations to date that a system to handle product liability cases will evolve in the near future. Many of the problems related to establishing jurisdiction center around the United States' system of federated government, which makes it difficult for jurisdiction to be moved from one district to another. In an effort to overcome this problem, some states have established long arm statutes that define jurisdictional limits. Some court tests have indeed defined very long arm statutes: In cases where foreign manufacturers have sold their products to American importers and later sold the products to end users, the courts have held that the foreign manufacturer was ultimately responsible, even though he did not actually conduct business in the United States. Just the fact that he knew the ultimate destination of his product to be the United States was sufficient grounds for including him in the court's jurisdiction.

In civil law countries, the question of jurisdiction is usually not as complicated as it is in the United States, but the concept of establishing jurisdiction is similar. Although the domicile of the defendant and the location of the event are universally understood, some foreign codes recognize personal jurisdiction based nationality. When this is the case, it is possible for a foreign national to be brought before the local justice system and tried because he caused injury or property loss to a national.

The bottom line for the exporter should be that, given a product liability problem, the foreign courts will find a way to establish jurisdiction and bring the defendant to court.

Once jurisdiction is established, the problem of serving proper notice becomes critical. Subpoenas that are served across international boundaries must meet the legal requirements for notice in both the country in which jurisdiction has been established and in the country in which jurisdiction for serving the subpoena will occur. Reciprocity between the two jurisdictions is imperative if a trial takes place and the defendant is found guilty and ordered to pay damages, because the foreign court will have to depend on the jurisdiction of the defendant's domicile for enforcement of a judgment at that time.

The Hague Convention on the Service of Judicial and Extrajudicial Documents in Civil and Commercial Matters has reduced a few of the problems inherent in jurisdiction. The United States and with twenty-seven other signatories have signed this agreement which minimizes the differences in legal systems between the United States and Europe by establishing central authority for the service of legal documents. In the United States, this centralized authority is the U.S. Department of Justice.

In certain civil law countries, documents are deemed served as soon as the plaintiff delivers them to the legal authority responsible for delivering them. In other words, it is not necessary to actually serve the defendant personally. In the United States, however, it is necessary to personally serve the defendant. The convention overcame this problem by agreeing to accept the American concept that service is complete if legal documents are mailed in a manner that requires a signature of receipt by the defendant. One proviso to this rule is that the state of destination must not object to this form of service. If it does, then service in this manner is not acceptable. Given the relations of the major industrial countries of Europe and the United States, approval by the state of destination is most likely assured.

The convention has wrestled with other problems inherent in international legal proceedings and continues to find areas of compromise. However, the problem of satisfying a judgment if the convicted party has no assets in the jurisdiction remains. Nonetheless, judgments issued in one member of the EEC's court are recognized by all the members of the EEC. Therefore, if an American has assets in England and is found guilty in France, his assets can be attached unless payment of the judgment is made.

Because of the high cost of international litigation and the uncertainty of jurisdiction, most joint ventures and license agreements, as noted earlier, contain clauses allowing for settlement of disputes by binding arbitration. It may also be wise to include clauses in such contracts establishing responsibility for product liability claims as well.[8]

FDA AND EPA RESTRICTIONS

There are not a great deal of restrictions placed on manufacturers or exporters of food and drugs. As long as the food or drug meets the specifications established by the importing government, U.S. manufacturers are exempted from the laws regarding mislabeling and adulteration. However, this does not apply to new drugs, whether for human or animal consumption. Questions regarding exportability of food or drugs should be directed to the FDA field office nearest the manufacturer.

The Environmental Protection Agency has very little to do with export, except in those rare situations where an American company wants to export its hazardous waste to another country. In these cases, it is necessary to notify the EPA and await the written approval of the foreign government for which the waste is destined. Unless the EPA receives this written approval, shipment of the waste will be denied.

OTHER POLITICAL CONSIDERATIONS

Other political considerations should always include the following:

If the exporter is considering shipping to a country without a convertible currency he should have a plan for a barter agreement so he can get some value out of his exports. Some time ago Pepsico entered into such a relationship with the U.S.S.R. whereby they provide syrup and the Russians pay in vodka. This avenue of trade is not suggested for the company that is new to foreign trade without the advise of competent international attorneys.

If the government of the country to be exported to has a history of instability, payment should always be made in advance of actual manufacturing, not just in advance of shipment.

If a country exhibits current political unrest in the form of revolution or rebellion, the exporter should make certain his payment is guaranteed before commencing production of the goods.

SUMMARY

The American exporter must be careful to respect his government's andtidiversion clause, making certain he always has a valid export license and includes the appropriate clause on his commercial invoices, export declaration, and bills of lading. Willful knowledge of diversion of technology or products important to the national defense can be cause for civil and criminal prosecution not only against the principal of the company, but also against the individual responsible for making the actual shipment.

From time to time, some foreign governments boycott another country or restrict trade for political reasons. If discrimination occurs against a country friendly to the United States, U.S. law makes it illegal to be a party to any transactions that further the restrictive trade practice. Again, the punishment for knowingly contributing to the furtherance of such activity leaves the company, its principals, and its staff liable to criminal and civil prosecution. The exporter should advise his staff that they must also report all instances of restrictive trade practices to the Office of Export Enforcement.

Strict attention to American antitrust laws should be accorded foreign commerce because antitrust statutes include foreign commerce, as well as interstate commerce. Of particular importance are any agreements such as exclusive production contracts, exchanging patents, market division agreements, and licensing agreements that could be construed as restrictive trade practices. Before any agreements are made with foreign companies, competent international legal advice should be sought.

Product liability laws long prevalent in the United States are becoming more common in other parts of the world, particularly Europe. European governments working in concert with the United States have recently broken down some of the barriers that have traditionally sheltered foreign companies from prosecution.

FDA and EPA regulations do not have much bearing on international transactions. The FDA will waive requirements on labeling and adulteration if the recipient country's laws are respected and met. The EPA only becomes involved in foreign trade if hazardous waste is being shipped abroad. In these cases the EPA will request a letter from the recipient country indicating its willingness to accept the waste.

Other political considerations faced by the exporter include his ability to receive payment for his products. In unstable countries or countries that do not have readily convertible currency, the exporter should always be certain to demand payment before commencing manufacturing of the goods being ordered. If this is not practical and if the exporter still wants to conduct commerce with the recipient country, he should enter into a barter arrangement with the foreign company and the consent of the foreign company's government.

NOTES

1. Gerard R. Richter, "Export Shipping Procedures," *International Trade Handbook* (Chicago: The Dartnell Corporation, 1963) p. 205.

2. *Restrictive Trade Practices or Boycotts Including Enforcement and Administrative Proceedings*, U.S. Department of commerce (Washington D.C.: U.S. Government Printing Office, May 1983), p.1.

3. Ibid., p. iv.

4. Ibid., p. iii.

5. Ibid., p.v.

6. *Export Administration Act*, part 387, p. 71.

7. Robert Charles Kelso, "Cartels and Antitrust," *International Trade Handbook* (Chicago: The Dartnell Corporation, 1963), p. 578.

8. From John E. Siegmund, *Increasing Product Liability Impact on International Commerce*, U.S. Department of Commerce, International Trade Administration, Superintendent of Documents (Washington D.C.: U.S. Government Printing Office, 1985), pp.79-81.

Appendix A
Abbreviations and Acronyms

A/B Term used in Swedish and Finnish to denote a joint-stock company.

ad val. European abbreviation for ad valorem which is a tax levied according to the value.

A.G. Term used in German to denote a joint-stock company; a close corporation.

Aktiengesellschaft A German privately held stock company.

A.m.b.H. A German limited liability company.

Anme. A French limited liability company.

A/R Against all risks; accounts receivable.

banq French for bank.

bbl. barrel

btto gross

B.T.U. British Thermal Unit.

Ca. Term used to denote a Portuguese company.

C.A. Term used to denote a Spanish company.

C.A.D. Cash against documents.

C.A.F. French term to denote cash against documents.

C & F Cost and Freight.

C & I Cost and Insurance.

CBD Cash before delivery.

cc Cubic centimeter.

c. de R. L. Spanish for limited liability company.

Ce. French term to denote company.

cia. Spanish term to denote a stock company.

Cie A French term to denote a stock company.

C.I.F. Cost, Insurance, Freight.

cm Centimeter.

C. por A. Term to denote a Spanish stock company.

cwt. British term for hundredweight; 112 lbs.

Directeur French term for manager, not director in the American sense.

DM. Deutsch Mark; German currency.

E.G.m.b.H. Term to denote a German limited liability company.

E.U.A. U.S.A.

E.V. German term to denote incorporated.

Fabbrica A factory.

Fabr. German term for a factory.

fr. French franc; currency.

GATT General Agreement on Tariffs and Trade.

gm. Gram.

G.m.b.H. German limited liability company.

Gomei Kaisha Japanese term for a partnership.

Goshi Kaisha Japanese term for limited partnership.

Kabushiki Goshi Kaisha Japanese term to denote a limited partnership with

shareholders.

Kabushiki Kaisha Japanese term to denote incorporated.

kilo kilogram; 2.2 lbs.

km. kilometer; 6/10 mile.

L. liter; 1.05 qt.

£ British currency; Pound Sterling.

Lda. Portugese and Spanish for a limited liability company.

lt. British term, long ton.

m. Meter; 39.37 inches.

m.b.H. German term to denote a limited liability company.

Messrs. French salutation; Gentlemen.

m.HH. German salutation; Gentlemen.

m.Hr. German for Dear Sir.

N.F. No funds.

N.V. A Dutch stock company.

OY Finnish term for incorporated.

Pf. German currency; pfennig; 1/100 of a mark.

prox. Next month.

P.T.T. French post office and telegraph.

Pty. British closed corporation.

S.C.P. Spanish term for a private partnership.

S.C.P.A. Spanish term for a civil partnership with shares.

Shokai A Japanese partnership.

Soc. French, Italian, or Spanish term for company.

Sociedad Spanish term for company.

Societe French term for company.

S.p.A. Italian term for corporation.

¥ Japanese currency; yen.

Appendix B
Commerce Department
Field Offices

ALABAMA, Birmingham—2015 2nd Ave. N., 3rd fl., Berry Bldg., 35203, Tel: (205) 264-1331.

ALASKA, Anchorage—701 C St., P.O. Box 32, 99513, Tel: (907) 271-5041.

ARIZONA, Phoenix—Federal Bldg. & U.S. Courthouse, 230 N. 1st Ave., Rm. 3412, 85025, Tel: (602) 254-3285.

ARKANSAS, Little Rock—Savers Fed. Bldg., Ste. 635, 320 W. Capitol Ave., 722201, Tel: (501) 378-5794.

C A L I F O R N I A , L o s Angeles—Rm. 800, 11777 San Vicente Blvd., 90049, Tel: (213) 209-6707.

Santa Anna—116-A, W. 4th St., Ste. 1, 92701, Tel: (714) 836-2461.

San Diego—P.O. Box 81404, 92138, Tel: (619) 293-5395.

San Francisco—Fed. Bldg. Box 36013, 450 Golden Gate Ave., 94102, Tel: (415) 556-5860.

COLORADO, Denver—Room 119, U.S. Custom house, 721 19th St., 80202, Tel: (303) 844-3246.

C O N N E C T I C U T , Hartford—Rm. 610-B Fed. Bldg., 450 Main St., 06103, Tel: (203) 722-3530.

DELAWARE, Serviced by Philadelphia office.

DISTRICT OF COLUMBIA Serviced by Baltimore office.

FLORIDA, Miami—224 Fed. Bldg., 51 SW. 1st Ave., 33130, Tel: (305) 536-5267.

Clearwater—128 N. Osceola Ave., 33515, Tel: (813) 461-0011.

Jacksonville—3 Independent Dr., 32202, Tel:

(904) 791-2796.

Orlando—75 E. Ivanhoe Blvd., 32802, Tel: (305) 425-1247.

Tallahassee—107 W. Gaines St., Rm. G-20, 32304, Tel: (904) 488-6469.

GEORGIA, Atlanta—Suite 504, 1365 Peachtree St., NE., 30309, Tel: (404) 881-7000.

Savannah—Fed.Bldg.,Rm. A-107, 120 Bernard St., 31401, Tel: (912) 944-4204.

HAWAII, Honolulu—4106 Fed. Bldg., P.O. Box 50026, 300 Ala Moana Blvd., 96850, Tel: (808) 546-8694.

IDAHO, Boise—Statehouse, Rm. 113, 83720, Tel: (208) 334-2470.

ILLINOIS, Chicago—1406 Mid Continental Plaza Bldg., 55 E. Monroe St., 60603, Tel: (312) 353-4450.

Palatine—Harper College, Algonquin & Roselle Rd., 60067, Tel: (312) 397-3000.

Rockford—515 N. Court St., P.O. Box 1747, 61110-0247, Tel: (815) 987-8100.

INDIANA, Indianapolis—357 U.S. Courthouse & Fed. Bldg., 46 E. Ohio St., 46204, Tel: (317) 269-6214.

IOWA, Des Moines—817 Fed. Bldg., 210 Walnut St., 50309, Tel: (515) 284-4222.

KANSAS, Wichita—River Park Pl., Ste. 565, 727 N. Waco, 67203, Tel: (316) 269-6160.

KENTUCKY, Louisville—Rm. 6368, U. S. Post Office and Courthouse Bldg., 40202, Tel: (502) 582-5066.

LOUISIANA, New Orleans—432 Intl. Trade Mart, No. 2 Canal St., 70130, Tel: (504) 589-6546.

MAINE, Augusta (Boston, MA. Districts)—1 Memorial Circle, Casco Bank Bldg., 04330, Tel: (207) 622-8249.

MARYLAND, Baltimore—415 U.S. Customhouse, Gay & Lombard Sts., 21202, Tel: (301) 962-3560.

Rockville—101 Monroe St., 15th fl., 20850, Tel: (301) 251-2345.

MASSACHUSETTS, Boston—10th Flr., 441 Stuart St., 02116, Tel: (617) 223-2312.

MICHIGAN, Detroit—445 Fed. Bldg., 231 W. Lafayette, 48226, Tel: (313) 226-3650.

Grand Rapids—300 Monroe N.W., Rm. 409, 49503, Tel: (616) 456-2411.

MINNESOTA,Minneapolis—108 Fed. Bldg., 110 S. 4th St., 55401, Tel: (612) 349-3338.

MISSISSIPPI, Jackson—300 Woodrow Wilson Blvd., Ste. 328, 39213, Tel: (601) 965-4388.

MISSOURI, St. Louis—120 S. Central Ave., 63105, Tel: (314) 425-3302.

Kansas City—Rm. 635, 601 E. 12th St., 64106, Tel:(816) 374-3142.

MONTANA, Serviced by Denver office.

NEBRASKA, Omaha—1st flr., 300 S. 19th St., 68102, Tel: (402) 221-3664.

NEVADA, Reno—1755 E. Plumb Ln., #152, 68102, Tel: (702) 784-5203.

NEW HAMPSHIRE, Serviced by Boston office.

NEW JERSEY, Trenton—3131 Princeton Pike, 4-D, Ste. 211, 08648, Tel: (609) 989-2100.

NEW MEXICO, Albuquerque—517 Gold, S.W., Ste. 4303, 87102, Tel: (505) 766-2386.

NEW YORK, Buffalo—1312 Fed. Bldg., 111 W. Huron St., 14202, Tel: (716) 846-4191.

Rochester—121 E. Ave., 14604, Tel: (716) 263-6480.

New York—Fed. Bldg., 26 Fed. Plaza, Foley Sq., 10278, Tel: (212) 264-0634.

NORTH CAROLINA, Greensboro—203 Fed. Bldg., 324 W. Market ST., P.O. Box 1950, 27402, Tel: (919) 278-5345.

NORTH DAKOTA, Serviced by Omaha office.

OHIO, Cincinnati—9504 Fed. Bldg., 550 Main St., 45202, Tel: (513) 684-2944.

Cleveland—Rm. 600, 666 Euclid Ave., 44114, Tel: (216) 522-4750.

OKLAHOMA, Oklahoma City—6601 Broadway Ext., Ste. 200, 73116, Tel: (405) 231-5302.

Tulsa—440 S. Houston St., 74127, Tel: (918) 581-7650.

OREGON, Portland—Rm. 618, 1220 SW 3rd Ave., 97204, Tel: (503) 221-3001.

PENNSYLVANIA, Philadelphia—9448 Fed. Bldg., 600 Arch ST., 19106, Tel: (215) 597-2866.

Pittsburgh—2002 Fed. Bldg., 1000 Liberty Ave., 15222, Tel: (412) 644-2850.

PUERTO RICO, San Juan (Hato Rey)—Rm. 659 Fed. Bldg., 00918, Tel: (809) 753-4555.

RHODE ISLAND, Providence (Boston, MA, District)—7 Jackson Walkway, 02903, Tel: (401) 528-5104.

SOUTH CAROLINA, Columbia—Fed. Bldg., Ste. 172, 1835 Assembly St., 29201, Tel: (803) 765-5345.

Charleston—17 Lockwood Dr., 29401, Tel: (803) 724-4361.

SOUTH DAKOTA, Serviced by Omaha office.

TENNESSEE, Nashville—Ste. 1114 Parkway Towers, 404 Jas. Robertson Pkwy., 37219-1505, Tel: (615) 736-5161.

Memphis—3876 Central Ave., 38111, Tel: (901) 521-4826.

TEXAS, Dallas—Rm. 7A5, 1100 Commerce St., 75242, Tel: (214) 767-0542.

Austin—P.O. Box 12728, Capitol Station, 78711, Tel: (512) 472-5059.

Houston—2625 Fed. Courthouse, 515 Rusk Sts., 77002, Tel: (713) 229-2578.

UTAH, Salt Lake City—Rm. 340 U.S. Courthouse, 350 S. Main St., 84101, Tel: (801) 524-5116.

VERMONT, Serviced by Boston office.

VIRGINIA, Richmond—8010 Fed. Bldg., 400 N. 8th St., 23240, Tel: (804) 771-2246.

WASHINGTON, Seattle—Rm. 706 Lake Union Bldg., 1700 Westlake Ave. N., 98109, Tel: (206) 442-5616.

Spokane—P.O. Box 2170, 99210, Tel: (509) 838-8202.

WEST VIRGINIA, Charleston—3000 New Fed. Bldg., 500 Quarrier St., 25301, Tel: (304) 347-5123.

WISCONSIN, Milwaukee—Fed. Bldg., U.S. Courthouse, 517 E. Wisc. Ave., 53202, Tel: (414) 291-3473.

WYOMING, Serviced by Denver office.

Appendix C
Official Languages
of Most Countries

Afghanistan,	English
Algeria,	French, Arabic
Argentina,	Spanish
Australia,	English
Austria,	German
Bahrain,	Arabic, English
Belgium,	French, Flemish
Bermuda,	English
Bolivia,	Spanish
Brazil,	Portuguese
Bulgaria,	Bulgarian
Cameroon,	English
Canada,	English, French
Chile,	Spanish
Columbia,	Spanish
Costa Rica,	Spanish
Cuba,	Spanish
Cyprus,	English
Czechoslovakia,	
	Czech, Slovak
Denmark,	Danish
Dominican Republic,	
Spanish	
Ecuador,	Spanish
Egypt,	Arabic
El Salvador,	Spanish

Ethiopia,	Amharic, English
Finland,	Finnish, Swedish
France,	French
Gambia,	English
Germany,	German
Greece,	Greek
Grenada,	English
Guadeloupe,	French
Guam,	English
Guatemala,	Spanish
Haiti,	French
Honduras,	Spanish
Hong Kong,	English
Hungary,	Hungarian
India,	Hindi, English
Indonesia,	Indonesian
Iran,	Farsi
Iraq,	Arabic
Israel	Hebrew
Italy,	Italian
Ivory Coast,	French
Jamaica,	English
Japan,	Japanese
Jordan,	Arabic

Korea,   Korean
Kuwait,   Arabic

Lebanon,   Arabic
Liberia,   English
Libya, Arabic, Italian
Luxembourg,   French

Martinique,   French
Mexico,   Spanish
Morocco,   Arabic, French

Netherlands,   Dutch
New Zealand,   English
Nicaragua,   Spanish
Nigeria,   English
Norway,   Norwegian

Pakistan,   Urdu
Panama,   Spanish
Paraguay,   Spanish
Peru   Spanish
Philippines,
               Tagalog,
English
Poland,   Polish
Portugal,   Portuguese
Puerto Rico,
               Spanish,
               English

Rumania,   Rumanian
Saudi Arabia, Arabic
Senegal,   French
Singapore,   English
South Africa,
               English,
               Dutch
Spain, Spanish
Sudan,   Arabic,
               English
Surinam,   Dutch
Sweden,   Swedish
Switzerland,   German,
               French, Italian
Syria, Arabic

Thailand,   Thai
Trinidad,   English
Turkey,   Turkish

Uganda,   English
U.S.S.R.,   Russian
Uruguay,   Spanish

Venezuela,   Spanish
Yugoslavia,   Slovene,
               Serbo-Croat

Bibliography

Application Procedure for ATA Carnets. New York: U.S. Council for International Business.

Del Mar, Alexander. *History of Monetary Systems*. New York: Augustus M. Kelley, 1969.

Export Administration Act of 1979. Title 15. Chapter III. Subchapter C. Code of Federal Regulations. Part 387, 1979.

Export Letter of Credit Checklist. Dallas: RepublicBank. n.d.

"Export Shipping Manual." In *International Trade Reporter*, (1236). The Bureau of National Affairs, Inc., July 25, 1987.

Goodearl, Arthur W. "Foreign Trade Documentation and Finance." In *International Trade Handbook*. Chicago: The Dartnell Corporation, 1963.

Instructions for the use of the Shipper's Export Declaration, Commerce Form 7525-V. U.S. Department of Commerce, Social and Economic Statistics Administration. Bureau of the Census. 1988.

Instructions to Buyer for Establishing the Letter of Credit. Dallas: RepublicBank. n.d.

International Mail. Publication 42, Transmittal Letter 83. U.S. Postal Service. Washington D.C.: Government Printing Office, January 2, 1976.

Keegan, Warren J. *Multinational Marketing Management*. New Jersey: Prentice-Hall, 1974.

Kelso, Robert C. "Cartels and Antitrust." In *International Trade Handbook*. Chicago: The Dartnell Corporation, 1963.

Lattimore, Owen, and Eleanor Lattimore. *Silks, Spices and Empire*. New York: Delacorte Press, 1968.

Letter of Credit Seminar. RepublicBank Dallas International Department. Dallas: RepublicBank, n.d.

Lightman, Joseph M. "Foreign Trademark Protection" In *Foreign Business Practices*. Treaties and National Laws: U.S. Department of Commerce. International Trade Administration. Washington D.C.: U.S. Government Printing Office, 1985.

Martinez, Charles. *Flow of Paperwork on International Shipments*. Houston: Harle Services, Inc, n.d.

"National Association of Councils on International Banking." In *Uniform Customs and Practices for Documentary Credits*. ICC Publication No. 400. rev.ed. 1983.

Restrictive Trade Practices or Boycotts Including Enforcement and Administrative Proceedings. U.S. Department of Commerce. Washington, D.C.: US Government Printing Office, May, 1983.

Richter, Gerard R. *International Trade Handbook*. Chicago: The Dartnell Corporation, 1963.

Shipper's Export Declaration. *International Trade Administration, Form 7525-V (3-19-85)*. U.S. Department of Commerce. Bureau of the Census. Washington D.C.: U.S. Government Printing Office.

Siegmund, John E. "Increasing Product Liability Impact on International Commerce." In *Foreign Business Practices*. U.S. Department of Commerce. Washington, D.C.: U.S. Government Printing Office, 1985.

Travaglini, Vincent D. "Foreign Licensing and Joint Venture Arrangements." In *Foreign Business Practices*. U.S. Department of Commerce. International Trade Administration. Washington D.C.: U.S. Government Printing Office, 1985.

U.S. Department of Commerce. *A Basic Guide to Exporting*. Washington D.C.: U.S. Government Printing Office, 1986.

Wellard, James. *Samarkand and Beyond*. London: Constable and Company, 1977.

Index

About the Author

ROBERT E. WEBER is President of the Weber Consulting Group, Dallas, Texas. He is founder and past president of Dallas-based Silverthorne Business Interiors and former vice president, international division, for Weber Marking Systems. His previous books include *Managing Your Renovation or Move to New Offices* (Quorum Books, 1987) and *The Greatest Ski Resorts in America*.